Fights & Flights with the Royal Naval Air Service

AIR-COMMODORE SAMSON AND FLIGHT-LIEUT. R. MARIX.

Fights & Flights with the Royal Naval Air Service

A Personal Account of Service with Armoured Cars and Aircraft During the First World War

ILLUSTRATED

Charles Rumney Samson

Fights & Flights with the Royal Naval Air Service
A Personal Account of Service with Armoured Cars and Aircraft During the First World War
by Charles Rumney Samson

ILLUSTRATED

First published under the title
Fights and Flights

Leonaur is an imprint of Oakpast Ltd
Copyright in this form © 2022 Oakpast Ltd

ISBN: 978-1-915234-76-6 (hardcover)
ISBN: 978-1-915234-77-3 (softcover)

http://www.leonaur.com

Publisher's Notes

The views expressed in this book are not necessarily those of the publisher.

Contents

Part 1: Armoured Cars (August–November 1914)

The Eastchurch Squadron Takes a Hand	7
Dunkirk	13
The Third "Battle" of Cassel	19
The Occupation of Lille	23
Car Reconnaissance and Some Uhlans	30
Morbecque and Antwerp	36
A Mixed Engagement at Orchies	42
We Make Use of a Trench	52
Excitement at Douai	60
The Evacuation of Antwerp	69
The Retreat from Antwerp	77
Roulers to Ypres	85
Poperinghe	93
Dadizeele	96
Co-Operation on the Roulers–Menin Road	100
Hollebeke and Ypres	106
The Last of Our Armoured Cars	114

Part 2: The "Iron Coast" (November 1914–February 1915)

Dunkirk Again	117

More Work with the 3-Pounder	122
The First Night-Bombing Flight	126
Two Fine Flights by Davies	135
Extension of Night Bombing	140
Our First Organised Air-Raids	146
Last Days in Flanders	153

Part 3: The Dardanelles (March to December 1915)

Tenedos	160
The "Landing"	171
Bombing Over the Peninsula	182
Imbros: The Death of a Friend	192
Kemal Pasha's Escape	201
The Maritza Bridge	207
The Evacuation	214

Part 4: The "Ben-My-Chree" (May 1916—January 1917)

Introducing the Ben-My-Chree	220
Aden and the Red Sea	227
Castelorizo, Beirut, Ruad, and Gaza	237
El Afuleh, Homs, and Adana	244
A Failure and a Success	254
The End of the "Ben-My-Chree"	261

Part 5: The North Sea

Yarmouth and Felixstowe	269

Part 1: Armoured Cars (August–November 1914)

Chapter 1

The Eastchurch Squadron Takes a Hand

After a period spent on the East Coast of England carrying out patrols against possible air attacks, my unit of the R.N.A.S. was ordered to proceed overseas, to co-operate with a brigade of Royal Marines who were to occupy Ostend.

My squadron was composed practically *in toto* from the R.N. Flying School at Eastchurch, which had been under my command since its start in 1912. The majority of the pilots were Eastchurch officers, and all the mechanics and working-party were from the same unit. They were all active R.N. ratings, who had joined the R.N.A.S., and had been with me, some since 1911, the rest since 1912 and 1913.

As regards personnel, therefore, my squadron had the advantage of high *esprit de corps*, and that mutual feeling of self-confidence engendered by some years of mutual work in aviation.

The pilots were: Lieutenant R. B. Davies, R.N., who was my First Lieutenant at Eastchurch, Lieutenant Osmond, R.N., Engineer-Lieutenant E. F. Briggs, R.N., and Lieutenant J. Courtney, R.M.L.I., who were all active service naval or marine officers; and Flight-Lieutenants Sippe, Dalrymple, Clark, Beevor, Rainey, and Lord Edward Grosvenor, who were direct-entry. R.N.A.S. officers. Captain Barnby, R.N.L.I., came as Camp Commandant, and Staff-Surgeon H.V. Wells, R.N., was our doctor; both were also aeroplane pilots.

Mr. Brownridge, a carpenter, R.N., was my repair officer, and what he didn't know about the repair and upkeep of aeroplanes wasn't worth knowing.

In addition to the pilots, the following officers, most of whom had been with us since the outbreak of war, were with the Squadron for transport, intelligence, and observing duties. They all held temporary commissions in the R.N.V.R.: Lieutenants W. L. Samson and F. R. Samson, two of my brothers, and Sub-Lieutenants A. Nalder, Glass, Huggins, and Bernard Isaac.

In addition to the aeroplane men, who were about seventy in number, I had twenty specially enlisted transport drivers. These had mostly been collected by F. R. Samson, and they were a first-class lot of men, the majority being very highly skilled motor mechanics and testers from the Rolls Royce, Wolseley, and Talbot motorcar firms. The result was that our transport was always kept in first-class running order.

I may add that among my aeroplane men were five or six whom we had taught to fly at Eastchurch. The whole lot were a splendid set of fellows, and were in fact the finest body of men it was possible to command. Practically every one of them had been personally selected by me, in the early days of naval aviation, out of volunteers from the navy. Never once were we let down by our men, and both in France and the Dardanelles they worked like slaves without a single complaint. In fact, during these periods I never had to deal with a single disciplinary offence. They were the very pick of the R.N.A.S., which means that they were absolutely second to none.

I must mention some of their names, although in the following pages you will come across them again in varying situations and events: Leigh, Bradford, Nelson, Keogh, Shaw, Cole, Platford, Bishop, Harper, Lawrence, Edmunds, Bateman, Brewe, Walsh, Palmer. What recollections their names bring back to my memory of aged aeroplanes worked on all night in order that they could fly in the morning, and of unreliable engines coaxed and tended so that they could carry us over the lines!

I am glad to say that a large number of these men now hold His Majesty's Commission as officers of the R.A.F.; but not one ever received adequate advancement.

As for the aeroplanes, the majority were old veteran servants of the Crown, and I doubt if anybody has ever taken to war such a heterogeneous crowd of machines. A modern Squadron Commander would have his hair turned grey trying to deal with the various types of aeroplanes and engines. They consisted of:

2 B.E. Biplanes, fitted with a 70-h.p. Renault engine.
2 Sopwith Biplanes, fitted with an 80-h.p. Gnome engine.
1 Blériot Monoplane, fitted with an 80-h.p. Le Rhône engine.
1 Blériot Monoplane, fitted with a 50-h.p. Gnome engine.

1 Henry Farman Biplane, fitted with an 80-h.p. Gnome engine.
1 Bristol Biplane, fitted with an 80-h.p. Gnome engine.
1 Short Biplane, fitted with an 80-h.p. Gnome engine.

The last in this list, the Short Biplane, was originally a seaplane, but its floats had been removed and a wheel chassis put in their place.

There were thus seven different types of aeroplanes and three types of engines.

The transport was an equally miscellaneous collection of vehicles, which had been hastily collected by Lieutenant F. R. Samson and Engineer-Lieutenant-Commander W. Briggs, of the Admiralty Air Department. It included ten touring cars, one of which belonged to F. R. Samson, and was fitted with a Maxim for antiaircraft purposes, two 5-ton Mercédès lorries, and eight London General Omnibus chassis, one of which was actually No. 2, so it must have been a veteran.

On the night of August 25th, 1914, I received a message ordering me to come up to London to see the Director of the Air Department at the Admiralty. This was Commodore Murray F. Sueter, C.B., who was the pioneer of airships. He was the active Chief of the R.N.A.S., and a splendid officer to work under, and during the long period in which I had dealings with him I always found plenty of encouragement and assistance from his department. He was in every way a real live man, to whom the R.N.A.S. owe a great debt of gratitude. His services have never been adequately rewarded, and jealousies kept him out of high command.

I got to his room about 10 p.m., and found there, Commander Clark-Hall. The commodore gave me orders to take my Squadron to Ostend, and start first thing in the morning. I reported that we were already at a moment's notice, and after discussing certain arrangements with Clark-Hall, who was going over on General Aston's staff, I set off back to Eastchurch, having first telephoned to Davies to have all the aeroplanes ready by dawn. The transport and men were to go over in H.M.S. *Empress*, a converted seaplane carrier, and a collier, which were both lying at Sheerness. Bill Samson was placed in command of the collier party.

After having a meal at the Hyde Park Corner coffee-stall, we went off in the car down to Eastchurch, and I am afraid we exceeded the speed limit on many occasions. Arriving there about 2 a.m., we found everybody collected in the mess playing poker. Nobody was desirous of going to bed, and all were keen as mustard on setting out to war as soon as daylight appeared.

About 3 a.m. I received a message saying that the Marine Brigade were not landing until the 27th, and we were therefore to postpone our departure until that day. This depressed everybody, as we were all suffering from the fear of the war being over before we could get a chance to take part in it. But fortunately, on the 27th we received orders to start, and after lunch we set off.

I was the first to start, flying in No. 50, an old B.E. Biplane, which I had flown for about ten months. As in those days there were no proper distinguishing marks for aeroplanes, I had arranged that each machine should fly a Union Jack lashed to one of its struts.

Every pilot was encircled with a couple of bicycle tyres acting as lifebelts, and carried a .45 automatic pistol. Grosvenor was in addition armed with a rifle. Briggs as usual carried a complete outfit of tools and various spare parts. He always went up into the air carrying a regular store of things, and we used to wonder how his machine ever flew with the weight of material it was loaded with.

The journey across was rather unpleasant, as we encountered a good deal of low cloud and some thunderstorms; but it would have taken something pretty bad to stop us that day. Making the French coast at Calais, I flew along past Dunkirk to Ostend, arriving there after a flight of an hour and a half, which in 1914 was very good time.

It was my job to find a landing ground, and the remainder had orders to alight where they saw me land. The only suitable spot I could see was the Leopold Racecourse, in the southern half of the town. This looked, and was, very narrow, and as the wind was across the course I had very little space for a landing. I got down all right, skimming over the surrounding house-tops, but ran into some railings at the far end, luckily without damaging the aeroplane, as I got her slewed round just before I hit. Jumping out of the machine, I tore up about 50 yards of railing, assisted by two Belgian civil guards, who appeared uncertain as to my nationality.

I had been fired at by rifles as I was coming down, and whilst I was waiting for the others to arrive, I found I was being stalked by a couple of marines, who were very disappointed to find I was a British naval officer. They had come over to Belgium to shoot Germans, and were simply aching to let off their rifles at the first opportunity. The next two to arrive, Osmond and Briggs, were received by a hot fusillade, but it was luckily not very accurate. By the time the others appeared I had sent out messengers to say we were on their side, and not *Huns*, and the remainder of my aeroplanes landed without being fired upon.

The only aeroplane that failed to arrive was Courtney's. He had alighted at Dunkirk with engine trouble, but got in next day. We found a much better aerodrome on the northern side of the harbour, and moved there the next day. H.M.S. *Empress* and the collier arriving during the morning, we soon unloaded our transport and stores, and started erecting an encampment. For the night we occupied an old Martello tower, camping out on the roof. We left that, next day, the 29th, for a bivouac which Brownridge had constructed out of some railway tarpaulins and canvas we had brought with us. Our camp had a very home-made appearance, and we were without any comforts; but this we didn't mind, as we were at last on active service and the weather was fine.

A naval airship arrived on the 29th, and as her landing party were without transport, we lent them some lorries. They were splendidly equipped for camp life, having bedsteads, ground sheets, etc., and as they were rather innocents compared to my band of pirates, I soon discovered that my men were very comfortable on the spoils of the airship people.

Our work consisted of reconnaissance flights over the area between Bruges, Ghent, and Ypres, and we made a considerable number daily without seeing anything very important. The country to be flown over, with its numerous very small fields, was bad from the aviator's point of view, as in case of a forced landing there was every chance of a crash.

It was soon apparent that if the Germans advanced upon Ostend, the Marine Brigade would have a very tough job to defend it. They were without artillery except what could be provided by the ships' guns lying off the port, and they only had about half a dozen machine-guns for the whole brigade. They depended on my motor transport for the supply of their outlying posts, being quite unprovided with any transport of their own except for some hand-carts. This showed a lack of foresight on the part of the responsible authorities.

On the 29th General Aston, who was in command of the brigade, sent for me, and asked me if I considered it feasible to carry out a motorcar reconnaissance as far as Thourout and Bruges. I thought it an excellent idea, and after consultation with my brother Felix we selected two cars for the job. My brother's car, which carried the Maxim gun, was taken for one, and a car with a wagonette body for the other.

The mounting of the Maxim was attended to so that horizontal fire could be obtained. Everybody wanted to come in the party, and it was difficult to decide whom to take. In the end I set off with Captain Barnby, Lieutenant Courtney, Lieutenant F. R. Samson, Mr. Brownridge—who said his carpentry knowledge would be essential for the success of the expedition—and four of the fiercest-looking Eastchurch men we had.

The enthusiasm we were received with all along the route, especially at Thourout and Bruges, was extraordinary. We first visited Thourout, where we halted at the Hôtel de Ville. The mayor quickly arrived on the scene, and we had a long interview with him, while our cars and the two sentries we had placed to guard the two roads leading into the square were the centre of an admiring crowd. The mayor told us that twenty German cyclists had passed through the town on their return from a reconnaissance to Ostend only about an hour before we had arrived. It was probably fortunate for us that they had left before our arrival, because we were not then the trained fighters that we became later. Leaving Thourout, we arrived at Bruges without encountering any Germans.

At Bruges the streets were crowded with people filled with the delusion, which with the obvious desire of deceiving the Germans we did not contradict, that we were the advance party of a large British Army. The civil guard hastily donned their uniforms on our arrival, and turned out bristling with weapons and valour. They used, we found out later, to be quick-change artists from uniform to plain clothes and *vice versa*, in accordance with circumstances.

Having gained some information in the town, we returned to Ostend. The whole party enjoyed themselves immensely, although some of the more bloodthirsty members were disappointed at not getting a fight. This trip made us consider the question of motorcar operations, and ideas were discussed for armouring the cars, Felix Samson especially being very keen on the scheme.

Chapter 2

Dunkirk

On August 30th orders were received for the withdrawal of the Royal Marine Brigade and the Aeroplane Squadron to England. This was not at all to our liking, as we all urgently desired to stay overseas. It was therefore a very depressed party that loaded up our stores and transport on board H.M.S. *Empress* and the collier. One touring car was retained to follow the aeroplanes along the coast to Dunkirk and embark from there. This car was put under the command of Lieutenant Bill Samson, who had with him an engine-mechanic and a rigger.

The same day the marines embarked and the aeroplanes started on their return journey. We all prayed for fog, but Dover reported that the weather was clear. Anyhow, I gave orders for all aeroplanes to fly low over Dunkirk and to follow my example if they saw me alight there.

I started off with the fixed determination that at the slightest excuse I would stop at Dunkirk. Luckily, on arriving there, a slight haze was present, so down I went, quickly followed by the rest of the squadron. Fortunately for us, though unfortunately for him, Edward Grosvenor made a faulty landing, and crashed his Blériot beyond all hopes of repair. He completely failed to appreciate the extreme joy I displayed at his accident, which gave me a peg on which to hang my plans.

By a stroke of luck, the French General Bidon arrived at the aerodrome, accompanied by M. Cavrois O'Caffrey, a Jesuit priest, who was later on to form a welcome addition to our personnel. I pointed out to General Bidon that here was a squadron second to none in the world, all ready to fight, and thirsting for blood; that with our assistance he could carry out extended reconnaissance, and thus largely increase the efficiency of his defence. He was so impressed by my description of our capabilities that he immediately put the telephones into action, urgently requesting that we should remain at Dunkirk to carry out operations with the French.

I next proceeded to Mr. Sarel, our consul, who immediately got on to the Foreign Office by telephone, and urged them to request the Admiralty to retain my squadron at Dunkirk, pointing out how important it was both for our amicable relations with the French and for diplomatic reasons.

Mr. Sarel, who remained consul at Dunkirk during the whole war, was not only a real friend and helper to the R.N.A.S., but rendered yeoman assistance to the Royal Navy. He kept up a splendid liaison between the French and English, and considering all he did he never received adequate reward.

Personally, I found many a difficulty smoothed out after going along to his office; nothing was too much trouble for him, and he remained constantly cheerful and optimistic. He had a rotten time of it during the intensive bombing and long-range shelling that took place during the last two years of the War; but nothing disturbed him. His name is one to be remembered when others who received honours and awards for far less are lost in obscurity.

Having obtained Mr. Sarel's co-operation, I myself sent a long wire to the Admiralty stating that the fog was too bad to allow us to cross the Channel. I said also that one aeroplane was badly damaged; but that we were repairing it, and that we could not leave it behind. I requested that my men and stores should be sent over. I further added that we had been asked to carry out flights by the French. I then sent two aeroplanes to carry out a reconnaissance towards Lille and Douai, realising that once we made a start, we would require some shifting.

For the next three days I suffered from a surfeit of wires from the Admiralty, which gradually ascended from "What is the delay?" to "You are to return to England immediately."

Happily, we could always raise a touch of fog over our bit of the Channel, and I constantly reported as a last resource "fog too bad to cross Channel." At last, just as things were getting desperate and I was fully expecting to be marched back to England under arrest, a telegram arrived to say:

> Samson's Squadron are to operate from Dunkirk, carrying out aerial patrols against Zeppelins and aeroplanes, and to carry out reconnaissance as required by the French general at Dunkirk.

The rest of our party with our stores and transport arrived shortly afterwards. The French military authorities gave me complete control of the aerodrome, and did everything possible to assist me. Nothing

THE AUTHOR AND BILL WILSON GOING UP AFTER TAUBES IN NO. 1210, DUNKIRK, 1915.

was too much trouble for them, and I am certain that if our operations had achieved little else, the *entente cordiale* resulting from our stay at Dunkirk was well worth it. Our quarters were very cramped at the aerodrome, and the majority of the aeroplanes had to be kept in the open, most of the hangar space being converted into billets for the men.

The officers had three small rooms, and we slept rather too close for comfort; our camp equipment was of the most primitive sort, none of us possessing camp-beds. This was my fault, as I had issued orders that no camp equipment was to be taken overseas, as I considered that "roughing it" was an excellent way to harden us all for a long campaign. Everybody cheerfully and loyally carried out the self-conditioning process, and no evil results occurred. Briggs used solemnly to dress himself in flying kit complete with sea-boots every night before retiring to bed. Some humourist put up a placard over his sleeping place, labelled "Captain Oates."

I started an office in a room belonging to a restaurant attached to the aerodrome. My office staff consisted of Mr. Smeeth, a retired naval master-at-arms, who in civil life was a bookmaker. He had been with me at Eastchurch before the war, and whenever any of us went to a race meeting, we generally managed to take Mr. Smeeth, with resulting good fortune, as he seemed to know every tout.

He was assisted by Mansell, yeoman of signals, who was simply invaluable. He also was a Naval pensioner, who had been a yeoman of signals with me on board H.M.S. *Philomel* in the East Indies. He had been employed for a year before the war as a shed cleaner in the R.N. Flying School at Eastchurch.

Our daily work was carrying out flights over the area enclosed by Ypres, Lille, Douai, Cambrai, and Valenciennes, looking for movements of German troops. This entailed some long flights in those days of slow aeroplanes. In view of possible forced landings, I started a motorcar patrol between Dunkirk, Cassel, and Bailleul, in order that a breakdown party would be in attendance on an aeroplane as soon as possible in case of a forced landing. Another reason for this road patrol was that it trained the personnel in view of the possibilities of motorcar reconnaissance becoming useful. Felix Samson was now working hard at plans for armouring motorcars.

On September 2nd Mr. Sarel asked if it would be feasible for me to take him to Lille, in order to have a talk with our vice-consul in that city. We started off during the morning, taking two motorcars, one of which carried a machine-gun. Besides Mr. Sarel, who was in uniform, I took Engineer-Lieutenant Briggs and the Rev. Cavrois O'Caffrey with three of my men. We had an uneventful journey as far as La Carnoy on the outskirts of Lille, where we were stopped by the local mayor, who stated that he had just heard that a large force of Germans had arrived in Lille.

Fortunately, there was a telephone in a house close by, and Cavrois O'Caffrey got through on the 'phone to the *prefecture* at Lille.

The secretary to the *prefect* answered the telephone, and stated that some Germans had just arrived. He could not say how many there were; but he thought only about thirty or forty; at the moment two officers were with the *Préfet de Nord* in the next room, and two soldiers were standing in the passage outside. O'Caffrey told him where we were, and then reported the situation to me. After consultation we considered that it would be quite possible to get into the *prefecture* unseen and capture the four Germans who were inside, as the remainder were in the front courtyard, and could not possibly see us if we came by a back way.

O'Caffrey got through to the secretary again, and told him what we proposed to do if the *prefect* agreed; as I did not like to do anything which might lead to reprisals on the town without first getting his permission. The secretary promised to try to talk to the *prefect*, which might be difficult to do without causing the Germans to suspect something. He said that the Germans were very violent, and he feared for the *prefect's* life, as they were demanding a large sum of money from the town.

We were soon rung up again by the secretary, who said he had managed to talk to the *prefect*, and the latter was adverse to an attempt being made, as although he had been very roughly treated by the Germans, even to the extent of being man-handled, one of the officers having seized him by the throat and threatened to hang him, he was frightened that if we kidnapped the German officers, the enemy would hold the town responsible and start reprisals.

Meanwhile, O'Caffrey, who had volunteered for the job, was sent into Lille by tram to find out how many Germans were in the town. As he was in plain clothes, he could do this with safety.

Whilst he was away, I disposed my little force so that we could deal with any Germans who came out our way. Mr. Sarel was very keen for some to come, so that he could have a little excitement, but as I wasn't very sure whether he would be treated as a combatant, although he was in consular uniform, I told him he must not take any part in a fight, since if he were captured, he might be hanged.

O'Caffrey was back in about an hour's time with the news that he had counted a column of 1,000 German infantry who had marched into the main square, and that some cyclists were being sent out on the various roads.

I sent off O'Caffrey and the consul, much to the latter's disgust, and waited with the other car for nearly an hour, hoping we should see some of the German patrols; but as none came along the Armentières road whilst we were waiting, I returned to Dunkirk. The reconnaissance had been useful, as it had shown the inhabitants that they were not being left at the mercy of the invaders, and that there was some force which might at any moment turn up and prevent them receiving the treatment dealt out to some of the Belgian towns and villages.

O'Caffrey had arranged with a Lille lawyer that the latter should come out daily to the spot where we had been waiting, and remain there between the hours of 10 a.m. and 3 p.m. to give us news of German movements in Lille, a friend of his remaining in Lille and telephoning any movements which took place in the former's absence. It was arranged that this gentleman should wear a white waistcoat, and he would stop any of my cars that came along, using the password "Eastchurch" as a guarantee of his *bona fides*.

Another man at Armentières was also found who promised to telephone to us at once if any Germans passed through that town.

Mr. Winston Churchill was very keen on attempts being made to attack the Zeppelin sheds at Düsseldorf and Cologne, and as the only possible starting-place was Antwerp, he issued instructions that a unit should be detached from my force to proceed to Antwerp. As it was necessary to make arrangements before sending aeroplanes there, it was decided to send the aeroplanes detailed for the work to Ostend, whilst Major Gerrard, who had been sent out to take command, went to Antwerp to see the Belgian authorities.

Three aeroplanes were all I could provide, and Courtney, Osmond, and Beevor were detailed by me as the pilots. They flew to Ostend on September 3rd, the necessary men and motor transport going there by road the same day.

This detachment reduced my available aeroplanes to five.

Chapter 3

The Third "Battle" of Cassel

On September 4th we had our first experience of a fight with motorcars. I had started out in the morning with two cars, one my brother's Mercédès, fitted with the Maxim, and the other a Rolls Royce, without any gun. Flight-Lieutenant Sippe, Lieutenant Felix Samson, and Sub-Lieutenant Alec Nalder accompanied me, while Armourer's Mate Harper, Able Seaman Matcham, Leading Shipwright Pratt, Stoker Wright, and my servant, Private Edmunds, Royal Marines, formed the force; most of us carried rifles.

Arriving at Cassel, which is 16 miles from Dunkirk, I was met by a *gendarme*, who said that General Bidon wished to speak to me on the telephone, which was in the *Gendarmerie* Barracks. The general said he had received confirmation that some German motorcars had passed through Armentières, and were coming in the direction of Cassel. He wanted me to intercept them. I immediately got on to Bailleul, which is on the Armentières-Cassel road, by telephone, and the post office there told me that one car had just left for Cassel with 6 officers on board. Some other cars, three or four—they were not certain how many—were outside the Hôtel de Ville. We dashed off in our two cars, telling the *gendarmes* to follow on foot if they wanted a fight.

I intended to try to get to a point on the Bailleul road where it made a sharp bend. This would provide me with concealment for our cars until the moment arrived for us to move out, and at the same time provided us with a straight stretch of road nearly a mile long along which the Germans would have to come, thus giving us plenty of room to fight. A better position could have been obtained, about half-way up the steep hill into Cassel, which would have placed the Germans, reduced to slow speed up the hill, at our mercy; but I wanted to avoid any risk of giving them a chance of talking about *francs-tireurs* and taking reprisals on the villagers, on the pretence that they had been attacked by civilians. In addition, in a fight close to the town there was great risk of some of the inhabitants being shot.

Before I proceed any further with my narrative, it may be of interest to my readers to know that there have been recorded in history two previous battles at Cassel: the first was the famous occasion when the Duke of York led his army up the hill and then led them down again; the other was a victory on the part of that most famous general, the Duke of Marlborough, so you will see that I was in good company.

The position I wanted to get to was 2 miles from Cassel, on the Bailleul side. Unfortunately, time did not permit of me getting there, as the Germans reached the corner first. As soon as they saw us, the German who was driving the car applied his brakes, skidded half-way round, and started reversing to turn completely. There appeared only one thing to do or they would escape us, and that was to stop and open fire. We couldn't use the Maxim whilst the car was moving, so I gave the necessary orders, and Harper opened fire with commendable promptness. The remainder of us took to the roadside and backed up the Maxim with our rifles. As soon as we started firing, the Germans jumped out of their car and made for the ditches at the roadside. The range was about 500 yards.

I told Harper to fire at the car, and the remainder to fire at the Germans, who were six in number. We hit one as he was making for cover, but his comrades dragged him into shelter. The action was quite a brisk one for a short time, as the Germans, who were armed with rifles, replied to our fire. Unfortunately, after having fired about forty rounds, the firing pin of the Maxim sheared, thus putting it out of action. The German driver then made a dash for his car, and getting it turned round in a moment disappeared from view round the corner; the other Germans made a dash for the car, dodging behind the trees at the roadside, carrying one of their number. We must have been bad shots or, what was much more likely, suffering from intense excitement, as all the damage we did was to wound another.

We ran after them to the corner; but by the time we got there we saw the car disappearing from view. Felix Samson and Sippe, who had been in the Rolls Royce and did not possess rifles, had been sitting at their posts during the fight exposed to most of the fire. They reported that they had been in most danger from a *gendarme*, up a tree about half a mile behind us, who had kept up a heavy and extremely accurate fire, accurate, at least, as far as we were concerned, as one of his shots hit the Rolls.

I didn't think it advisable to pursue the Germans, as, for one thing, we wouldn't have been able to catch them before they got back to Bailleul, and, for a second reason, we were not strong enough, now our Maxim was out of action, to put up a fight against the additional three or four carloads that were at Bailleul. I determined therefore to lie in wait at the corner, hoping they would return reinforced.

After waiting about ten minutes or so a veteran captain of *gendarmes* arrived complete with wife in a large covered motorcar. He said he had come to fight at my side, having raised a little army of ten *gendarmes*, armed with carbines, who shortly came upon the scene. *Madame* and the limousine then retired from the battlefield, and this sporting old *gendarme* captain, who was quite sixty-five or more years of age, armed by the way with the longest-barrelled pistol I have ever seen, disposed his army behind the hedge, and we awaited with confidence the possible return of the enemy.

Within a quarter of an hour further help arrived on the scene, one of our old cars appearing with Barrett as driver and Sergeant-Major Bishop, Royal Marines, who stated that General Bidon had sent them out to reinforce me. This seemed rather a meagre sort of support to have been dispatched; but still, Bishop was a well-trained soldier and a first-class marksman, which was more than some of us appeared to be. I may say that everybody claimed to have wounded the two Germans who were seen to be hit. The time passed by with one or two false alarms; but as after nearly a two hours' wait no more *Huns* appeared, and finally a telephone message came from Cassel to say Bailleul post office reported that the Germans had all gone back towards Lille, we returned to Cassel.

Bailleul post office said that two Germans were wounded, and they had seen blood dripping from the car when it arrived back from Cassel. They also said that after this car's arrival the Germans held a consultation and then all left for the direction of Lille within two or three minutes; also, that they had evidently been shaken, and expecting an attack, as they had not waited to load up a lot of wine they had collected from the village.

We had a tremendous reception from the inhabitants of Cassel, who had enjoyed a splendid view of the little engagement from their commanding position on the hilltop. It was most embarrassing; but at the same time, I was pleased that they had seen Germans running away, as it would remove that 1870 feeling, which there is little doubt the Germans still produced in the minds of civilian Frenchmen. There is little doubt that this fight gave us a prestige in the villages outside Dunkirk far greater than its results called for, as of course it got tremendously exaggerated. That it had impressed the Germans out of all proportion there is no doubt, probably because the six German officers had reported that they had run up against tremendous odds. Otherwise, it seems difficult to understand why they did not push on their reconnaissance, considering the numbers they had at Bailleul.

General Bidon was very pleased indeed with our efforts, and said that he considered motorcar patrols on the roads most useful and productive of good results. He asked me to carry them out as frequently as possible.

Whilst this car work had been going on, my aeroplanes were equally busy making flights trying to locate the Germans in the neighbourhood of Lille, Cambrai, etc. Many flights were made on September 1st and 2nd, including one flight as far as the Schelde River looking for a Zeppelin that had been reported; but this subsequently proved to be a false alarm.

On September 3rd Dalrymple Clark made our first bomb attack. He was on a reconnaissance to Douai and fortunately carried bombs. Close to Douai he saw about forty Germans near a wood: coming down fairly low, he let go a 16-lb. bomb at them. This he saw caused two or three casualties. On the evening of September 4th, after my return from Cassel, I went up in my aeroplane, No. 50, to see if I could locate any Germans along the road between Lille and Bailleul. About midway between Armentières and Bailleul I sighted three motorcars, and about forty to fifty Germans halted on the road. I dropped two small bombs at them from a height of 2,000 feet; but missed with both of them. This party were evidently waiting for any of my cars which might come along.

CHAPTER 4

The Occupation of Lille

During the night of September 5th General Bidon sent for me and said he had received intelligence that the Germans were about to leave Lille, and in fact a good many of them had already marched out. He heard that there was every chance of some transport wagons being left behind. He intended therefore to send some infantry to Lille, going by train as far as it was possible, and a squadron of cavalry was setting out as far as Bailleul to act as supports. He required me to take some motorcars and escort the infantry back from Lille. Having only one machine-gun, I borrowed two from the French, and the general kindly lent me four French artillerymen to man them.

I issued orders for an early start with a strong force, and we started off with four motors, three of them armed with machine-guns, six officers, ten of my own men, and the four Frenchmen. This gave the force quite an international appearance, and was an excellent method of strengthening our *entente* with the French at Dunkirk. The inhabitants *en route* were also highly gratified at seeing this co-operation between the English and their own army.

Just outside Bergues, which is only 5 miles from Dunkirk, we passed a squadron of cavalry trotting along the road with patrols out in the fields at each flank. Thinking at the time this was only an extra precaution, meaning a further supporting force at Cassel, I went on past them without asking where they were going. Afterwards I discovered that this was the squadron of cavalry supposed to go as far as Bailleul. In reality they never got as far as Cassel, nor did the infantry go to Lille, as we found out later on.

As we were uncertain if the Germans were still in occupation of Lille, I used every precaution in approaching the town. Our march routine was gradually getting more efficient, as every trip we made tended to develop the proper tactics to be used by motorcars. I soon discovered that the correct way to proceed was for the cars to keep station approximately 70 yards apart, and, every time they halted, for them to stop at alternate sides of the road; for instance, the leading car always stopped on the left side of the road, the second car on the right-hand side, the third car on the left-hand side, and so on.

This not only gave each car a chance of getting its gun into action, but also provided turning space for each. The method I developed of going through villages was for the cars to halt outside and for the leading car to turn round and back into the village. When the leading car had got to the first houses it stopped, and the others then went through; the leading car then turned round and took up its proper position. In going through towns, the cars were in close order, because we found that we were likely to lose touch with each other if we did not keep close together.

The chief dangers I expected were when passing through woods or ascending steep hills, and for these I adopted the following routine. The leading car used to go at full speed through the wood or up the hill and stop at the end; the others then followed in turn. This precluded an ambush having a sitting target at the cars, and also placed us in a good fighting position.

If we came to a stop for any purpose, the cars were always turned half-round, and men were always stationed on each flank about 50 yards away from them.

It must be borne in mind that as the cars were unarmoured, we were very vulnerable to attack by a few determined men firing from a house or in ambush. Even when the first armoured cars arrived the crews were still exposed.

These precautions I found to work very well in practice, and my opinions on the subject were strengthened by an instance later on, when a party of my cars, under the command of an officer, got badly mauled through neglecting to take these precautions, two marines being killed by German cyclists firing from very short range behind a hedge.

An aeroplane was detailed to escort us, flying well ahead, with orders to come down low and fire a Verey light when over us if any enemy were sighted. This duty was carried out by Dalrymple Clark. There seemed great possibilities in this combination of aeroplane and car.

In the outskirts of Lille, we came across our friend of the white waistcoat, who reported that the Germans had left Lille at an early hour that morning. They consisted of 2,000 infantry and 80 cavalry. The nearest force of the enemy to Lille were some cavalry at Tournai. Taking our friend on board to show the way, we went on into Lille and made for the *prefecture*. This is in the big square, which is nearly as big as Trafalgar Square, with the *prefecture* at one end. The *prefecture* is a very large and imposing building, with a courtyard facing the square.

Some warning of our approach appeared to have been given, as the spot was packed with people, who thronged round the cars when we stopped in front of the official block of buildings. We got through the crowd, and took the cars into the courtyard, lining them up in line abreast, facing the square. The *gendarmes*, at my request, kept the roadway in front of the building clear of the populace, so that we were afforded a clear exit in case we had a fight, although I didn't much look forward to one with this seething crowd of civilians in the way.

Practically the whole of Lille appeared to be here; they were most enthusiastic, cheering, singing, and shouting out "*Vive l'Angleterre.*" I did everything I could to impress the people with our discipline and military behaviour, placing four of my men as sentries in a line behind the railings, and one man standing by each machine-gun. Our sentries stood like Guardsmen, and even when beautiful French girls came on the scene, and sponged their faces and brushed the dust off their clothes, they stood like lumps of granite.

Inside the courtyard were collected as nice-looking a bunch of ladies as I have seen for a long time. Mostly the relations of the Government officers, they were overwhelming my people with refreshments, both edible and liquid. Leaving Davies in charge of the party, I went inside to see the *prefect*. His room overlooked the square and courtyard, and both provided an interesting scene.

He was very pleased to see us, and said that our arrival had reassured the town to a most extraordinary extent, demonstrating to the people that they were not entirely at the mercy of the enemy. He then told me of the brutal treatment he had received at the hands of the Germans, showing me marks made on his throat by the fingers of a German lieutenant who had nearly throttled him. They had gone so far as to lead him out to hang him from a balcony, and he said he had only been saved from this terrible fate by the coolness of his secretary, who told the German that the *Préfet de Nord* was one of the chief officials in France, and that his murder was a serious matter, not lightly to be undertaken.

The *prefect* gave me the German officer's name, and told me if I ever came across him, I was not to let him go. I promised I wouldn't. The *prefect* then went on to say that the Germans had been quite worried over the fight at Cassel, and they had got the idea into their heads that there was a large force of English there. Two German officers had been wounded in the fight, one seriously and the other only slightly.

There were, he said, about fifty French and some few English wounded in the town; they had been left there by the Germans, and if I signed a proclamation to say I had taken the town, they could be evacuated to Dunkirk, otherwise the town would be held responsible. I therefore made out and signed the following proclamation:

> To the Authorities of the City of Lille,
> I have this day occupied Lille with an armed English and French force.
>
> C. R. Samson,
> Commander R.N.
> Officer-in-command of English Force at Dunkirk.

I added the latter sentence in order to impress upon the Germans that there was a large force at Dunkirk.

This proclamation the *prefect* ordered to be printed immediately and posted up all over the town. The wounded were then sent off to Dunkirk by train.

After a stay of about two hours, we went to the Hôtel de Ville to see the mayor. We got a civic reception, and were received by the whole Council; *en route* to the Hôtel de Ville we were cheered to the echo by the crowd and pelted with flowers, chocolates, and cigarettes. I remained at the Hôtel de Ville until late in the afternoon, and as by then it was discovered that the Germans had not left any transport behind, and that there was no chance of any French troops being sent to Lille, I reluctantly decided that I ought to return to Dunkirk.

We had an ovation on our return journey through the streets, and our cars were full of flowers, chocolates, and cigarettes; the dense crowds cheered themselves hoarse, and one felt rather like I imagine a Roman General used to feel on being given a triumph.

The only mishap was when an excitable individual threw a bottle of beer at me which smashed the wind screen and gave me a severe blow on the jaw; I rather fancied he must have had German sympathies.

On our return to Dunkirk General Bidon was most complimentary concerning our expedition, which he considered had been of great value.

The Cassel fight showed the immense possibilities of motorcar combat, and also demonstrated its difficulties and limitations. We saw that it was essential to protect the engine and the crew. I got permission from the Air Department for the "*Forges et Chantres de France*," the big shipbuilding firm at Dunkirk, to turn one of our cars into an armoured car, and my brother Felix Samson designed the armour protection. One of the difficulties he encountered was to protect the radiator and at the same time allow of an adequate flow of air into it for cooling purposes. He achieved this by using two hinged doors, which were operated by the driver. The doors were left open until we went to action stations, when they were closed; if the action was a long one the driver could open the doors very slightly, when a good flow of air was provided. This device is used to this day (1930).

As it was impossible to obtain armour-plate, we had to use boiler-plate, and tests showed that it would keep out English rifle bullets from over 500 yards. The weight of the plate was of course a heavy load for the car, so that we were forced to keep the area of armour down to as small a size as possible. In the end we were provided with an engine completely protected, gear-box protected, and the tyres protected from end-on fire. There was protection for the crew from ahead and astern, and also broadside fire when they were lying down.

This armour, as we suspected at the time, provided more moral than material protection.

One great asset was that the car looked very fierce and warlike, and no doubt the Germans considered it more invulnerable than it really was.

The first car we armoured was my brother's 45-50 h.p. Mercédès. The men quickly dubbed it the "Iron Duke" in compliment to the Grand Fleet flagship, and this name stuck to it to the end. The second car we put in the works to be armoured was a 50-h.p. Rolls Royce. Meanwhile, I had applied to England for armour-plate, and we got out a design for a properly protected car.

The two French machine-guns were mounted on two of the cars, and this raised our fighting force to three machine-gun cars.

The next outing we had was to make a further trial of reconnaissance with a motorcar and an aeroplane in co-operation. Dalrymple Clark went in the 80-h.p. Short Biplane, and I went in one of the cars carrying a machine-gun. We passed through Cassel and Bailleul, and about 2 miles on the Armentières side of Bailleul we saw a car approaching us from Armentières at full speed. We stopped and went to action stations which entailed two men with rifles in the ditches at the side of the road. Seeing our warlike preparations the advancing car stopped, and a civilian jumped out and ran towards us at full speed with his arm outstretched.

When he got to us, he was so out of breath that it was some minutes before he could speak. He then presented me with his card, which showed he was a barrister. He was terribly excited, very voluble, and rather difficult to understand.

It boiled down, however, to an urgent demand for us to follow him and kill some Germans who were going from Lille to Douai. He said he knew a road by which we could cut them off. I thought it advisable before we commenced the attack to find out how many Germans there were. Finally, I discovered that he thought there might be between two and three thousand, with two batteries of artillery, but, as he naively explained, "What are numbers compared to your machine-gun?" Personally, I thought about 2,000 Germans rather a tough proposition for four Englishmen and one unreliable old Maxim, and I regretted that we could not carry out the slaughter he desired. He was very crestfallen and said, "But I will come too." I am afraid we left with him a bad impression of our fighting capabilities.

I signalled to the aeroplane to scout to the south-east, and she discovered a large force of Germans on a road about 3 miles from us, going towards Douai. We returned to between Bailleul and Cassel and telephoned the intelligence to French Headquarters at Dunkirk. I also telephoned to my aerodrome to send out another aeroplane with bombs; but unfortunately, this aeroplane failed to locate the Germans, who had evidently halted in a wood or a village.

It was clear that this motorcar work was daily gaining in importance, and that it would be more efficient if I could go out with a stronger force. I therefore wrote to the Admiralty asking that fifty marines should be sent to me for motorcar operations. Mr. Winston Churchill fortunately was taking interest in our work, and with his usual custom of backing up any enterprise that was beginning to show signs of life, he decided to send me a large force of marines and also at the same time ordered a considerable number of motorcars to be armoured. He also started enlisting officers and men for an Armoured Car force. In this work he was backed up by Commodore Sueter, another live member of society, who did not suffer from hidebound ideas.

One day a sentry came to me and reported that a gentleman was outside asking to see me.

A very dapper gentleman he turned out to be, dressed in a Savile Row blue serge suit, with a yachting cap. He said he was Baron de Forest's *chef*, and that the baron, who was shortly arriving to join up with my command, had dispatched him in advance to prepare quarters for him.

I said, "Well, here are our quarters, and the baron can have that corner by the window. Outside under that bit of tarpaulin is the officers' kitchen; you are just the man I have been longing for, so trot round there and see what you can do about our lunch."

He didn't seem unduly delighted at the idea, and said he couldn't start at once, as he had left his clothes in the town. Also, he would have to telegraph to the baron.

Foolishly I let him depart.

Everybody was delighted at the idea of being provided with a real live cook, as up to date we had suffered from the ministrations of our amateur sailor cooks, who, although willing, were by no means professors of the culinary art. But this was the last we saw of our *chef*. He fled to England never to rejoin us.

CHAPTER 5

Car Reconnaissance and Some Uhlans

We carried out aeroplane reconnaissance daily, watching movements of German troops along the roads.

On September 8th I received a reinforcement of 250 Royal Marines, under the command of Major Armstrong, one of the finest officers I have had the pleasure to have under my command. He was always game for anything, and was coolness personified in a fight. He died a soldier's death at the Dardanelles. The other marine officers were Captains Graham, Lathbury, Coode, and Williams; they were all first-class fighting men, keen and energetic. The marines were simply splendid; but as they were all reservists and pensioners, they were rather too old for motorcar work; but they were stout men when it came to a fight.

My efforts were now concentrated on training the marines in motorcar fighting, and in keeping up our motorcar patrols as an adjunct to our aeroplane reconnaissances. I got into touch with Captain Goldsmith, of the G.H.Q. Intelligence Department, who was sent by General Macdonagh. Through his efforts I was put in control of the *gendarmes* in the villages in the zone I was operating in, and Captain Richard, of the Boulogne *Gendarmerie*, was placed at my disposal.

By this time, with the marines and *gendarmes*, I was gradually getting command of a large force. I therefore intended to clear the country between Arras, Amiens, and Douai of the parties of Germans who were terrorising the inhabitants, and also to give the Germans the idea that a large British force was guarding the approaches to the coast. At this time the Germans were in force at Arras, Albert, and Douai, and at times in Lille; but there were many parties of them wandering about patrolling and scouting round about Béthune, Hazebrouck, Armentières, and St. Pol.

Incidentally, several of them were robbers of the worst type. It was out of the question to attack the large towns, as it would lead to street fighting and probably result in the burning of the town. Moreover, our force was always too small, owing to the small number of cars available even when augmented by three or four French ones carrying the *gendarmes*.

I tried a couple of drives, using *gendarmes* on foot, and the cars going on a converging route in order to try to surround some parties of cyclists that had been located. We failed in our endeavours, although the *gendarmes* nearly got one party.

It was on September 12th that we got our next fight. I was carrying out a reconnaissance which took me through Cassel, Hazebrouck, Aire, Lillers, Chocques, Béthune, to the outskirts of Lille, and thence to Houdain, Bryas, and St. Pol, and I was nearing Arras when at the Auberge de la Maison Rouge a civilian on a bicycle informed me that a part of twenty *Uhlans* were in the village of Savoy. I had with me four cars and twenty-four officers and men. As I wished to avoid a fight in the street, which would have been to our disadvantage, I blocked the entrance of the village with a scout, and proceeded along a lane to the west of the village.

Unfortunately, when the *Uhlans* broke cover, they were out of range from the cars, and as we could not get any closer to them, I sent some marines, under Captain Coode, to try to cut them off. The *Uhlans* then saw one of the cars, and being fiercer than the usual run of their tribe, they started to charge towards it; but they thought better of it when they got closer, evidently seeing the rest of us. They halted, so we opened fire; but the range was too far to do much damage. As soon as we started firing, they bolted across-country and disappeared. We thought we had wounded one, as he nearly fell off, and was being supported by a comrade.

We went on then towards Arras, and lay in ambush for nearly two hours about 2 miles outside the town. The only thing that happened though was the arrival of a most extraordinary-looking motorcar, apparently about one of the first half-dozen ever built. It came from Arras, and when the occupants saw us, it came to a stop and out jumped a most beautiful lady dressed in Red Cross clothes. She said she had come out to pick up the wounded, as she had heard that a big fight had taken place. It seemed a peculiar business, as Arras was in German hands, and I felt certain she was a spy, but she couldn't get much information, as only one touring-car was visible. I didn't see any use in taking her prisoner, as she may have been quite genuine; anyhow, she would have been a nuisance.

We spent that night in Hesdin, where we put up at a most comfortable hotel, the men and cars being put in the *Gendarmerie* Barracks. The mayor provided a wonderful dinner for my men of about five courses, with wine, coffee, and liqueurs. We were equally well looked after at the hotel, where the proprietress couldn't do enough for us.

This was perhaps due to the presence with me of Capitaine Richard, commanding twenty *gendarmes*. He was a great man for arranging our food and looking after our comfort. We always lived well when he was of the party, meals of the first order springing up all over the country at his slightest gesture. The *gendarmes* were in cars provided by local amateurs who, dressed as they were in plain clothes, would have suffered the extreme penalty if they had been captured; but this didn't seem to deter them.

Having mentioned plain-clothes fighters, I will here record an incident I saw in Belgium later on. I was proceeding along a road not far from Ghent, when I heard firing close at hand. I went to the direction it came from, and discovered a civilian standing on a bridge over a canal; between his legs was a bicycle, in his hands a rifle. On the opposite bank of the canal, along the tow-path, were four *Uhlans* on horses. The civilian had already killed two, and as we arrived, he dispatched the others.

Having completed the job, he got on his bicycle and pedalled past me, raising his hat as he passed. I stopped him, and said he oughtn't to do such a thing, as only soldiers were supposed to shoot the enemy. He replied that he was a retired Congo official, and having seen his family murdered by Germans, he was getting a bit of his own back. The doctors had refused to pass him for service, so that he had to carry on a private war.

The next day I continued our sweep from Hesdin, reinforced by the arrival of Major Armstrong and Davies. We had eleven cars altogether, and I intended to operate and clear up the country between Doullens, Arras, and Albert, getting into Doullens about midday. We passed through the town, and on speeding up to climb the hill out of the town on the Albert road we suddenly came across six *Uhlans* riding into us at the cross-roads. I never saw them myself; but the second car nearly ran into them.

The *Uhlans* bolted into the fields and made across-country, where of course we couldn't follow them. Luckily, when we got to the top of the hill on the Albert road, we sighted them again, and although we couldn't get the machine-guns on to them, we got out of the cars, and opening fire with our rifles at about 500 yards range, we hit five of them. Three were killed, and one was picked up severely wounded. We took him to a hospital in Doullens, where he died without recovering consciousness.

It rather made me feel a brute seeing this poor fellow dying, and war seemed a beastly business. He looked half-starved, and appeared as if he had been on short rations for a long time. It was quite a repugnant job searching him whilst he was passing away from this life; but it had to be done. Goldsmith, who could read German, found from his papers that he belonged to the 1st Squadron of the 26th Dragoons, Würtemberg. He had a little child's atlas with which to find his way about the country. The map of France was about 3 ins. square, with only the names of half a dozen towns on it. Later on in the day, the *gendarmes* reported that the fifth *Uhlan* had given himself up: he was slightly wounded. This one stated that the Germans had put a price on my head.

I remained up the Albert road about a mile from Doullens until late in the afternoon, hoping that some Germans would come along to see what had happened to their patrol. We were in a splendid position, with a view over miles of country; but no enemy came into sight. I therefore returned to Dunkirk, arriving there late that night, and found that I had missed seeing Lord Kitchener and Winston Churchill, who had come over on this day.

Next morning General Bidon, the Governor of Dunkirk, sent me out to co-operate with some French Infantry, who reported that they had engaged a force of 300 cavalry who had a machine-gun section and a battery of horse artillery. We set off with three cars, carrying machine-guns, to try to intercept the Germans, who were reported to be going towards Bailleul; a French staff-officer came with me. Unfortunately, the Germans had too big a start, and we kept on getting conflicting reports from civilians leading us to go on a wild-goose chase. Passing through Steenwoorde and Strazeele, still in chase, we got close to Laventie, where I received intelligence that the Germans had halted and taken up a position in front of a wood.

The country we were now in was very bad from our point of view, as it was all small fields with high hedges, and numerous cottages and farmhouses, blanketing our fire and providing excellent positions for dismounted cavalry. Getting as close to them as I dared, I decided that an attack upon them in their present position would be a fatal policy;

we would be certain to get a hiding, and most likely lose our whole force, which consisted of twenty men all told. I therefore fell back about a mile to a position at some cross-roads which gave us a good chance of inflicting some damage upon them, if they followed us up.

Placing the cars so that each had a good field of fire, I sent out two parties of riflemen. well ahead on each flank, and took up a position myself in a windmill, from where I could see the country for miles all round. We waited here for nearly two hours; but the Germans evidently were not inclined to come and test our fighting powers, and moved off.

I then returned to Cassel, where we remained for the night, in case they decided to make a reconnaissance once more in this direction.

The next day I was reinforced, and sending Sippe off to Morbecque to look for an aerodrome there, I went to St. Pol, Doullens, and Acheux, and then along the Doullens—Arras road close to Arras. We found Arras occupied by about 800 Germans. We sighted some of their patrols; but they didn't give us a chance of getting to close quarters, as we naturally were handicapped by having to keep to the roads.

At a railway station close to Arras, whilst I was telephoning along the line, a crowd of civilians collected round the cars; and on coming out I found one of my *gendarmes* had arrested an old man whom he had seen writing in a notebook. I examined the book, and as it was full of varied notes concerning movements of *gendarmes*, state of the roads, and some remarks about our cars, I took the man along with us, leaving him in the charge of the Mayor of Doullens, with instructions for the mayor to send him to Dunkirk. There was little doubt in my mind that the man was a spy, although the mayor said he knew him well, and that he was a most reputable citizen. His case was investigated at Dunkirk by the French authorities; but they considered the evidence insufficient, and he was released.

We came back *via* St. Pol, where I was to leave my *gendarmes*. Our arrival there was in the nature of a triumph, as the *gendarmes'* families lived there, and they were all heroes after the Doullens episode. The crowd was most embarrassing, as it would force bottles of wine on us, and then somebody started making speeches, and one or two of the old ladies commenced kissing the *gendarmes* and then started to carry out the same operation on my men. The young good-looking females seemed to be left out of this performance until one of my younger officers bestowed a chaste salute on a very pretty one. Then the epidemic spread, and I could only stop it by starting the cars off.

There is little doubt that our constant patrols kept the whole region enclosed by a line passing through Cassel, Hazebrouck, Aire, and Hesdin clear of Germans, and undoubtedly saved Boulogne and other open towns on the Channel from being rushed and attacked by the enemy. It must be remembered that during this period, the only places that were garrisoned were Dunkirk and Calais, and that the remainder of the country was absolutely open to the Germans. The Germans were undoubtedly misled as to the strength of my force, and were unaware that I was totally unsupported. I think that we deserve some little credit for saving a number of towns and villages from serious damage, and the inhabitants from ill-treatment.

I constantly received assistance from the postal employees, who were very prompt in informing me of the presence of Germans.

The *gendarmerie* are worthy of every praise for the manner in which they kept to their stations, generally carrying on their usual duties in plain clothes.

A remarkable feature was the lack of appreciation of the value of the telephone displayed by the Germans, as one would have thought they would have destroyed all telephone lines, thus hampering my work.

One day, whilst coming back from a motorcar reconnaissance, driving alone with Nalder, having sent the rest of the party on ahead, I came across a car standing at the roadside evidently in trouble with a puncture. I stopped to see who they were. The party consisted of a lady and two men in civilian clothes. As they appeared to be rather amateurs at the job we did the work for them, and then stayed and had tea with them, as they were provided with a Primus stove and a tea basket. The lady was a most delightful person and cheery to the last degree. They said they were going to Paris.

Leaving them, I went on to Dunkirk, where I reported at the French H.Q.; having seen the general, a staff-officer spoke to me, and said, "If you ever come across a lady who goes by the name of Madame B——, and who is driving a blue two-seater car, shoot her without compunction. She is a most dangerous spy." He described her to me, and I really hadn't the heart to tell him that not only had I met her, but I had helped her on her way.

I would personally have hated to have shot her.

CHAPTER 6

Morbecque and Antwerp

Meanwhile, a disaster had occurred to the aeroplanes detailed for the Zeppelin attacks. They were still at Ostend, whilst Gerrard was in Antwerp making arrangements for the flight. These arrangements included an advanced refuelling base, which was to be guarded by Belgian armoured cars under Baron de Caters, the well-known racing motorist. While this was in progress a very strong gale had wrecked all the aeroplanes. The Air Ministry then ordered me to take charge of the flight, which had up to date been on detached duty under Gerrard. I had to provide them with the best aeroplanes we could scrape up from my Squadron. I sent Gerrard the three best machines we had, one of them being No. 50, my own, which I had flown for over a year.

It was a great wrench parting with her; but the Antwerp scheme was all-important. I fully expected never to fly her again; but fortunately, she was returned to me after Antwerp fell, and I flew her during the remainder of our stay in France, and also at the Dardanelles, where she was the sole survivor of our original 1914 machines. She went right through the Dardanelles Campaign, doing a lot of useful work, though at the last I must say I only flew her occasionally simply for old acquaintance' sake.

In order to save the long journeys from Dunkirk I now moved to new headquarters at Morbecque, installing them in an old *château* close to the Motte au Bois Château, which Sippe had found, about 3 miles from Hazebrouck, along the Béthune road. The *château* was in rather a dilapidated condition, but anything with a roof on it suited us in those days. The officers and office staff occupied the house, whilst the men lived in tents in the garden. I had quite a strong force at Morbecque, consisting of about 180 marines and 30 R.N.A.S. ratings.

Living at the Château Motte au Bois was Madame la Baronne de la Grange, who had remained there all the time. When various parties of Germans arrived, her behaviour had so impressed them that they had left the village untouched.

I saw a great deal of Madame de la Grange. She was a most indefatigable worker for the Allies throughout the war. Several distinguished soldiers, including Lord Allenby, stayed at her house during the war, and she used to treat them as her guests. I did my humble bit in later years by assisting to get her rewarded with the Legion of Honour and *Croix de Guerre*.

Several years after the war, she came to see me at Malta. She hadn't changed a bit, just the same energetic charming *grande dame*, with a wonderful memory.

Major Armstrong soon got the place into a state of defence, digging trenches all over the estate and rendering it unsafe to walk about at night, if nothing else. Some of his works were most ingenious—three large trees, for example, alongside roads, with their trunks practically sawn through, which could be made to fall across and block up the road if some men pulled on a rope. The two armoured lorries were placed at the cross-roads each night, with a party of men on board each; and an armoured car was kept fully manned on the road outside the house throughout the night.

These armoured lorries were made by the "*Forges et Chantres de France*" to the designs of Felix Samson and myself, with the idea of providing protection for a force of Infantry who could accompany the cars. The armour was boiler-plate, and in practice at short range it was of little use, but effective at long range. Twelve marines could be taken in each, and loopholes were cut in the sides for rifle fire. The lorries carried the weight very well, but in practice they were found to be too slow to keep up with the cars. This handicapped the cooperation between cars and infantry; and we eventually went back to the scheme of carrying the riflemen in light touring cars.

In addition to our defensive arrangements, patrols were daily carried out by a section of cars; and a cyclist force was raised from the marines. This consisted of twelve men under the command of Bill Samson. At first, they were not capable of going on very long patrols, owing to the advanced age of the cyclists, and their strong objection to exceed a speed of about 5 miles an hour, and also to the reluctance they displayed in passing *auberges*; but in time they developed into quite an efficient unit, and did some useful reconnaissance work through the Nieppe Forest. O'Caffrey started a boy scout service, collecting a number of youngsters of all ages who knew the country well.

We provided each with a bicycle and paid them 1 *franc* a day. They were most useful, as they could get into places which were occupied by Germans without fear of capture. On one or two occasions these boys brought us valuable information.

A convenient field close to the *château* provided an excellent aerodrome, once we had cut down some of the high trees which surrounded it. I intended to keep the headquarters flight at Morbecque with the intention of carrying out from there the patrols over Douai, Cambrai, and Valenciennes.

The aeroplane organisation now was as follows:

Headquarters flight at Morbecque. This sounds grand, but at this time only consisted of No. 42.
One flight at Dunkirk, to carry out patrol against hostile aircraft over the Coast Zone.
One flight at Antwerp for the Zeppelin Sheds attack.
One flight in the course of organisation standing by to go to Lille when the French or English should occupy that town.

The aeroplane repair depot was kept at Dunkirk. The armoured cars and motor transport were stationed at Morbecque.

The whole of the Morbecque force were practised daily in the operation of moving camp, and we were soon well enough trained to be on the road within half an hour, with everything loaded up in the lorries. When we moved to Morbecque, the majority of the marines had marched from Dunkirk on foot, in order to give them some march practice. They arrived in very good condition after the long journey, which was very creditable, taking into consideration the veteran character of the force. They were a splendid lot of men, and what they may have lacked in activity they amply made up for in marksmanship and steadiness in action.

Shortly after our arrival at Morbecque, the new type of armoured cars arrived from England in driblets of twos and threes. The armour protection had been designed at home, without consulting us; and we did not like the finished article at all. It is funny how often the man on the spot is overruled by the man in the office at home. The engine and chassis were very well protected; so was the driver, who was stowed in a little house; but the rest of the crew were totally unprotected. I considered this a very faulty design, as protection should be afforded to the crew; otherwise, any man behind a hedge could pick them off with ease. The chassis used were Rolls Royce, Talbot, and Wolseley.

Of these the Rolls Royce proved by far the most reliable and suitable.

Major Risk, Royal Marines, who belonged to the R.N.A.S., and had been an old Eastchurch pilot, came out in charge of the first lot.

Another arrival was Lord Annesley, who was sent out with his own car, which he had armoured himself in some local garage. With him came his driver, Ryan, who became two years afterwards my coxswain in H.M.S. *Ben-my-Chree*, after he had gone through the Dardanelles campaign with the old squadron.

Annesley's armour was a very comic home-made affair. Although as far as design went it was excellent, it was only soft iron, and very inadequately secured to the car; bits of armour used to drop off every now and then, and somebody unkindly said that Annesley must have been in the old-iron trade. We soon removed his armour, and his car was used for despatch work. Annesley himself was a great fellow, and we soon found him indispensable.

At Morbecque I had the following officers with me: Osmond as First Lieutenant, Staff-Surgeon Wells, Briggs, Bill and Felix Samson, Lord Annesley, O'Caffrey, Armstrong in command of the marines; while Lathbury, Graham, Coode, and Williams were the other marine officers.

I had a great disappointment one day, as I received a message from England to say that a new aeroplane was being sent over to me. I determined to keep this for my own use, and told Dunkirk to send it on to Morbecque when it arrived. I was in the office when Osmond dashed in and said: "Commander, here comes your new machine." I ran out to the aerodrome, and was in time to see it smashed beyond repair. The pilot had made a very bad misjudgement, and had come in over the trees far too high. He touched the ground about twenty yards from the opposite side of the aerodrome, and naturally went full tilt into a tree; with resulting complete deletion of my new aeroplane. He hadn't hurt himself. What I said to him need not be repeated. Afterwards he did splendid work in the war, but I don't think he has ever forgotten the first time he met me.

On September 16th the French told me that a new Maurice Farman seaplane had just arrived at Boulogne from Paris. They were very keen to get it taken away from there owing to the risk of capture, for it must be remembered that there were absolutely no troops at Boulogne, and it was for a long time quite on the cards that raiding parties of Germans could have come into the town and done what they liked. In fact, the danger of this was so apparent that the British Naval authorities had evacuated the town. I told the French that I would fly the seaplane to Dunkirk and use it, until its rightful owners claimed it.

We found the seaplane waiting all ready for us, on the beach with a Farman mechanic in attendance; it was a two-float type, fitted with a 100-h.p. Renault engine. After some delay we started off, a French officer coming as my passenger. It was pretty late in the evening before we got away, and darkness came on before we had passed Calais. It was the first time I had ever flown a seaplane at night, although I had often done night flying in aeroplanes. I was rather handicapped, being without any lights at all with which to look at the instruments, and also it being to me a new type of machine; in addition, we were rather worried about the reception we might meet with on arrival at Dunkirk, fully expecting to be greeted with a hot fire.

We got in, however, without any trouble, and I alighted safely inside the harbour. I was rather pleased with myself until my French friend embraced me. It was his first flight.

On September 17th I decided to go to Antwerp myself to see how the preparations for the attack on the Zeppelin sheds were getting on, as the affair seemed to be hanging fire. The Air Department were anxious that it should be attempted as soon as possible. As we were so hard up for aeroplanes—what we had being required for reconnaissance patrols—I went by motorcar, and selected Sub-Lieutenant Bernard Isaac to drive me there in his Daimler. He was commonly called the "Old Man," presumably because he had very little hair on his head, and he was getting on in years also. We had a most interesting journey to Antwerp, and Ghent struck me as full of the most beautiful buildings. The road was an awful one to travel on, being mostly *pavée*. Close to Antwerp we found barbed-wire entanglements being erected; they looked deep enough to stop anything.

We had some trouble at the bridge of boats because we had not the password for the night; but a little talk with a Belgian officer provided the missing word, and we managed to get across it into the town. We went to the St. Antoine Hotel, where Gerrard met us, and I made the final arrangements for the flight. He had got everything organised, and was only awaiting a favourable day. The "Old Man" and I had a most excellent dinner that night, although it was rather spoilt for us, as we felt a very shabby pair of individuals in comparison to the other guests at the hotel, who were all in evening dress.

The British Minister with his family and the Legation staff were seated at the next table to ours, and I must confess I felt very much ashamed of my war-worn uniform. I had a long talk with the minister that night after dinner, although I was so tired that I kept on falling asleep; he gave me the impression that Antwerp would never be taken. It fell three weeks later, however.

The aeroplanes at Antwerp now consisted of 2 B.E. Biplanes and 1 80-h.p. Sopwith Biplane; 2 Sopwith Tabloids were daily expected to arrive from England.

On the 18th a move was made on the part of the Dunkirk garrison, a battalion of infantry being sent to Lille. This made the road between Lille and Cassel fairly safe from *Uhlan* raiding parties.

Some very valuable reconnaissance work was carried out between September 18th and 22nd by my aeroplanes and motorcars, Major Armstrong, with a force of five cars, getting very close to Cambrai. In fact, he got closer to this town than we ever did either before or after; he had a small fight with a German patrol.

On September 22nd the long-expected attack was made on the Zeppelin sheds. Four aeroplanes started out from Antwerp, flown by Major Gerrard, Lieutenant Collet, Lieutenant Marix, and Lieutenant Spencer Grey, the latter carrying Lieutenant Newton Clare as passenger. They started soon after daylight. The weather was very suitable at first; but they ran into a fog at the River Roer, which extended as far as the Rhine.

Collet was the only one who located his objective, and he made a splendidly determined attack on the Zeppelin shed at Düsseldorf. Unfortunately, he was too low for his bombs to function, as at his low altitude combined with the height of the shed sufficient time was not permitted for the safety fan of the bombs to unwind, thus preventing the explosion of the bomb when it hit. One of the three bombs that missed the shed exploded just outside the door and killed two or three soldiers.

All the aeroplanes safely returned to Antwerp.

CHAPTER 7

A Mixed Engagement at Orchies

On September 20th the Right Hon. Mr. Winston Churchill came over to Dunkirk, and a conference, which I attended, was held at the French Headquarters to decide upon the methods of carrying out attacks on the German Lines of Communication in the zone including Cambrai and Valenciennes.

It was felt that with my motorcar force and the French garrison at Dunkirk something might be achieved.

Mr. Churchill was very keen on attempts being made, as he evidently considered that successful raids might affect the situation at the Front. The cars alone could not achieve very much; but working with the support of artillery and infantry certain important points like railway bridges might be attacked and destroyed.

After considerable discussion it was decided that a force consisting of a brigade of French Territorial Infantry with a Squadron of Algerian Volunteer Cavalry, popularly known as Goumiers, and a battery of *soixante-quinze* field guns were to proceed to Douai and operate from there.

I was placed at the disposal of the general-in-command, with as big a force of cars as I could muster. Some of my aeroplanes were to be based at Douai as soon as it was considered safe to use the aerodrome at that place.

General Plantey, Second-in-command of the Dunkirk garrison, was placed in command of the force. He was a very gallant soldier with a great deal of colonial service, and I found him a most delightful man to serve under, deeply appreciative of anything that one could do, and always helpful in difficulties. The failure of our little enterprise was, I consider, by no means his fault. Meanwhile, Brigadier-General Sir G. Aston, Royal Marines, had arrived at Dunkirk, shortly to be followed by his brigade of marines; the same force and commander with whom we had been at Ostend.

I was placed under General Aston's command, as far as ground operations were concerned; but exercised independent command as regards aeroplane work.

I left Morbecque on September 22nd with a strong force of cars, two of them with boiler-plate protection, and two heavy lorries similarly armoured. Major Armstrong, Captain Lathbury, Captain Williams, of the marines, Lieutenant Bill Samson, Lieutenant O'Caffrey, Sub-Lieutenant Nalder, Lord Annesley, and the ever-present Staff-Surgeon Hardy Vesey Wells were with me, and the crews consisted of sixteen R.N.A.S. and twenty-seven marines.

We all expected that we were about to take part in some tough fighting, as there was little doubt that the cars would have to undertake the *rôle* of advance guard in the attacks which the force were intended to make. I certainly considered that we would meet tougher opposition from the German infantry than we had encountered up to date from their cavalry. As far as I could judge, my little party were full of fight, and simply aching for a scrap.

Arriving at Douai at 8 a.m., I found the French had already detrained, and I was immediately summoned to a conference held at the railway station. Here I found General Plantey with his staff, consisting of two old friends of mine, one a Naval officer. It was decided to make attacks on certain sections of the railway line.

Whilst preparations for these attacks were being made, the cars were to carry out a reconnaissance towards Cantin, Somain, and Bagnicourt to clear up the situation.

One battalion was immediately dispatched to Orchies, about 8 miles from Douai. I left Douai with eight cars, all carrying machine-guns, two of them with boiler-plate protection, and two cars with marines. On arriving at Lewarde, I received information that there was a party of cavalry in Aniche, and a large body of cavalry about 2 miles outside Aniche on the Valenciennes road.

Leaving the remainder of my party in a good position at some cross-roads about a mile from Aniche, I went off with my two armoured cars and another one to see what we could do.

On reaching the outskirts of Aniche I took a side road, intending to go right round the town to the Valenciennes or German side of it, in order to get what Germans there were in Aniche between me and my main body, who were well concealed, and also hoping to cut off the Aniche Germans from their main body. Unfortunately, the citizens, who were all hiding in their houses, rushed out immediately they saw us and started making such a terrible noise, shouting out "*Vive les Anglais*," etc., that all the hopes of a surprise were at an end.

The only thing to do was to go full speed for the main square of the town, where I heard there were some *Uhlans*. Off we set, and dashing into the square we found five *Uhlans* leading their horses up the Lewarde road. Directly they heard us they left their horses and ran into houses. We got in some shots before they could reach shelter and killed three of them. The horses bolted towards Lewarde, and I hoped they would be picked up by my main body, who would then see that we were in a fight.

We now came under a hot fire from close quarters, as some more Germans were in houses only about 20 or 30 yards off us; they were able to shoot right down into the cars from upper-storey windows. I jumped out of the car for the double purpose of giving "Ginger" Walsh ample room to work his gun, and also to try to get a shot off with a rifle grenade at a German who kept popping out of an upper window and firing a revolver at us. Nalder, my driver, got hit in the knee by a bullet which penetrated the armour, and he was in a bad way.

After about three minutes of this excitement, we silenced the opposition, principally through some good work by Lathbury, who got off a Lewis-gun burst at some Germans who kept exposed a bit too long.

Civilians now called out to us that a large party of cavalry were coming up; so, I decided to withdraw from the square and fall back upon our main body, well satisfied with our reconnaissance. Nalder was very badly crippled, and after he had turned the car round he collapsed.

Walsh and I had rather a job getting him out of the driving seat, so that I could take the wheel; two others of our little party were wounded. We returned to our main body by the same route as we had come; arriving at their place of concealment, I found that they had got four of the horses. I was rather pleased at this capture, as I have always been a horse lover. One of the horses, an English thoroughbred, was an officer's charger, the others were troop-horses. The charger I kept for myself, and he went through France and the Dardanelles with me.

Wells, after examining the wounded, said that Nalder was badly hurt, as his knee was one mass of small punctures from bits of the soft iron armour. He immediately sent him and the other two, who had only received slight wounds, off to Douai in the ambulance with a report of our fight. I found that I had spoilt my overcoat, as somebody had shot a couple of holes in it, without touching me.

On examining the cars, we found them riddled with bullet holes; but all fit for action. The boiler-plate was as we had feared worse than useless at short range.

I remained between Lewarde and Aniche, hoping the Germans would come on, as we were in an excellent position, with a good field of fire along three roads. An amusing feature was the steam tram, which continued to ply between Aniche and Lewarde; it made two trips whilst we were there, each time bringing us back information of the Germans, who were stated to be about 300 strong, and were occupying the outer houses in Aniche. The tram driver told me we had killed three and wounded four or five. The driver was so keen on his intelligence work that he even ran a special trip.

After waiting an hour, we saw two German cyclists coming along the road. I gave orders not to fire until they were right on top of us. To our disgust they stopped when about 200 yards off, turned round, and pedalled back to Aniche. As after another thirty minutes nothing happened, I took three cars and set off to get into Aniche by a side road that approached it from the opposite direction to that we had used before.

We went along expecting to run up against the *Huns* every minute, but reached Aniche without a sign of them. Pushing on into the town, we heard that they had left about half an hour ago, in the direction of Valenciennes. I therefore returned to my little army, and carried on with our reconnaissance as ordered without coming across any more signs of the enemy.

General Plantey was pleased with the results of our tour, and said that we had done what would have taken his cavalry three or four days.

That evening a French infantry patrol brought in a German motor-bus, which they had ambushed close to Flines de Raches, which is about 4 miles from Douai.

The half-dozen Germans in it had got separated from their convoy, and, losing their way, had got on to the wrong road. The bus was of covered type and single-decked; its interior was a most gory spectacle, as the Germans had put up a stout fight, and the French had finished them off with the bayonet.

General Plantey presented me with the bus; but unfortunately in the partial evacuation next day, it was included in the vehicles that left, and I never got hold of it again. Its log-book provided most interesting reading, as it recorded the daily runs in the first advance of the Germans through Belgium.

Douai was a delightful town, with remarkably fine buildings, clean streets, and some very high-class shops. The Hôtel de Ville, in which the general established his headquarters, was a most imposing building, possessing a large courtyard. The inhabitants were still in occupation of the town, apparently following their usual vocations, and on the surface paying little attention to the war; at least that was the impression that I gained.

Going into a barber's shop to get my hair cut, I asked the operator how the Germans had behaved when they were in the town.

"*Oh, mon Capitaine,* they were terrible; the *cavaliers* used to walk their horses on to the pavements and make them dance."

This didn't strike me as being a hideous crime to commit; but on the contrary as providing a most interesting spectacle.

He went on to say that now the Allies had arrived all would be well, and Douai would now be quite safe from further trouble. I didn't spoil this satisfactory state of mind by hinting that our arrival would probably stir up things a bit.

The staff proposed that we should take up our quarters in the barracks; so being of an inquiring mind I went to have a look at them before accepting the offer. They were a fine-looking lot of buildings, but the Germans had used them; one look at the barrack rooms was sufficient, as the evidence of recent German occupation was quite enough to deter the strongest. I therefore requested that we might have a second choice; so, we were given the use of a big school. This proved ideal, as it was very clean, and had an excellent courtyard, surrounded by a high wall, which provided space for all our cars.

Early in the morning next day, September 24th, intelligence was received that the Battalion of the 6th Regiment of Territorial Infantry, who had occupied Orchies in order to guard the route between Lille and Douai, were being heavily attacked by two battalions of Germans. The message said that the French were being hard pressed and reinforcements were asked for.

General Plantey sent for me, and ordered me to proceed at once to Orchies with all my cars and three French cars, and see what I could do. He said he would send further reinforcements as soon as possible. I set off with six cars, some protected, the others not, and the three

French cars, one of which had a gun.

At Raches I met a French cavalry patrol, who reported that some German infantry had got across the Douai-Orchies road at Bois des Flines. Going on, until I was close to this wood, I halted and sent Armstrong with two cars to proceed a short distance along the Faumont road, whilst I went on along the Orchies road, hoping, if the report was correct, that we would get the Germans between my two parties. I left orders with Armstrong to wait in position for half an hour, then to follow me on to Orchies.

As I got to the junction of the Auchy-Orchies and Douai-Orchies roads, I saw part of Orchies in flames, and heard heavy rifle fire coming from the direction of the town.

As the situation was obscure, I left one of my cars with the three French cars, in a good position overlooking the town, with orders that they were to await Armstrong's arrival, and then tell him that I required him to take up a good position with the cars and cover the Auchy-Orchies and Douai-Orchies roads, and the southern approaches to Orchies.

With the remainder of my force, which consisted of the two protected and an unprotected car, together with Wells and his ambulance, I set off into the town to see what could be done. As soon as we got to the outskirts, we came across a French soldier who, on being questioned, said he was on his way to Douai for reinforcements. I said: "We are the reinforcements."

He replied: "*Pas assez, encore plus,*" or words to that effect. Anyhow, he seemed in a great hurry, so we let him go. Luckily, round the next corner I came across a second one, also looking for reinforcements. I made him get on to my car, and come along to show me where his pals were.

I went on a bit farther towards the sounds of heaviest firing, rather like the old general, Napoleon, I believe it was, who said, "You were never wrong if you went towards the sound of cannon." Passing through the centre of the town, I got towards the south-east corner, all the time undergoing a fairly brisk fusillade which seemed to come from all directions. Eventually, I came across some French infantry occupying the lower rooms and courtyard of a large house; as they would not come out, I went on a bit farther, in my endeavour to locate the enemy. I soon found the latter, who were lining a railway embankment; as far as I could discover, the only Frenchmen actively engaged were a party of about forty, under Captain de Maroguerye, who were holding out amongst some cottages on the outskirts of the town.

I left two of my cars with them, and then went on with the third car for about 200 yards towards the enemy, where I could get some shelter behind a house, with at the same time a good field of fire. I sent Bateman and Walsh to guard my left flank, and then opened fire with my machine-gun on the Germans, who had started to advance from the railway embankment.

Our fire caught them completely by surprise, and was very effective, as we were at close range on their flank. They halted, broke, and ran back to the embankment, leaving a number of dead behind. I then got the other two cars up into action, and Captain de Maroguerye with his stout band came up to my position.

I decided that the only thing to do was to attack, and attack quickly, whilst the Germans were still shaken as a result of our fire. We were too few at present, but remembering the Frenchmen I had seen farther back in the town, I felt that if we could collect some of them, we might try an attack. So, I sent off two of the doughty Frenchmen to collect as many as they could, as I intended to advance in five minutes. Meanwhile, I told Maroguerye, who had placed himself under my command, to spread his men along behind a low wall.

Before my time-limit expired I found I had about 200 Frenchmen, so considering this a sufficient force Maroguerye and I hastily organised them into three lines. After a brief explanation of the plan of attack I ordered "fix bayonets," and then leading the first line, I advanced upon the Germans, making short rushes of about 20 yards, with each line in turn; whilst one line advanced the others kept up a heavy fire. My cars kept up with us along the road on our left flank. The Germans of course were firing at us the whole time, but, as the results proved, they were very wild.

Unfortunately, just as we were still about a hundred yards short of our objective, the Germans fled to a wood, which was close behind; it was bad luck, for my Frenchmen were now full of fight, and we were about to complete our attack with a bayonet charge. I now had quite a job stopping my little army from chasing after the Germans into the woods, which I didn't consider advisable, as the enemy were undoubtedly in superior force, and my crowd would have lost all cohesion.

The cars of course would have been of little assistance in the woods, and without their moral support the future was uncertain. I therefore halted at the railway embankment and organised my force for either defence or another attack.

I counted eighteen dead Germans between the embankment and our first position; our losses were one Frenchman killed and two wounded.

Personally, I thought we had done pretty well, as these old Territorials could not be expected to carry on like regular troops, especially as there was only one officer in evidence. Concerning this fact, I later reported to General Plantey. The general was very upset, and immediately caused an investigation to be made. He was, however, very pleased with Captain Maroguerye, who had undoubtedly behaved with resolution, and had obviously determined to hold his ground to the last. His behaviour was all the more creditable as he was a bit of a veteran. I now set about clearing up the situation and preparing for the future.

I sent off one of my cars back into the town with orders to send out to me any troops found, and then to go on to the high ground behind the town, where I had left my other car. If Armstrong was there, he was to be told to collect all the Frenchmen he could, and organise a defensive line where he was. Thus, he could provide me with a position to fall back upon, or additional support in case I advanced.

Armstrong, who had just arrived, sent in the three French cars to scour the town; luckily these cars got a view of the Germans who had been fighting us, and saw them retiring from the wood. The cars opened fire with their machine-gun, and killed about a dozen.

Whilst I was waiting, a battery of artillery arrived from Douai, escorted by about thirty cavalry. The artillery took up a position close to Armstrong, and seeing large bodies of Germans retiring, they opened fire on them, and on the wood in front of me. This finally finished the Germans, as they cleared off in the direction of home; some of them didn't reach home, as they tried to cross some open ground which was within range of my cars' guns.

I sent word to the artillery to cease fire, as some of their shells were coming close to us. Meanwhile, the cavalry charged across-country in fine style, going past my right flank. What they were charging at, or what subsequently happened to them, I don't know, as I couldn't see from where I was, and never saw them again.

This account may be somewhat involved; but it must be remembered that the whole situation was obscure, and I had to deal with things as they came, with rather a vague idea of what force I had. A message was now brought, asking me to go to the post office, as General Plantey wished to speak to me on the telephone.

Arriving at the post office, I found the sole occupant a young girl, who said she had remained at her post during the whole fight. She was remarkably calm and collected, and I feel sure she would have sold a stamp or sent a telegram just as sedately as she did on ordinary days. She certainly provided an example which others had not followed.

I was immediately put through to General Plantey, who asked me to explain the situation. I told him that we had driven off the Germans; but that I didn't think it advisable to advance, as they were in superior force, and my troops were a bit uncertain and untrained. I said that if I remained with my cars, I could hold the town; but if I left, the infantry alone could not do so.

The general said that he wanted the artillery sent back to Douai immediately. I replied that I would have to send a strong escort of infantry or some of my cars, as there was every chance, according to my latest information, that the Germans would get across the Douai road.

He decided therefore that I should remain in command of the whole force, evacuate Orchies, and retire to Douai.

With the invaluable help of Major Armstrong, I got our little army, which now consisted of almost 350 infantry, a battery of artillery, an ammunition column, the French cars, and my own cars, organised for the march.

Armstrong went off as advance guard with four cars to the Flines de Raches to hold the cross-roads. I then sent off 100 infantry along the main road with flanking parties in the fields. Five minutes after they had started, I sent off three batches of twenty infantry with orders for each one to halt when they had reached certain points of the route and await the arrival of the artillery, after which they were to follow it on, with my two remaining cars and the French gun car acting as rearguard, and intending to follow on when the artillery had got 2 miles along the road.

The main body had hardly gone ten minutes when I discovered parties of Germans advancing across our old friend the railway embankment and entering the town. Opening fire, we killed four or five; this stopped their further advance, until we started off to rejoin the main body, which I found halted at Coutiches.

After half an hour's rest I once more started off the whole force, remaining behind as before to cover their rear.

Although we kept on seeing small parties of the enemy, we did not have any further fighting, as the Germans, evidently not appreciating our machine-guns, were content to keep at long range. They satisfied their martial ardour, however, by burning Coutiches after we had left it at dusk.

Soon after I left Coutiches O'Caffrey arrived bearing an urgent message from the general to say that Douai was being attacked, and that he wanted me to send him the artillery as quickly as possible. I therefore ordered the battery commander to trot the rest of the way to Douai; at the same time, as the situation was obscure and I received three reports to say that the French were falling back from Douai, I sent O'Caffrey to Douai with two cars and half the Infantry. The remainder of the force I used to escort the ammunition column, whose horses were very tired, to Le Forest, where they would be in touch with the troops at Lille, whilst at the same time in a good position either to retire or return to Douai at daybreak.

Having seen this party safely into Le Forest, I returned to Douai with the remainder of my cars.

On arrival there I found things had quietened down, and the German attack had petered out: probably it was only a reconnaissance in force.

The whole incident was rather interesting from the point of view of a British naval officer commanding an Allied force in a shore battle. Personally, when I joined the navy as a naval cadet, I never anticipated that I would have to fight as a soldier, especially in command of Frenchmen.

CHAPTER 8

We Make Use of a Trench

Next day I made a long reconnaissance with all my cars to Arras. We had no fighting during the trip, and only saw one small *Uhlan* patrol, who escaped us by galloping across-country.

In Arras I found a battalion of colonial infantry with a squadron of Algerian cavalry. As at Douai we were totally unaware of their presence there, I telephoned to General Plantey telling him that this force had just arrived, but would only remain in Arras for a few hours, as they were momentarily expecting orders to retire. As far as I could gather, they were acting as flank guard for a French division, which was being hurried up in the direction of Lens. I got back to Douai about 3 p.m., meeting *en route* my old friends the French cars, who were very pleased with themselves, as they had fallen across a patrol of *Uhlans* and killed three of them.

Having made my report to the general, I sent off my men to have a rest, as they were all fagged out, and proceeded to follow their example myself. I had hardly laid down, when I was called to the telephone and asked to go round to H.Q. Going there in the Talbot touring-car with Felix Samson and Lord Annesley, I found the general had left for Le Racquet, leaving word for me to follow, as he was about to attack the Germans in that sector, and would like me to see the fight. Sensing trouble, I telephoned to Armstrong to get a section of cars ready, and come out with them to Le Racquet as soon as possible. Meanwhile, the three of us set out after General Plantey.

Arriving at a spot about 2 miles from Douai, I found an artillery duel proceeding, and the general standing on the road behind a trench with about 500 infantry lying down in the fields on either side of the road.

Our guns were about a mile behind us, firing high explosive and shrapnel at the crest of a hill, about 1,000 yards away on our left front.

The German artillery, apparently about 1¼ miles distant from us, was replying to the French guns, with every now and then a shell in our direction. When the general saw me, he said he was pleased we had arrived, as we could be of great service. He required a reconnaissance carried out to Cantin to discover what force the enemy were in.

This seemed an extremely unpleasant job to tackle, as Cantin was a village about 3¼ miles away, directly along the road we were on. It appeared perfectly evident that between us and Cantin there were not only the German guns but plenty of German infantry. I must confess that the three of us did not at all relish the idea of ambling into the whole German Army and the local Von Kluck, in a touring car; but the job had to be attempted, if only to keep up the reputation of the R.N.A.S.

After an examination of our arsenal, which we found to consist of two rifles with ten rounds of ammunition, and three automatic pistols, we set off, passing through the two trenches that guarded the road.

About 100 yards beyond the trenches, we found a side-road which branched off to the right for about 300 yards and then followed parallel to the main road. This was just what we wanted, so we followed it.

After going about a mile, I saw a farmhouse close to the roadside on the top of a slight rise; as it appeared to be an excellent spot for the Germans to be occupying, I did not relish the idea of passing it in a car until we had made certain that it was tenanted or otherwise. I therefore stopped when we had got within about 1,000 yards of it, and Annesley turned the car round to face Douai.

My brother and I then proceeded on foot, each taking a rifle. When we had gone about 300 yards, I left my brother as a connecting file and went off myself across the fields towards the farmhouse.

I must explain that the main road here was about 400 yards from our side-road, and that the intervening country consisted of a turnip field; our by-road was slightly below the level of the turnip field, probably about 2 feet or so. I had not gone on more than another hundred yards when I saw a body of cyclists about forty strong pedalling along the main road towards Douai.

I immediately knelt down and fired three rounds at them, and to my delight dropped the two leaders; at the same time Felix opened fire and bagged another. I then ran back towards the car. Felix, having expended all his ammunition, waited for me, and then we ran like hares for Annesley, with bullets buzzing round us like mosquitoes. Annesley afterwards said that we were surrounded with little clouds of

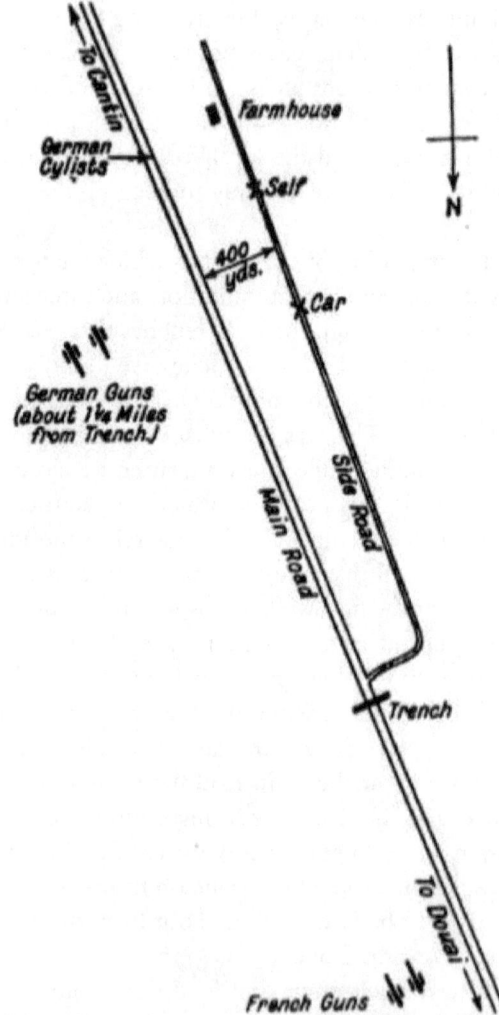

SKETCH MAP OF POSITION ON THE DOUAI—CANTIN ROAD.

dust kicked up by the cyclists' shots at us.

Arriving at the car, we found that a French car had come on the scene. It had a *mitrailleuse*; but they would not open fire, although Annesley had refused to let them fall back. I got into the French car and opened fire with the machine-gun on the Germans, who by this time were behind the trees on the main road.

After expending nearly all our ammunition I decided that the situation had got beyond our capacity to deal with, as the Germans had begun an advance towards us through the turnips. We therefore got on board our cars, and dashed back towards our trench. On arriving there we found that it was held only by a sergeant with about thirty men. There were no signs of any further troops.

I got rid of the rest of the machine-gun ammunition on the Germans, who were now advancing through the fields on either side of the main road. Meanwhile, I dispatched Annesley in our car to Douai first to get hold of Armstrong and bring him out with all my people, and then to tell General Plantey that our reconnaissance had ended up in a battle.

Having no more machine-gun ammunition, Felix and I joined the thirty-one Frenchmen in the two little trenches, where we kept up a hot rifle fire on the Germans, who evidently had been reinforced; but our party, who were unmistakably the better shots, were more than holding their own, and in addition we scored by being in a trench, whilst they had little cover. In about ten minutes the doughty Armstrong arrived on the scene with three cars and ten of my marines, including Sergeant Davis.

As the road only permitted of one car getting into action at a time, my brother got into the leading one and having turned it round, he most gallantly stood on the step and steered it backwards until close up to the trench. Whilst he was doing this, the Germans concentrated their fire on the car, and Felix had a warm time, totally exposed as he was; but once he had reached the trench, and the machine-gun could open fire, the German fire was mastered.

It was rapidly getting dark; therefore, as we were by now only wasting ammunition by continuing when we could only see the enemy by their flashes as they fired, I ordered the cars out of action. I then sent Armstrong back to Douai with two cars to ask for Infantry to be sent out to take over our position, and also to guard our flanks.

It appeared that there were no troops except ourselves outside Douai, and there seemed no reason why the Germans should not carry on a general attack if they felt like it. It was certainly not my job to remain out here; but I decided to remain until somebody-else arrived. Felix, myself, Sergeant Davis, ten of my marines, and the thirty-one Frenchmen occupied the trench. Every now and then the Germans fired a few shots, to which we replied.

We all felt quite happy in the trench until Felix asked Sergeant Davis if the parapet would keep out a bullet. "God bless you, sir, a bullet would go through it like through a pat of butter," Davis replied. This slightly damped our spirits.

After about half an hour or so some French Infantry arrived, having been collected by Armstrong. I turned over our position to them and returned to Douai in the armoured car, which I had kept in reserve.

The Germans must have been poor marksmen, as not one of us had even a scratch; the cars, however, were fairly plastered with bullet holes.

Going round to the general, I found him rather depressed, as things were not going any too well, and he was not receiving much support from some of his command. He asked me to telephone to General Aston, our marine general at Dunkirk, and ask him to send out a battalion of marines to Douai, as he felt that with this stiffening something might be achieved. General Aston, however, refused to agree to this, as his force was not yet organised, and he didn't want to split it up.

Personally, I will always regard this as a fatal mistake, as if the marines had been sent, we could easily not only have held out at Douai, but made some vigorous attacks upon the enemy's line of communications. As will be seen, we lost Douai.

General Aston went on the say I was to return to Morbecque with my force, as the Douai operations had now obviously failed, and that I would be more useful elsewhere.

I didn't like to leave General Plantey, and persuaded General Aston to allow me to leave behind a section of cars at Douai to provide some moral and practical support to that tough old warrior. The next day, September 26th, after a cordial farewell to General Plantey, who promised to telephone through to me if he wanted assistance, I left for Morbecque. Arriving there, I found General Aston, and we had a long talk about the future.

It was decided, rather against his will, that I should continue to occupy Morbecque; but he would support me by sending a battalion of marines to Cassel, so that if heavily attacked I would have some force upon which to retire.

I felt quite happy about Morbecque, as with my cars and other arms I had no fears of being surprised. I did everything possible to prevent this happening, also to keep a close watch on the country, and to keep open the route to Douai. Bombardier Brown and another marine were stationed at Béthune telephone exchange in order to form a link between that town and myself. In addition, I kept an armoured car and an armoured lorry with eight marines at Béthune during daylight hours ready to mop up any patrol that came near, and to provide a close reinforcement for any of my patrols or my Douai detachment. Daily patrols of cyclists and armoured cars were sent all over the country.

Meanwhile, we carried on as much aeroplane work as we could, and made, amongst other reconnaissances, two bomb attacks on the railway line between Cambrai and Valenciennes.

On September 27th Captain Williams, who was at Douai in command of three Rolls Royce armoured cars of the new Admiralty pattern, which provided practically no protection for the crew except for the driver, had a fight with five German cyclists about three-quarters of a mile east of Lewarde.

The Germans took cover behind a haystack, so it became an Infantry affair, as the cars could not get into action. Williams soon won a victory, although the Germans put up a stout fight. One German was killed and four wounded and taken prisoners. Our casualties were Petty Officer Harper and Able Seaman Walsh seriously wounded, and Captain Williams slightly wounded. Harper and "Ginger" Walsh were two of my best men, and Walsh had always formed one of my car's crew.

Unfortunately, when Douai fell, they were both too bad to be moved, and they were the first Eastchurch men to be taken prisoners by the Germans.

Cavrois O'Caffrey was with Williams in this fight, and his medical knowledge gained as a Jesuit missionary came in very useful.

Both the fight and the reconnaissance were really good work, as Williams had got well behind the German outpost line.

As it was evident that a stronger force was required at Douai, I sent off Armstrong with Captain Lathbury and Felix Samson with three armoured cars as reinforcements, meanwhile recalling Williams, whose wound kept him out of action for some little time, to Morbecque.

On the 28th I had a crash in old No. 42. This aeroplane was really on her last legs; but as we were so woefully short of aeroplanes, we had to use her. As soon as I left the ground the engine stopped dead. I was faced with the alternative of attempting a turn which would have landed her in some trenches full of marines or of charging the trees in front of me.

I chose the trees, and luckily managed to find a soft one. The aeroplane remained hung up in the branches about 30 feet in the air, and I escaped without a scratch; but No. 42 had flown her last flight.

It was then decided to send a battalion of our marines to Lille. As some of them were going by road, I received orders to guard the route. I sent out all my cars to cover the road, and in addition Bill Samson with his cyclists was dispatched to Bailleul, and from there to return towards Cassel until he met the marines. I set off in a touring-car, later in the day, accompanied by Major Risk, with the intention of seeing that our patrols were doing their job, and also to inspect Lille aerodrome, as I was going to send Davies there with a flight of aeroplanes to work with the marines.

It was a lucky thing I set off, as when I had got about 3 miles from Bailleul I came across some lorries loaded with marines. They had come to a stop and the marines were debussing at full speed and lining the hedges. I asked what was the trouble, and was told that some German cyclists were coming along the road. Suspecting who these were, I jumped out and got to the leading marines, arriving just in time to stop them opening fire upon Bill and his elderly marine cyclists, who were solemnly pedalling along, well satisfied with life after a good meal at the Bailleul hotel.

All the arrangements for guarding the route had worked admirably, and once more armoured cars had demonstrated their utility.

Risk and I went on to Lille ahead of the marines, and after visiting the aerodrome, which I found to be a first-class one, we went to see Nalder in the hospital. He was in good spirits, although he had been through a bad time. He was delighted to see us, and more so when he heard that the marines were going to occupy the town, as well as some of the old squadron, who would see that he wasn't abandoned a second time.

Getting back to Morbecque, I got on the telephone to Armstrong, who was having plenty of work at Douai.

He had been out on patrol all day with a troop of volunteer Algerian cavalry nicknamed Goumiers. They were all well-to-do farmers, and were perfect walking arsenals, bristling with every conceivable type of weapon. They were mounted on their own little Algerian ponies, provided with the high perched-up saddle of the country. Certainly, if fierce looks went for anything, one felt some sympathy for the *Uhlan* who came across them.

Near a little village called Gouy Armstrong ran up against some Germans who were occupying two or three cottages; unfortunately, he found it impossible to get the cars close enough to them to do anything, so the job had to be left to the Goumiers, who advanced across the fields.

Through some misunderstanding the resulting action led to the retreat of our Allies. The French subaltern in command displayed great bravery in order to encourage his men. He rode up at a walking pace in full view of the enemy, under a very hot fire, to within about 300 yards or so of their position, halted, and lit a cigarette, and then rode back at the same leisurely pace.

Armstrong told me that it was the finest display of courage he had ever seen. Unfortunately, it was of no practical use.

CHAPTER 9

Excitement at Douai

On September 29th I sent Davies with three aeroplanes to carry out work from Lille, and, in support, some armoured cars under Captain Coode, Royal Marines. Davies's aeroplanes made some excellent flights and obtained good intelligence.

Rainey was missing for three days; but turned up again merry and bright as usual, having had an exciting time with Belgian cyclists and *Uhlans*. Owing to an engine failure he had to make a forced landing, and spent a lively two or three minutes dodging an *Uhlan* round and round his aeroplane, having unfortunately left his pistol in his seat; he had some close shaves from the German's lance. Luckily, just as the situation was getting rather too exciting even for Rainey, some Belgian cyclists arrived and dealt with this *Uhlan*. The aeroplane had to be burnt, as a large body of Germans appeared.

On the evening of the 29th Armstrong telephoned to me that he did not like the situation at Douai, as they were practically in a state of siege, and he thought there was every likelihood of a serious disaster. I immediately set out for Douai with two armoured cars and three touring-cars, at the same time telephoning to Coode at Lille to stand by to go to Douai.

Arriving at Douai, I found that General Plantey was not at all happy as regards the situation. He was very pleased to see us, and said that our presence there would encourage his troops, who, it must be remembered, were all Territorials of uncertain age; he was also very short of officers, and those he had were mostly insufficiently trained.

On the day after my arrival General Plantey sent me out to see what the situation was on his left flank. I carried out a long reconnaissance with my full force, and got into Orchies without finding any Germans. At Auchy, which is about 3 miles from Orchies, I found a battalion of French Infantry, and after a consultation with their colonel it was decided to send a company to Orchies. I therefore went back there, and going through the town got to the position where we had started our fight on September 24th, intending to stay there until the French infantry were in position at the cross-roads behind the town. Whilst waiting for the French to arrive I determined to try my new rifle, and with Armstrong spotting I fired half a dozen shots at a tree. Everybody was at peace with the world, when *ping, ping, ping,* came some shots in reply from the direction of my target. Everybody ran for cover.

We soon settled the opposition, though, as we opened fire with a machine-gun, sweeping in an arc through the trees ahead of us where the shots had come from. Nothing further happened, although we spent another half-hour in position. The French by this time arrived, and I went back to Douai.

The situation now was that there was a battalion between Orchies and Auchy, and nearly 5,000 infantry with one battery of artillery in Douai. As far as I could see there were no outposts outside the town except at Le Racquet, all the remainder of the troops being inside the walls of the town. This appeared to me to be a bad sign. During the evening the Germans shelled Le Racquet, and I was sent out in case an infantry attack followed; but this didn't eventuate, and we suffered some shelling for nothing. I went to bed that night fully expecting some hard fighting next day.

We all slept in our clothes, and I put our school in a good state of defence in case we had a night attack; I felt we could hold it against quite a strong force.

I found that I was perfectly right in my surmise, as the morning found us guarding the barricades at the Ponts de Valenciennes and Cambrai. These barricades were the most comic affairs, having been put up at the last minute, and mostly consisted of wire mattresses and a paving-stone or two. Certainly, they provided no protection. After waiting at these spots for over an hour, and seeing the infantry gradually dwindling away, I came to the conclusion that we would soon be left to fight alone. I telephoned to Captain Coode at Lille to come to Douai at once with his three cars.

I then reported to General Plantey that it would be impossible to hold out with the cars unsupported by infantry, as the Germans would get into the houses, and experience had shown that for house-to-house fighting cars were of little use. It was essential that infantry should occupy the houses near the barricades to prevent the enemy from getting behind the cars. I strongly impressed on General Plantey my opinion, which was either to fall back out of the town and occupy the high ground behind it, or to debouch from the town and attack the enemy. In either operation we would stand a good chance of success, as the armoured cars would prove valuable weapons in a fight outside the town walls; but penned in inside the town, they were seriously handicapped. If the cars had been properly designed, affording protection for the crews, they would, of course, have been fairly useful for street fighting.

After a consultation with his staff and myself, the general decided to evacuate the town, and take up a position behind it on the high ground, where we would be in an excellent place to hold out until the arrival of the reinforcements who were reported to be arriving at Lens and Arras.

The general said that he would depend upon me to guard the retirement of his force along the Hénin-Liétard road. This I guaranteed, as the road passed through country which was very suitable for our style of fighting, and I reckoned that over this sort of ground each car was equal to a company of infantry. I immediately sent off the cars to various points along the route. I had by now no less than eleven fighting cars, about two-thirds of them being armoured. Captain Coode having arrived with his section, I remained at a position about a mile behind the town with two cars, whilst Armstrong went about halfway between the main road and Le Polygone to prevent the enemy advancing through Dorignies.

As soon as I reported we were in position the evacuation of the town commenced, and the wounded, ammunition, and transport were all passed safely through.

When we had got the majority of these away, I received orders to escort them to Hénin-Liétard and Lens. I therefore sent off all my cars except four to carry out this work, keeping these latter with me.

We were very pleased to see arrive from the direction of Beaumont a cavalry patrol of three *cuirassiers*, who stated that they were a reconnaissance patrol from a cavalry division which was close to Beaumont. This meant that reinforcements were within 6 miles of Douai. I sent a car in with this report to Douai, and the car returned with orders from the general for me to come into Douai, as he had decided to hold out in the town. I therefore returned to Douai, sending word to Lathbury to keep a section of cars at Hénin-Liétard until night-time in case the French, who were reported to be detraining at Lens, advanced along that road to Douai. I told him to hold out at this important position in case we were surrounded at Douai, a situation which I considered practically certain to happen, as my party were the only troops preventing the enemy from working round behind the town.

When I arrived at H.Q. I immediately saw the situation was very bad; practically the whole of the infantry were congregated in front of H.Q., which was at the Hôtel de Ville, and in the main square. The artillery were in a street just behind. The morale was apparently getting low, and altogether it seemed that no defence was being put up; everyone appeared depressed and uncertain. I reported to the general, who ordered me to stay with him, saying that he considered the cars as his best fighting unit, and wished to keep them in reserve in order to save the situation, if possible.

Urgent requests for assistance having come in at 4.30 p.m. from the Pont de Valenciennes, he ordered me to send a car there to reinforce the post. I sent Captain Coode with one armoured car; this left me with one armoured and two unarmoured cars, one without a machine-gun. My whole force consisted of Armstrong, Coode, eighteen men, and our armament of two Maxims and one French machine-gun.

At 4.35 p.m. some Germans who had got into the town started firing at the Hôtel de Ville from the house-tops. I dispatched Armstrong with three marines to climb the clock tower to see if he could locate them. Whilst this was going on a German aeroplane flew over the town, causing some panic amongst the infantry, who seemed to expect bombs.

Just before 5 p.m. Captain Coode's servant, a private of marines, arrived on a bicycle. He was wounded in the arm, and reported that Captain Coode was having a bad time of it, being practically surrounded, and that the French had fallen back. The enemy were getting into houses behind the car; and he urgently requested reinforcements. I reported this to the general; but he could not do anything. I therefore decided to recall Captain Coode's party, as I considered that the only thing to do was for my force to collect and stick together in readiness for the curtain to rise on the last act of the drama.

As Captain Coode's servant volunteered to go back with the message, and as he knew the route, I sent him to Coode with written orders to rejoin me at the Hôtel de Ville. I also sent a messenger to recall Major Armstrong from his lofty perch. Both parties were with me once more in a very short space of time. Coode's car was nearly out of ammunition, and he had another man wounded; but they were full of fight, and said if the infantry had backed them up, they could have held the gate.

Coode reported that the Germans were swarming into the town, without any resistance being made on the part of the infantry. I again went to the general and asked him what he proposed to do, suggesting that it was not too late to fall back out of the town; I pointed out that otherwise it was certain that the infantry would either be killed off like sheep or that they would surrender. I had telephoned to Morbecque about 4.30 p.m. and told Briggs, who had answered the 'phone, that it was extremely unlikely that we would get out of Douai, and that the situation looked very black. I told him to organise the defence of the aerodrome and to send out a strong force of cars to Béthune next morning, as the Germans would be certain to push on after taking Douai.

I told Armstrong that we must keep together, and that if the French surrendered, we would try to break through. He cordially agreed with this, as he, like me, hated the idea of being included in the surrender. It was beastly waiting there doing nothing, surrounded by a mob of infantry who were waiting for the Lord knows what.

At 5.25 p.m. the end came. A shouting mob of cyclists and infantry in a state of panic rushed into the courtyard of the Hôtel de Ville, yelling out that we were surrounded, and that the Germans had taken the Pont d'Esquerchin. I went to General Plantey and said that the only thing to do was to recapture the bridge and drive the Germans away from that sector. He agreed, and said that if I would lead the way with my cars, he would follow with those of the troops he could get to fight.

There was no doubt that if we did not do something a wholesale surrender was certain. I strongly objected to being mixed up in that, as if the force had surrendered, we would have had to surrender also; I felt certain that if we could only start a fight the morale would improve, and that we would have every chance of extricating the whole force from its predicament. From my experience with these troops, once they got a lead they would fight like hell.

I led out our cars therefore from the Hôtel de Ville, and forcing our way through crowds of Infantry and civilians, we reached a corner where I found about 400 infantry. I alternately implored, swore, and ordered them to follow us against the enemy, but only one came jumping on the step of the last car. From this corner a straight street

400 yards long led to a bridge over the canal, which was held by the Germans. I must confess that as we went along this road I certainly thought that here was the end of our little party; and I felt very guilty at bringing Armstrong, Coode, and the other fine fellows to death for no purpose except to keep up the Pride of the Service.

The fact that the infantry would not come on after us made us very fierce, and I am certain, speaking for myself, that this feeling of anger made us far braver than we had felt at first. When we had got to within 100 yards of the bridge a hot fire was opened on us. I took the cars to the head of the bridge and then halted them, and we opened fire along the roadways which ran on both sides of the canal and along the road ahead of us. I ordered the marines out of the cars on to the roadway, and told them to keep up a hot fire on the Germans who were on the opposite bank.

Going myself with Platford on to the bridge, I saw some *Huns* had got on board two barges which were alongside the far bank and emptied my magazine at them. I can remember to this day the sound one of their bullets made as it hit the girder alongside my face. We were so excited that I am afraid our fire was very wild; but it certainly made up for lack of accuracy by its volume, our three machine-guns firing like mad.

We kept at this game for about five minutes, when I saw the Germans clearing off in all directions. I ordered cease fire, and all aboard the cars. I then led the cars at full speed along the main Hénin-Liétard road, intending to get to the position we had held in the morning, as from there we could cover the retreat of the French and command the approaches to the Pont d'Esquerchin.

The car I was in was totally unarmoured, having simply a wagonette body. It had suffered a bit in the fight through the second car running into it during the excitement at the bridge; but it was still in working order.

We had lost no men killed and only had one wounded, besides the two already hit.

I knew that in front of us there was a double trench across the road which entailed cars stopping and reversing to get through in the gap left between the two trenches. Just short of this obstacle was a side-road leading towards Beaumont. I determined if we met the enemy at the trench to hold the corner at the side-road as long as we could, hoping that the infantry would follow on. This side-road would be the line of approach of the cavalry division reported close to Beaumont.

BILL SAMSON AND FRENCH OFFICER AT DOUAI.

ARMOURED LORRY AT DOUAI.

On arriving at the corner, we encountered a very heavy fire coming from the trench and the high ground close to it. It would have been useless to have attempted to go on against that, so we stopped at the corner, where we got some shelter from a cottage, and opened fire with the machine-guns on the two armoured cars, whilst the rest of us lay down on the road and kept up a hot fire with rifles.

We held out at the corner for nearly fifteen minutes until the Germans opened fire with field guns from Le Polygone. The situation then got too warm, as shrapnel was bursting all round us, and the cottage was quickly demolished by high explosives. I therefore gave the order to retire, and we jumped on board the cars and went along the Guincy-Esquerchin road. After we had put a mile between us and the corner, I halted to see how we had fared. Our casualties now consisted of eight men wounded.

All the cars had many bullet marks; but no serious damage had been done to them except that one of the armoured cars had a bullet through its radiator, causing it to lose practically all its water.

We only had about 200 rounds of ammunition left, and were running pretty short of petrol, otherwise all was well with us.

I felt very pleased at our endeavour to save the situation, and thoroughly thankful that I had managed to get my party away. I also considered that we had done everything we could to open a line of retreat for the infantry, and that we had held out at the corner as long as was feasible.

As it happened, we had cleared the way for the French, for the general got 2,500 infantry out of the town across the Pont d'Esquerchin, and keeping close to the canal bank had got them well clear of the *Huns* without firing a shot whilst we were fighting them at the corner. I am afraid that a good number remained in the town and were captured.

To proceed with our narrative, we went along for another mile, when we came across a squadron of Goumiers under a colonel, to whom I narrated what had happened at Douai; he told me that the cavalry division was close at hand. He turned back with his cavalry and followed us towards Beaumont. Just short of this village I came across the cavalry division. I went up to the general, who was a fine martial figure surrounded by an escort of *cuirassiers* with steel breastplates, and after I had told him what had happened, I said that there was every probability of the Douai force having surrendered, but there was a chance of them having got out whilst we were holding the cross-roads.

He recommended that I should return to Morbecque and report to General Aston, and added that he was not pushing on any farther, but was going to retire to Beaumont. I therefore went through Beaumont to Béthune and back to Morbecque, where we were received as if we had risen from the dead. Briggs told me that they had fully expected never to see us again.

I went to bed after telephoning to General Paris, who had relieved General Aston in command of the marines. General Paris sent the following report to the Admiralty:

"Commander Samson and all ranks appear to have behaved very gallantly in difficult circumstances, and I consider his action was perfectly correct."

I also received a letter from General Bidon, of which the following is a translation:

St. Pol,
11th November, 1914.

My Dear Commander,
Since our escape from Douai I have not yet thanked you for all that you have done for the force I commanded. It was thanks to your energy, to your indomitable courage, and to the noble officers and men under your orders, that we were able to resist several times the incessant German attacks and carry out the mission which had been confided to us.

I have reported highly on your merit to M. le Général de Maudhuy, C.-in-C. of the 10th Army. It is in his name, as well as mine, and also on behalf of the Army of France, that I thank you for the brotherly aid which you have provided....

(Signed) Plantey,
General.

P.S.—I will never forget, my dear commander, how you placed yourself at the head of the troops to force the passage with your machine-guns."

CHAPTER 10

The Evacuation of Antwerp

The next day General Paris sent for me and gave me orders to stand by to proceed to Antwerp with the whole of my force. The aeroplanes would of course fly there, and the cars would have to escort seventy motor-omnibuses that had just arrived at Dunkirk.

On October 1st a new section of armoured cars had arrived from England; they had been sent straight to Lille, arriving there at 7 p.m. the same day. The commanding officer was Lieutenant-Commander Josiah Wedgwood, M.P., R.N.V.R. He soon showed that he was a fighter of some determination, and quickly grasped the essentials of armoured-car operations. By this time a drill book had been produced from notes that I had supplied, and this book was, I believe, found of good use; anyhow, if you followed its advice, you had the advantage of starting with some reliable data to work on.

Between September 28th and October 3rd, the aeroplane flight at Antwerp was busily engaged carrying out reconnaissance flights and bomb dropping, Gerrard, Collet, Spencer-Grey, and Marix being the pilots. Lord Carbery, who had a bad crash, was sent home.

On October 3rd I sent off practically the whole of my aeroplanes to Antwerp, Davies, Peirse, Courtney, Osmond, Beevor, Rainey, and Sippe flying there from Morbecque, Dunkirk, and Lille. We turned over our camp at Morbecque to the Oxfordshire Hussars, and then I went to Dunkirk with eleven armoured cars, half a dozen armed with machine-guns, carrying altogether 120 marines.

At Dunkirk the seventy motor-omnibuses were handed over to me to escort to Antwerp.

These omnibuses had just arrived from England, most of them having been taken directly off the streets. The drivers and conductors, who were all volunteers, were practically all in plain clothes, only one or two having achieved either a uniform coat or cap. One I remember, who possessed a large and open type of countenance, had a sailor's cap, which was far too small for him, perched on the top of his head; but what they lacked in discipline and uniform they made up for in driving skill and cheerfulness.

By 2 p.m. I had marshalled my procession. The problem of escorting such a large convoy was a difficult one; but I solved it by sending on sections of armoured cars to cover certain portions of the route with orders to rejoin the convoy when we had passed their patrol area. I divided up the remainder of my cars, placing two sections amongst the omnibuses and using the remainder as an advance-guard and rear-guard respectively. The marines I placed in parties of ten in every sixth omnibus, so whatever part of the long line was attacked an escort of cars or marines was sure to be close at hand.

The omnibuses kept splendid station, and rumbled along at a steady ten miles an hour; the clouds of dust they kicked up were appalling, and the only comfortable position was the one I chose, *i.e.*, in front of the procession. After we had gone about 20 miles, I discovered that no arrangements had been made about food for the drivers, who had not had a meal since the day before. I therefore dispatched the invaluable O'Caffrey and the equally competent Lathbury to go on ahead and collect all the food they could at Ghistelles; they came back loaded up with bread and sausages: this solved the food problem. We arrived at Bruges about 7 p.m. and I determined to stop the night there, as it was not advisable to move our large convoy by night.

All the buses and cars were driven into the barracks at Bruges. It was a very tight fit, and Captain Leafe, the officer in command of the omnibuses, told me it would take hours to get them out again and lined up on the road. It certainly appeared likely to be a tough proposition, but I told him we would leave it to the drivers, and I was justified in my opinion, as within twenty minutes from the word "go" they had all got their buses lined up in the road outside the barracks; it was a wonderful exhibition of skill, and could only have been done by men with years of experience of driving in the London streets. At 5 a.m. we were again on the road.

When we got near to Antwerp, I determined to make an impressive entry to hearten up the inhabitants, so I got all the armoured cars at the head of the procession and then halted the convoy so everybody could have a brush up and remove one or two of the layers of dust from their persons.

Our entry was really a grand sight, as the eleven armoured cars

CONVOY OF MOTOR OMNIBUSES AND ARMOURED CARS ON THE WAY TO ANTWERP, 1914.

followed by the two armoured lorries looked extremely shipshape and warlike. The streets were crowded with people, who cheered us to the echo. The martial look of the procession was rather spoilt by the number of children and other civilians who scrambled on to the buses; but still it cheered up the inhabitants.

I took the whole procession to the aerodrome, where I turned over the omnibuses to the Marine Brigade. I found most of the aeroplanes had arrived, and a trainload of our stores was expected to arrive from Dunkirk that night. Having made all arrangements for the men and parked the cars at the aerodrome, I reported to General Paris, and then went into the town to find a bed, taking Bill Samson with me. I was done to the world, as I had had practically no rest since September 29th. I got to bed about 1 a.m., at an hotel, leaving my car outside.

At 3 a.m. I was awakened by Lord Annesley, with orders for me to proceed to the front line with all the armoured cars, as an infantry attack was expected. I sent Annesley with orders for the cars to get ready, and hastily getting into my clothes I drove off to the aerodrome; unfortunately, I lost my way in the dark, and by the time I got to the aerodrome I found the cars had left in the direction of Lierre. I picked up Lieutenant Osmond, Leading Seaman Bateman, and my driver Barrett—a very doughty warrior, this latter fellow—and getting out along the Lierre road we soon came across the armoured cars who were in Bouchet village, having received orders to remain there in reserve.

I reported at H.Q. of the Marine Brigade, and received orders to go to Colonel Parsons, who was in command of a Battalion in the front line at Lierre. He was in a small cottage, and I found that he was very keen to get a machine-gun to support a platoon of marines who were holding a trench by the bridge over the River Nethe. As it was still dark there was a good chance of getting the gun into position before daylight.

We set off in the car with Captain Richards, the adjutant; and leaving the car hidden behind some houses, Osmond, Bateman, Captain Richards, his orderly, and myself, crept along the empty streets through piles of broken glass and rubbish carrying the Lewis gun belonging to the car and a dozen charges of ammunition. We arrived at the head of the bridge, which had been partially demolished, and got into the end house overlooking the river. The Germans were on the opposite side of the river, and the marines were holding a trench a little to the right of our house. We got upstairs and found an attic window which gave a good field of fire. We soon fixed up the Lewis gun, and seeing some pillow cases we began to fill them with earth from the garden.

Hard at work in the garden, I did not notice dawn was on us and was only awakened to the reality of my position by a German firing two shots at me from the other side of the river. As he was only about 60 yards away, he must have been a rotten shot, as he missed me; I was inside the house like a flash. We now found ourselves in an awkward predicament, as it was essential for Richards and myself to get back to our respective Units. There was no way of getting out of the house except through the street door and along the street; for about 50 yards, we would be in full view of the enemy until we reached a side-street. We tried to breakthrough into the next house, but could not do it.

The longer we waited the less we liked the job. Drawing lots who should be the first, which was the desired part, we set off, without attracting the enemy's attention. We were all glad when we reached the friendly shelter of the side-street, and rejoined the car. Osmond and Bateman stayed in the attic and got some *Huns* with their gun. They got back in the evening after having expended all their ammunition.

Going back towards Bouchet I found Bill and Felix Samson with four armoured cars drawn up on the main road; they reported that they had been ordered to stay there in support. As the cars were totally exposed, I placed them on a side-road and put the men in the ditch. The Germans were now shelling the road very heavily with big stuff; 8- and 12-inch shells were bursting all round us, and things were getting rather sultry. A kite balloon was up, evidently controlling the German shell-fire. Close in rear of us was a Belgian battery.

After we had been in the lane for about twenty minutes shells began to drop fairly close, evidently being registered on the Belgian guns; the shells burst closer and closer to where we were. All this time my two brothers and myself were standing in the lane close to its junction with the main road in order that we could see if any messenger came along the road with orders for us. Suddenly a salvo of shrapnel burst right on us. Extraordinary to relate, we three were absolutely untouched; but the men who were crouching in the ditch suffered heavily, two men being killed and four wounded.

The cars were started up and the wounded placed on board. I sent the cars off with all the party to a village about 2 miles farther back, where Armstrong was waiting with my main body. Felix Samson and my driver Barrett made two trips, taking the wounded, and had some narrow shaves whilst doing so, a fragment of a shell removing the flagstaff which was lashed to one of the lamp-brackets.

Bill Samson came with me along the main road towards Lierre, where I could be in a position close to Battalion H.Q. in case the cars were required. Walking along the road I got hit by two shrapnel balls, receiving wounds in the back and foot. Luckily, neither was severe, although I lost a good deal of blood. After an hour I received orders to take the cars back to the aerodrome; so, walking back along the main road I got to Armstrong and we returned to our aerodrome.

I must say that the big shells we had been encountering made us feel rather depressed, as it seemed rather a hopeless job defending Antwerp with the few old and obsolete guns that the Belgians possessed against the big siege howitzers that the Germans were employing; it was certain that if the enemy got across the river at Lierre they could soon reduce Antwerp to ruins. There was little doubt that the defending force was far too small to hope to keep the Germans from crossing, once they were ready to attack.

The Belgian infantry were worn out, and required a rest and refit. The marines, splendid as we knew them to be and as they proved, were too few and too old to be able to hold out for long. The naval division arrived during the day; but it did not impress us as a fighting unit of much value, being badly equipped, and with very little training. The armoured train, with its 4.7 inch-guns, was our only heavy artillery which was of any use. Big naval guns were arriving, but it was doubtful if they could be mounted in sufficient time to assist.

There was, moreover, every sign that the Belgians desired to fall back from Antwerp, and thus save the remnants of their army. The one bright spot was the arrival of Mr. Winston Churchill, who was full of cheery optimism regarding the situation. It was certain that the longer Antwerp could be held the better it would be for the armies in France, as large numbers of Germans were being held up in the siege; and in attacking our lines of communication through Lokeren and Ghent.

I used to find the streets of Antwerp a most depressing sight, thronged as they were with Belgians; beautifully dressed ladies were apparently carrying on their usual life, shopping and promenading as if the siege was a minor affair altogether. To one who realised that any day these same people might be exposed to shells from the biggest of guns, this could not fail to make one wonder what would happen to them all.

Staff-Surgeon Wells and Surgeon Graeme Anderson, two of my

doctors, did splendid work organising a casualty clearing station and attending to the wounded, both British and Belgian. Dean, who drove their ambulance, deserved every credit for the way he constantly went up and down the Lierre road under heavy shell-fire. The Germans concentrated on this road, and a journey along it was not a joy ride, as I found to my cost, as I had to go along it at least half a dozen times a day, to report to General Paris. My aeroplanes did all that was in their power to assist the defence, bombing the German guns and Infantry continuously; everybody worked at full pressure, especially Peirse, who was wounded by shrapnel. I had a couple of flights myself over the German lines.

On October 6th it was decided that the evacuation of Antwerp would take place as soon as possible. I received orders to get the aeroplanes and cars away by dawn on the 7th. Certain aeroplanes were to be left to the last in order to carry out an attack on the Zeppelin sheds at Düsseldorf and Cologne. Spencer-Grey and Marix, with two Sopwith Tabloids, were detailed for this. We had a terrible job getting our stores away, as I only had the two armoured lorries and the armoured cars. One section of armoured cars was sent to Ghent to escort Mr. Winston Churchill on his journey through there to Ostend. Wedgwood's section was already at Ghent co-operating with the Belgians.

Everybody worked like slaves during the evening and night of the 6th, and by dawn we had got all the aeroplanes away except the two Tabloids and Sippe's B.E., which had magneto trouble. Some of the aeroplanes which were under big repairs had to be smashed up, as it was impossible to get them in flying trim.

All my marines and stores were dumped on the South side of the Schelde, and at 5 a.m. the sole occupiers of the aerodrome were Bill Samson, Sippe, Osmond, Marix, and Spencer-Grey, with Leigh, a chief petty officer mechanic, three other men, and myself. We left a car to attend on the Zeppelin strafers and take their mechanics away. I left about 6 a.m., telling Sippe, who was still suffering from engine trouble, to fly back if he could, but if not to destroy his aeroplane before the Germans arrived.

I found the approaches to the Bridge of Boats full of dense crowds of civilians escaping from the town; we had a hard job getting through, but got across the bridge at last. I soon found the unperturbed Osmond, nicknamed Sondon (*i.e.*, "*Sans Dents*," or without teeth), sitting in the midst of our stolid party of marines and mechanics. We loaded up the two lorries and cars with what they could stow, and sent them off with orders to dump the men and stores at Ghent, and then return for the rest.

Leaving Osmond at the dump with a small guard and a couple of cars in case they had to make a bolt for it, we went on to Ghent, soon picking up our party, but making slow progress owing to the road being full of infantry and refugees. The latter were a sad sight; in fact, I always think a crowd of refugees quite the most depressing and disheartening spectacle of war that it is possible to see.

We got to Ghent at last, and after reporting to the Belgian general I took the cars to the Leopold Barracks, where we unloaded them, and sent them back to Osmond.

Luckily, we had not been there half an hour when six armoured cars arrived; they turned out to be Wedgwood's section. He was full of elation, as he had had some good fighting close to Termonde. I soon checked his martial ardour by sending him with his cars loaded up with our gear to Bruges and thence to Ostend. With Wedgwood was Lieutenant Tom Warner, Royal Marines, a marine of the old school, who had risen from the ranks. This was my first meeting with Warner, who was to become one of my stoutest assistants in armoured-car work, and as Armament Officer with me in France and the Dardanelles. He was always cheerful and full of energy and resource, a real old pirate of the first order. He always used to repeat with delight our first conversation in the Leopold Barracks, which was as follows:

Self: "I haven't seen you before."
Warner: "No, I have never struck you before, sir."
Self: "Well, see you well don't."

CHAPTER 11

The Retreat from Antwerp

We got Osmond and all our stores to Ghent, and out of Ghent that night, and arrived in Ostend on the morning of October 10th pretty well tired out.

I established the cars at the racecourse and telephoned to Longmore, who was in charge at Dunkirk, to send the aeroplanes to our old aerodrome at the racecourse.

I then proceeded to report to General Sir H. Rawlinson, who was in command of the IV Corps, with his H.Q. at the harbour railway station; his infantry, the wonderful 7th Division, were between Bruges and Ostend. He told me to get all my aeroplanes ready for reconnaissance work, and to give my cars a stand-off for the rest of the day.

O'Caffrey had as usual arranged splendid quarters for us in the Terminus Hotel at the harbour railway station, and I found myself the occupier of a fine bedroom and bathroom; of the latter I made good use. After an excellent dinner I was sent for by Sir H. Rawlinson, who told me he wanted me to go towards Antwerp and find out what had happened to General Paris and his force; he gave me a dispatch to take to General Paris, which I was to read and learn off by heart. It contained orders for General Paris, and showed the disposition of the IV Corps. I felt very flattered at being chosen for this duty, which I realised would be a difficult job.

I left orders for Wing-Commander Longmore to come to Ostend and take over command in my absence. I determined to take the three best armoured cars I had, and picked out three Rolls Royces.

In deciding on my companions, I had no hesitation in selecting Major Armstrong, as I knew his sterling worth. In addition, I took Lieutenant Aspinall, the least tired of the armoured-car officers, who had all had a very strenuous time. I realised that it would be a tough job to get through owing to the congested nature of the roads, thronged as they were with refugees and stragglers.

At 8 p.m. I reported to General Sir H. Rawlinson that I was ready to start. I found him in conference with Generals Byng and Carden, men whose names are now household words. General Rawlinson insisted on ordering in some champagne, and told me to destroy my dispatches if there was any danger of getting caught. This mission was my first duty under the command of this famous general, and I look back with pride and pleasure on my service under him; if there was ever a white man to serve under it was General Rawlinson.

Always cheery and optimistic, full of human sympathy and understanding, he stands out in my mind as the greatest man I served under in the war, a commander you felt you would do anything for. I came into contact with him continuously for the next month, and I never once saw him downhearted, even in the worst periods at Ypres; personally, I never left his presence without feeling that we were bound to win; he was worth an army corps himself.

General Byng and General Carden also impressed me very strongly. The former I came under on a good many occasions, and I found him a splendid general to serve, having that same saving grace of understanding that was possessed by Sir Henry. They were a trio of doughty fighters, and they undoubtedly saved England and France by their stand at Ypres.

We set off at 8.30 p.m., the three generals coming out to see us start. We got to Eecloo in good time, using by-roads to avoid the stream of refugees. Here I obtained the services of a Belgian smuggler, who knew the roads along the frontier. We soon got blocked in a mass of carts and vehicles, and as it was impossible to proceed with all three cars, I sent Aspinall back to wait at Bruges with one car. We then went on at a snail's pace through the most distressing scenes; everybody was hurrying to Ostend to escape the *Boches*, and everybody imagined the *Uhlan* close on his heels.

The one bright incident in the night was encountering some English nurses, who had two omnibus-loads of wounded. They were a splendid advertisement for the English race, absolutely unperturbed, calm, and competent, amid the surrounding mob of panic-stricken people. They impressed me more than I can say. Their one job was to get their wounded charges safe to Ostend, and that they would do it was evident to the most casual observer. I had one day whilst at Antwerp paid a visit to their hospital with Armstrong to see Coode and three of our wounded men. On that occasion I had been very favourably impressed with their work and competence. Meeting them on the retreat increased my admiration for them.

Just short of Selzaete we found that the crowd was worse than ever, the road being blocked by carts; I therefore sent back the second car, as it was all we could do to get one through. It took exactly one hour to get through the town. The smuggler was sent back in the Second car, as he reported that he was suffering from some terrible illness, and was rolling about on the floor boards holding his stomach. We diagnosed it as *Germanitis*.

An interesting sight in Selzaete was a Belgian machinegun battery, provided with dog teams. These faithful animals looked done to the world; but whilst we were waiting to get through a block in the traffic, I noticed that they had enough energy to fight, as two teams got too close together, with resulting argument on the dogs' part.

At the bridge over the canal the first signs of an organised rearguard were found, some Belgian infantry and *gendarmes* being stationed to guard the bridge. They had mined it, and were standing by to blow it up. The officer told me that the king and queen were sleeping in a house close to the bridge. The road leading to their house was guarded by some mounted *gendarmes*. I doubt if Their Majesties could have obtained much sleep with that din going on.

After having got about three miles beyond the bridge we were hopelessly blocked by some broken-down carts. Armstrong and I then decided we could get on much quicker on foot, so we told Bateman to take the car back to Bruges, and wait for us there. We two set out, hoping every minute to come across the marines. We soon got past the last of the refugees. One party were rather humorous.

About six soldiers were in a small car of very archaic design; it was suffering very badly from engine trouble, and kept on stopping. They would get out and tinker at the engine, and get it going again. Then they would all get on board, and it would go along for about 10 yards, and then give up the ghost again. Out would jump everybody, and work on the engine would recommence. The engine would restart and stop again. They could have walked far quicker than the car was taking them. One of them informed us that the marines were on the railway line to the north of us, and that the Germans were close at hand, and we would run into them if we went on in the direction we were going.

As we had little chance of getting to the marines before daylight, I decided to return to Selzaete, and see if it was possible to get through to them by telephone. We made good time back to Selzaete, getting a lift in a cart, and arrived there before daylight.

Getting to the railway station, we ran the stationmaster to ground in his office, and by use of his telephone got on to the next station to the eastward, where I got into communication with a Marine officer, who told me that a large number of marines and naval division were waiting at the station for trains. They were all very tired and hungry; one brigade of the naval division were still well behind, and they didn't know for certain where they were.

In Selzaete railway station I found two trains complete with engines and staff; and after exercising considerable persuasion and appealing to their patriotism, I got the railway people to despatch these two trains to pick up the English troops. Another smuggler was found and sent off in one of the trains to act as guide in case they were held up. I then telephoned to the Belgian Army Staff at Ghent, and asked them to send as many trains along to us as they could.

One train soon returned loaded up with our men; they were very tired, and all wanted food, which we were unable to provide, and I hastened the trains off to safety.

Two more trains soon arrived from Ghent, and were sent on to embark some more troops; meanwhile, I carefully burnt my dispatches. Armstrong, who had gone out to see what was happening in the town, came back and said that some English had gone through in two cars towards Bruges; the only troops now left in the town were two squadrons of Belgian guides cavalry, and a company of infantry holding the bridge.

There were some motor-omnibuses in the town, and a few on the far bank of the canal; these turned out to be my old friends. Armstrong went out, and finding Captain Leafe told him to get them on the move as soon as possible. This was difficult to do, as they were short of petrol, but after some trouble and dividing up the petrol between them we got most of them *en route* to Bruges, leaving four or five behind. The king and queen were still in their house, and did not leave until 6 a.m. No finer example of courage or calmness, amidst the surrounding panic, could have been shown than was displayed by Their Majesties.

The queen drove off in a rather dilapidated motorcar, the king on horse-back, with an escort of mounted *gendarmes*. I was deeply stirred at seeing this evidence of how Royalty behave in times of great danger. Here they were practically the last of the army, with only about two hundred fighting men between them and the Germans. Personally, I felt greatly relieved at seeing them start.

About this time Colonel Tom Bridges, of the 4th Hussars, and Colonel Dallas, G.S.O.I of the IV Corps, arrived in a Rolls Royce, and a Métallurgique. I was delighted to see them, as I was relieved of any further responsibilities. Colonel Bridges, who had already made a wonderful name for himself in the war, immediately set about collecting food in the town to give to the troops, who were arriving in the trains. Armstrong and I assisted at this, and did our best to distribute it during the few moments the trains remained in the station. About 6.30 a.m., we got news that the Germans had reached the railway line, and had attacked a train; we could not find out what had happened to the troops in the train, and of course no more trains could be sent out.

After this we could do nothing more to help, so Armstrong and I sat in the stationmaster's office and had some food. We were both thoroughly played out, and I for one felt that all I wanted was to go to sleep for twenty-four hours; we were so tired that I didn't worry whether we were the last people in Selzaete or not. I suspected that we were pretty nearly the rear-guard, as I had seen the *gendarmes* doing a flit.

From my experience of war up to date, you always had about half an hour to spare after the *gendarmes* departed before the first *Huns* arrived. I felt quite secure, as we had two cars, and I knew that Colonel Bridges would not go without us. Whilst I was dozing off a civilian arrived, and waking me up said that a British officer of high rank had fallen off his horse and was in the lunatic asylum on the other side of the canal.

I told Colonel Bridges, and he let me have his car. Armstrong and I set off. Crossing the bridge, we found a picket, the last of the army, standing by to blow it up. We made them promise not to do it until we came back, or until the Germans actually came in sight. We had not gone a hundred yards when we met a cavalryman, who said he had sighted some German cyclists coming along; this made us hustle. We found the lunatic asylum, and going inside discovered Colonel Ollivant, G.S.O.1 of the marine brigade, lying in bed. He was suffering from concussion. We had a hard job getting him out of bed and into his clothes, and I am afraid we were not good valets—anyhow, dressing an unconscious man is not an easy job; but I did not relish having to swim the canal, as it was rather a chilly morning. We got across the bridge in time, and I was very glad when we had put the river between us and the enemy.

In a quarter of an hour, we all set off for Eecloo in the two cars. We stopped that night in Eecloo, and went on next morning to Bruges, where I found that Reggie Marix had just gone off in my car to Ostend. This made me rather anxious to have a few words with him; but I found Captain Williams with some of my cars in the town, and taking one I got into Ostend, where I reported to General Rawlinson.

On arrival I heard the story of the successful attack on the Zeppelin sheds. The party we had left behind had a most adventurous time. At about 11.30 p.m. on October 8th the enemy had commenced to shell Antwerp. Spencer-Grey, who was in command, got the aeroplanes out of the shed and placed them in the middle of the aerodrome, where he considered they had less chance of being damaged by shell-fire. The weather was too misty for a start to be made until 1.30 p.m. on October 9th, at which time Spencer-Grey and Marix set off in their "Tabloids."

Spencer-Grey got to Cologne, but found it obscured by mist, and he could not locate the Zeppelin sheds; he therefore dropped his bombs at the railway station. He got back to Antwerp at 4.45 p.m. At 8.30 p.m. the enemy commenced shelling the aerodrome, and two aeroplanes, his own and Sippe's, were both put out of action by shells. It was therefore useless to remain any longer, and he started off with the mechanics in a motorcar for Ostend.

Marix, who had Düsseldorf for his objective, achieved a great success. He let go his bombs from 600 feet and scored direct hits with both of them; he had the gratification of seeing the roof fall in and flames shoot up into the sky, proving that he had destroyed the Zeppelin.

He encountered a very heavy fire from machine-guns, and his aeroplane was hit in numerous places; 20 miles short of Antwerp, close to the Dutch frontier, he was forced to alight owing to running out of petrol. Abandoning his aeroplane, he got into Antwerp after a most adventurous journey, going some of the way by bicycle and some by a railway engine. He got away from Antwerp in the motorcar.

We were all very pleased at Marix's success, and he and Spencer-Grey richly deserved the D.S.O.'s they were awarded. Thus, the squadron now possessed four D.S.O.'s after six weeks' fighting. Not bad going for a small unit.

During my absence Wing-Commander Longmore had done yeoman service in collecting and reorganising the units of my command.

The situation was as follows:

> The depot was at Dunkirk, under Lieutenant Chambers.
> The advanced depot for armoured cars was established at the Leopold Racecourse, Ostend.
> One section of armoured cars was working with the 3rd Cavalry Division at Bruges.
> The remainder of the armoured cars, eight in number, were at Ostend. Nine aeroplanes were in flying condition at Ostend. Two or three more aeroplanes were at Dunkirk in various stages of repair.

We were all in good condition for further service as regards personnel and material, except that we were very short of heavy tenders. The latter was a serious handicap, as there was every chance of a move being made.

I now received orders to place myself under the command of General Sir H. Rawlinson.

I cannot start on our further experiences without expressing what a debt of gratitude I felt to the officers and men under my command during the trying operations of the last three weeks. We were always on the go, without a home, without any idea where we were going to next, without food sometimes, always without adequate transport; that we had kept going was solely due to the way all ranks had pulled their pound and a bit over. The one and only complaint I ever heard was from old Mr. Smeeth, who complained to me once that he would like a good meal of eggs, beefsteak, and beer.

The pilots at Antwerp were Gerrard, Davies, Peirse, Sippe, Beevor, Chambers, Osmond, Bigsworth, Marix, and Newton Clare. With the cars, my two brothers, Aspinall, Isaac, Warner, Major Armstrong, Major Risk, and Wedgwood, had been invaluable.

Staff-Surgeon Wells and Dr. Anderson had worked like Trojans, and Wells, although he had got to the end of his tether, turned to like a hero during the retreat from Antwerp and was my right-hand man; without his aid I could never have reached Ostend without losing half our gear.

The men had all been splendid, especially Keogh, Leigh, Bateman, Shaw, Dean, and Platford. Old Mr. Smeeth and Mansell had somehow kept the office going all along, and it used to be the constant joke of the squadron seeing Mr. Smeeth settling himself comfortably in as soon as we arrived anywhere; he had a faculty for seizing on the best room in any house we fixed upon as H.Q. and unpacking the scores of books and ledgers he travelled with. Everybody knew that as soon as Mr. Smeeth came and reported to me that the office was ready, the next moment we would have to go somewhere else. They had a light tender which was called the office car, and if you were out of food, you could always be sure that they had plenty.

Ostend was crowded with refugees from Antwerp and other parts of Belgium, and most distressing scenes were seen in the streets. I know no more depressing sight than people who have abandoned their homes. Some had all their worldly possessions with them; others seemed to have saved nothing except what they stood up in. The harbour railway station was simply packed with a seething mass of humanity trying to get on board the few steamers which went to England. The hotels and shops were meanwhile doing a roaring trade, and the commercial instincts of the shop-keeping class appear fully developed in times like these.

My office had been installed in one of the waiting-rooms, and Mr. Smeeth had a hard job to do his work under the constant stream of inquirers who came in demanding a passage to England. Small fishing-boats appeared to be reaping a splendid harvest, taking people across the Channel, and even rowing-boats were booked up in case the Germans arrived.

Officers and men of the naval division were frequently coming into the town in parties of twos and threes dressed in civilian clothes. Some had escaped through the German lines; others had got in after crossing the Dutch border. I remember a German aeroplane flying over the town one day; it caused great excitement, and everybody fired at it, including the *gendarmes*, two of whom were seen to discharge their revolvers at it after taking careful aim. They must have been optimists, these *gendarmes*, as the German was flying at about 7,000 feet.

CHAPTER 12

Roulers to Ypres

The IV Corps were now ordered to fall back; and on October 12th I received orders to leave Ostend. My instructions were for one section of armoured cars to work with General Byng's 3rd Cavalry Division; the remainder of the cars were to follow H.Q. IV Corps to Thourout, and remain close at hand in readiness for any work required. General Sir H. Rawlinson sent for me, and asked if it was feasible for the aeroplanes to keep with the troops in their retirement, and carry out continuous reconnaissance, working from extemporised landing-grounds. I answered that wherever H.Q. went I would guarantee that the aeroplanes would stick to it; and right well they did so.

We were rather pleased with our work, as an R.F.C. Squadron which had arrived at Ostend had reported that it was impossible to do this, and moved to Dunkirk. The R.N.A.S. thus kept up their reputation. Sir Henry told me in 1915, when I visited him, that he would never forget the way my aeroplanes had stuck to the IV Corps and carried out reconnaissance in filthy weather under the most difficult circumstances.

Placing Davies in command of the five aeroplanes, I ordered him to follow us to Thourout on the 13th; but if he saw no landing mark there, he was to go on to Roulers. I left a few men with him, also a lorry and a touring-car. Lathbury, I placed in command of the detached section of cars; he set off on the evening of the 12th and carried out some really good work before he rejoined me at Ypres. He actually got into the outskirts of Commines, which was in the hands of the Germans, and obtained some excellent information. Some of this was the result of a telephone conversation he had with a German cavalry officer. The German, being quite deceived by Lathbury's excellent command of the language, thought he was talking to a compatriot.

I set off at 6 p.m. with all the heavy transport and the remainder of the cars. We stopped at some little village for a meal. There was the choice of two *auberges*; unfortunately, Armstrong chose the wrong one for the officers, and we had a most scratchy repast. The men I later discovered had fared much better.

At a very late hour we arrived at Thourout, and settled down comfortably or otherwise in billets. The rain now started, and continued to fall during the whole of the retreat.

Early in the morning I received orders to go on to Roulers.

I sent a motorcyclist back to Ostend with orders to Davies to carry out certain aeroplane reconnaissances, and then land at Roulers.

Leaving Armstrong to bring on the convoy, I set off in my car, accompanied by Morrison, my faithful motorcyclist. He was a most experienced rider, having been a star turn at Brooklands and in Tourist Trophy races. His job was to stick close to my car, which he carried out to the letter, never being more than a yard off my rear mudguard. Nobody envied him, as I had a nasty habit of sending him off ahead whenever we came to a doubtful village or wood, where there might be some Germans.

Arriving at Roulers, I had a difficult task in finding a suitable place to turn into an aerodrome, the country being cut up into tiny little fields. After searching for over an hour, I received a message from Sir Henry to say he could see a suitable spot from his point of vantage up in the church tower. This I found to be a comic sort of racecourse; it was quite big enough, but the surface was more like a marsh than an aerodrome. Anyhow, it had to do, and placing the landing signal we awaited the arrival of our aeroplanes. The steady downpour was making the ground worse and worse, and it soon became a question as to whether it would be more suitable for seaplanes than aeroplanes.

Marix and Peirse arrived with their aeroplanes during the forenoon, followed by Davies and Collet in the afternoon. They reported that Briggs had had a nasty smash, and was coming on with the car; but as the day dragged on no signs of Briggs were evident.

Late in the evening I received a message from Corps H.Q. to say that a patrol had brought in two suspicious characters, who claimed to be part of my command, but they doubted their statement, and thought they were spies. Would I come round and have a look at them? When I got there, I found the two suspects were Briggs and Beevor. I did not feel surprised at the suspicion they had been treated with, as they looked a most disreputable pair. Briggy, in his flying kit, at the best of times looked a holy terror, and Beevor was a tough-looking customer; their experiences had not added to the charm of their appearance.

They had set off from Ostend in Briggs's Blériot; leaving the ground, they had gone out to sea to gain height in order to clear the buildings. When about 300 yards out to sea, the engine had stopped, and they had to take to the water. Luckily, they escaped unhurt, and were able to swim ashore. Briggs was most crestfallen at losing his old Blériot; but much more so at the loss of his tool kit. This mysterious bag seemed to contain everything from a King Dick spanner to a complete spare engine, and everybody at Eastchurch always said that Briggy kept it up to date by abstracting tools from their cars. Popular report said that he used to take it to bed with him.

Armstrong, after bringing along the convoy, set out to do a bit of scouting with the cars, and soon ran across a German patrol whom he engaged; but they got away across-country.

Roulers was a beastly little town, and the persistent downpour rendered it even worse. My billet was distinctly uncomfortable, and I had a tight squeeze to get all my party into it. I shared a room with four others, and naturally claimed the bed. One look at the latter, and I determined discretion was the better part of valour and decided to sleep on top of it instead of inside. Taking off some of my outer clothing, which was soaked through, I soon fell asleep; but not for long was I left undisturbed. In fact, so used had I become to never being left to sleep, that I doubt if I could at this date have slept for more than three hours at a time. On this occasion I only had about an hour, being routed out at 2 a.m. with a message to go round to H.Q.

I had rarely felt less inclined for war when, having struggled into my wet clothes, I walked round to H.Q. I soon cheered up, however, as the general was at his cheeriest. He gave me orders to move at once, as the Germans were pushing on pretty fast.

The cars were to escort the army transport to Ypres, except one section, which was to operate with the 3rd Cavalry Division. The aeroplanes were to make reconnaissances as soon as it was light, and then go on to Ypres and alight there. The cavalry were to be at Ypres at 7 a.m. and the infantry would arrive about 10 a.m. or so.

I returned to my dwelling, and got all hands on the move. I have seldom seen a more piratical-looking crew; but the spirit was willing, and everybody was soon ready for the next job.

Davies, Peirse, Marix, and Collet set off to the so-called aerodrome;

I told them to start off as soon as it was light and search the roads thoroughly between Roulers, Menin, Ypres, and Lens; then to fly to Ypres and look out for my landing signal.

Armstrong, I detailed to go off with the cars and escort the Army transport. Briggs was to get the aeroplanes away, and then come on to Ypres with the aeroplane ground party and the aeroplane stores.

I set off to Ypres, to discover an aerodrome, with three cars, taking Bill and Osmond.

We had an uneventful journey, except when taking a wrong turning and seeing my mistake I did a sharp turn at the last minute and ran into the faithful Morrison. Fortunately, the collision didn't harm him or his bicycle. Arriving at St. Jean, a little village on the outskirts of Ypres, I found an excellent field close to the main road; I dispatched Bill in one of the cars to Roulers to inform Davies, in case he had not already started, where I had found a landing-ground.

My party now consisted of Osmond and five men, with two cars, one carrying a Lewis gun. We quickly filled in two ditches and removed a few hummocks; then I went to a little *auberge* to see if I could obtain some sheets with which to make a landing signal. I found a dear old lady, who insisted on me taking her best sheets. She absolutely refused any payment, apparently considering that this was her contribution towards the war. I am afraid that she underwent a terrible time during the severe fighting which took place at Ypres.

In addition to the sheets, she provided us with a real breakfast, which we badly needed.

At 7 a.m. I sighted three of my aeroplanes. They flew over close to our field, and regardless of the landing mark, which they probably could not see, they flew on over Ypres and disappeared from sight. After waiting a short time, I set off to discover where they had landed. Passing through Ypres I could see no sign of our cavalry, who should have arrived in accordance with the time table. The inhabitants were very jumpy, as they said a large force of German Cavalry had only just left. I felt distinctly anxious at this, as I feared that my aeroplanes would be in trouble.

Luckily, as we arrived at the railway station, we came across Reggie Marix, whom I was very glad to see; but found that he was just as delighted to see me. He said that he and Peirse had failed to see our signal, and had alighted in a field close at hand; Davies had continued on to Lens. We all went on to the field, which was alongside the road. There I found a crowd of civilians, amongst whom was an agent of police in plain clothes; they all said that a large party of *Uhlans* were close at hand. The obvious thing was to remove the aeroplanes to my original field. Peirse quickly got into the air; but Reggie's engine refused to start.

I now got a bit anxious, as it seemed certain that the Germans would make an attempt to bag such a valuable prize as an aeroplane. Sending Barratt with one car back into Ypres to await the arrival of our cavalry, and bring some out immediately they appeared, I took the other car farther along the road, and disposed my little army in a position which provided some protection for the aeroplane.

Leaving one man at the Lewis gun, the three others and myself got into the fields on either side of the road; Osmond and Marix were left at the aeroplane to take out the sparking plugs. The Agent of Police, who had a bicycle, formed a useful scout, as I sent him along the road to see if he could discover signs of a hostile advance.

After about a quarter of an hour, Barratt came back and reported that there were no signs of our cavalry. On my cursing him for coming back instead of remaining in Ypres, as I had told him to do, he cheerily replied, "Oh, I thought you were going to have a scrap, sir, so I came back as soon as I could to see it."

Good fellow, Barratt. His great delight in life were the many bullet-holes in our car, especially a broken mudguard caused by a shell splinter, which latter he refused to have mended, and for months I suffered mud in my face. I liked him except when he loaded his revolver, when he was an extremely unpleasant companion, as he was distinctly careless with it, insisting on driving with it in one hand, until one day I found it pointed at my head; then I told him if he ever loaded it again before we actually got into a fight, I would send him back to the base at Dunkirk. If I was to be shot, I preferred it to be done by a German, and not through exuberance.

We remained in our position for over an hour, although it seemed much longer, with our energetic scout continually coming back *ventre à terre* and reporting Germans coming along the road, sometimes 4, sometimes 100. Fortunately, they never actually arrived.

At last, two car-loads of my aeroplane hands arrived, and I felt that now we were in sufficient strength to advance and see if we could find some of these elusive Germans.

Taking two cars and twelve men, I went about two miles along the road, but failed to locate any enemy, so returned to the aeroplane; here I found a troop of our dragoons had appeared on the scene. I therefore left them to the work of looking for the enemy. Leaving Marix with the twelve aeroplane men, with orders to locate the engine trouble, I returned to Ypres to look for Sir Henry's Headquarters.

On the way in we saw a German monoplane coming along at only about 2,000 feet altitude; evidently the Germans were ignorant that the English had arrived at Ypres, as otherwise they wouldn't have been so low. Whilst waiting for it to come over us, we heard a fusillade start from the town; we did not open fire until it was directly over us, when we fired at it with the machine-gun and volleys from our rifles.

The aeroplane suddenly put its nose down and glided down, evidently hit; jumping into the car, we dashed off in the direction it was taking.

We were somewhat delayed by getting into a *cul-de-sac*, and having to go by a round-about road; but eventually ran it to ground in a ploughed field. General Montgomery, and several soldiers, mostly Headquarters clerks, were already on the scene.

The monoplane, a D.F.W., was practically undamaged, and had only one bullet hole in it. Examination could produce no reason for its descent, as the controls and engine were in working order. General Montgomery, on seeing me, said, "Here you are; you are the man I want; the aviators have escaped into that wood. Will you go and search it with these clerks of mine?"

Marshalling this mixed force, I started to beat through the trees. I regretted that I was leading the way when I found that the man who was following in my footsteps had his rifle at full cock with his finger on the trigger, and in addition had a beastly habit of keeping it steadily aimed at the small of my back. I therefore reorganised our little section by taking his rifle and giving him mine, which was unloaded.

We thoroughly searched the wood, but found no signs of the Germans. I left Osmond with a couple of men to remove the engine, which was a new Mercédès. I sent it to England next day, as it might be of value to our Air Department, being of the very latest type. Osmond burnt the aeroplane, as it was of no use to us.

Late that night the German pilot and his observer were caught by a mounted Belgian *gendarme*, and brought into Ypres. I attended their examination, which was carried out by the provost-marshal. They were a very woebegone pair, and quite the opposite of what one expected German aviators to be. They were both terribly scared, and were only too willing to say anything. On arriving at H.Q., I found that everybody had brought the Taube down, including Sir Henry

Rawlinson, who had seized my brother's rifle, and fired five shots at it with the cut-out closed.

The only man who couldn't claim it was the anti-aircraft Pom-Pom captain, who was in a fearful rage because he had failed to get his gun into action, through being obstructed by the crowd of generals, etc., all shooting at the Hun. The total bag was counted up to be I Hun aeroplane, 5 sparrows, 3 windows, and most of the telegraph-wires in the main square. My cars did great work this day, as after escorting the transport they had gone out on reconnaissance under Armstrong, Lathbury, and Williams.

Lathbury got right into Commines totally unsupported, and brought back valuable information.

Williams had a good fight, and brought back ten prisoners and reported he had killed nine. Major Armstrong brought in six prisoners and reported killing seven; he could have got more, only unfortunately his gun failed at the critical moment. To complete an excellent morning's work two more prisoners turned up from a most unexpected quarter, Marix arriving with a captain of *Uhlans* and a trooper. He had captured them in the following manner. I had left him with a party guarding the aeroplane; but to a man of Marix's disposition a long wait was rather boring, so he had set off to see if he could come across any *Uhlans* who might still be lurking in the neighbourhood. He took with him eight men, including Private Edmunds, my servant, and Gunner Allen, one of our old Eastchurch marines, and went towards a *château* in which *Uhlans* were reported to be.

Placing his party so that they surrounded the building, he advanced towards it with Edmunds and Allen. Before he had got within 200 yards of it more than twenty Germans dashed out, some mounted, others on foot. He opened fire and gave chase. The Germans on horseback got away; but the ones on foot were not so lucky, as their horses, which they made for, were behind a haystack, and it developed into a foot race between Marix and the Germans who could get there first.

The chase resulted in the death of one German and the capture of the officer and one trooper, who surrendered. The officer was very angry when he saw the small numbers of the party who had defeated him. Marix handed over to me the German captain, who was very punctilious, and I turned him over to the provost-marshal.

General Sir H. Rawlinson was very pleased at the work the cars were doing, and in a letter to the Admiralty, dated October 14th, stated:

I must write a line to express my very sincere thanks for your kindness in allowing me to keep the armoured motors and aeroplanes under Samson. They have all done excellent work. The armoured cars pick up half a dozen prisoners a day, and have instilled a holy terror into our opponents. We could do with double the number of them. Samson and his aeroplanes have obtained us the most valuable information.

CHAPTER 13

Poperinghe

On the 15th I installed our aeroplanes at Poperinghe finding a good field there; we also made Poperinghe my headquarters. The cars were kept in the main square, whilst the officers and men were billeted in various houses surrounding it. A sentry was kept on guard over the cars and lorries day and night; the drivers carried out this duty. As the majority of these men were newly joined from civil life, they had had little training in military duties, although several of them had been under fire in the armoured cars.

One night Felix Samson, on going round to see if everything was correct, found that in place of one sentry there were two on guard. Being greatly struck with this excess of zeal, he sent for Chief Petty Officer King, his chief assistant, and incidentally his chief pirate when we ran out of tools, etc.

> *Felix*: "I am very glad to see how keen our drivers are in guarding their cars; two of them keeping sentry-go instead of only one."
>
> *C.P.O. King*: "Well, sir, the real fact is that some of them aren't so brave as the others, and they feel less lonely at night if they have a pal with them because of ghosts."

I was in close touch now with the aerodrome and Corps H.Q., which was installed at Poperinghe. October 16th was spent reorganising my command. The aeroplanes were put under Lieutenant Davies and the cars under Major Armstrong, and Captain Courtney was sent to take over command of the depot at Dunkirk, Chambers having been recalled to England.

On the same day a welcome addition to my force arrived in the shape of a 3-pounder Vickers Semi-Automatic gun, mounted on a lorry.

Warner, Felix Samson, and myself had worked out the design, and the job had been carried out by the *"Forges et Chantres de France"* at Dunkirk. The mounting was excellent, and neither mounting nor lorry gave any trouble whatsoever.

One section of armoured cars was working during the 16th with the 7th Infantry Division, but were not engaged.

We nearly made a good haul on the 15th, as an Army Service Corps convoy of lorries arrived at Poperinghe, and left their lorries on the main square whilst the officers and men went to have a meal. As we were lamentably short of heavy transport at that time I sent for the worthy Bateman, and he in a few moments converted the markings on two of the lorries to R.N.A.S. Unfortunately, as he was getting well into the third one, the rightful owners arrived, and wanted to know what he was doing. Bateman's pained surprise was worth pounds to see; but they never found the first two, which were spirited away to the aerodrome. We always noticed afterwards that Army Service Corps heavy transport never left their lorries without a strong guard whilst in Poperinghe.

The aeroplanes carried out some good reconnaissance work daily, and although we generally could only muster three aeroplanes in working order, we obtained plenty of intelligence for the IV Corps.

On the 17th we had a chance to try our 3-pounder gun on the enemy, and right well it performed. Corps H.Q. sent me to report to the 3rd Cavalry Division at Zonnebeke, as they had asked for some armoured cars. Arriving there, I reported to General Byng, who sent me to General Kavanagh, who in turn sent me to the 2nd Life Guards at Westroosebeke. I had the 3-pounder on the lorry, one armoured car with a Maxim, and a touring-car.

I found the regiment in the village with outposts holding trenches round the outskirts. On reporting to Colonel Wilson, he said he wanted to get into Oostnieuwkerke, which was reported to be held by the Germans, to see if they could recover the body of Captain Robin Duff, who had been killed on the 16th. They found that they couldn't do the job by themselves, as there were Germans in farmhouses covering the approaches to the village.

I went out along the Hooglede road with a troop of Life Guards guarding my left flank. At the junction of this road and the road to Oostnieuwkerke I came to a stop, as there were some Germans in a farmhouse covering this latter road. I got the 3-pounder into action against this farmhouse, and after half a dozen rounds the Germans bolted; we got a few rounds into them with the armoured car's Maxim, but they quickly got into cover. I was very pleased with the 3-pounder, as we discovered that it was ideal for this type of work.

The shell had a fuse with sufficient delay action to permit of it passing through the walls of a house and detonating inside, and the lorry kept as steady as a rock. Leaving the lorry at the cross-roads with the cavalry, I pushed on to Oostnieuwkerke with the armoured car and the touring-car; four Life Guard officers came with me. Two hundred yards short of the village I left the armoured car, where it could cover our advance, and went on with the Life Guard officers to the first cottage. Here we found an inhabitant, who told us that the *burgomaster* had buried Captain Duff.

Whilst we were going to the grave, which was close by, a patrol of Life Guardsmen was sent into the village. Having visited the grave, there was nothing more to do, so I sent back the four officers in my car, whilst I stayed behind with the armoured car to cover the cavalry patrol. We had not long to wait, as we soon saw some German cyclists coming along the Roulers road; from where we were they provided a fine target, although the range was about 1,100 yards, and we seemed to cause some casualties. Hearing our fire, the cavalry patrol of three men and a sergeant came cantering back.

Allowing them ample time to regain the troop near the cross-roads, we followed them to the 3-pounder and dropped a few shells from it at the Roulers road. I found in a farmyard a long ladder which I used to enable me to get to a spotting position on the roof of a cottage. As this ladder was just the thing I had been looking for, we took it along with us, and it formed part of the lorry's equipment for many a day. As we were no longer required by the 2nd Life Guards we went back to report to General Byng, who sent me back to Poperinghe.

CHAPTER 14

Dadizeele

On the next day, October 18th, I had quite an interesting time. General Byng sent me out with a troop of the Royals to carry out a reconnaissance through Dadizeele and along the Roulers—Menin road. Major Joe Laycock, of the IV Corps staff, came with me to have a chance of shooting a *Boche*. I took Warner, Osmond, and Bill Samson with the 3-pounder lorry and two armoured cars.

Warner acted as gunlayer to the 3-pounder, a job he kept throughout; he was a very fine shot, and would not let anybody else fire it. Armourer's Mate Hughes and Gunner Platford were his chief assistants, and Private Edmunds always used to come as well. With this doughty four one felt confident to take on anything. The equipment of the lorry consisted of four tins of petrol, ninety-six rounds of 3-pounder ammunition, a Lewis gun in case we had a fight at close quarters, the ladder for fire observation, 3-pounder spare-part box, and sundry ropes and tools with which to get the lorry out of the mud if she got into it. In addition, Warner insisted on carrying enough food on board to feed an army. Barratt always used to follow the procession in my car, as I preferred to travel in it until we got to the scene of operations.

We picked up Captain Carrington, of the Royals, at General Byng's H.Q.; he wanted to see the cars in action, so we got him on board the lorry. He was unfortunately killed shortly afterwards. We had to wait for the troop of Royals, so I ordered a halt about I mile outside Dadizeele, as we couldn't carry out our plan properly without their assistance.

The idea was for the cavalry to get round each side of the village; when they were in position the two armoured cars were to go in, the 3-pounder lorry taking up a position where we could command the approaches from the south and east. We hoped in this way to get a good bag. As the Cavalry were behind time, I determined to have a look towards Kezelberg, where it was reported that the enemy were holding a windmill. I hoped to find a suitable position for the 3-pounder to shell this place whilst the armoured cars and cavalry came down by the road.

Leaving the cars, Joe Laycock and I went on foot up into a wood about 500 yards on our right flank. I left word for eight marines to follow us in five minutes.

Getting into the wood, we found we could see Kezelberg from the top of a pile of bricks. Laycock and I climbed up the pile, therefore. I hadn't been there a minute, when I felt that there was something doing, so I looked round, and there, not 100 yards away, were two *Uhlans* sitting motionless on their horses with their backs towards us. As luck would have it, I was without a rifle, a thing I never had previously left behind. The marines were nearly in sight of the Germans, who did not see them. I signalled to the marines to lie down, and then Laycock and I as quietly as possible descended from our bricks, and stole to the marines.

Reaching them, I pointed out the *Huns*, who were within 150 yards of them. Notwithstanding my endeavours to keep them quiet, the marines when getting into position to fire at the *Uhlans* made so much noise that the pair of them looked round and got the shock of their lives. Horrible to relate, they bolted through the trees under a heavy and inaccurate fire, escaping scot-free.

Laycock's remarks were unprintable. He finished up with, "Anyhow, commander, you did show me some *Boches*, as you said you would; but I am damned if I like going out on reconnaissance with you, if you are in the habit of squatting down admiring the view with a Hun a yard off."

The cavalry then arrived and went after the *Huns* like a pack of hounds. It was a fine sight to see them galloping round the thickets, and galloping up to likely spots and then tearing away again, hoping to make the Germans, if there were any, open fire.

Whilst they were doing this, we went into Dadizeele all ready to shoot anybody, and we very nearly did, as we suddenly came across a troop of Northumberland Hussars, who said that they had been there for over an hour, having come in from the north. I didn't explain that we too had been just about to carry out the capture of Dadizeele with horse, foot, and artillery, quite on the scale of a major operation of war. Anyhow, we collected the Royals and decided to get into the main Roulers-Menin road with the cars, whilst the cavalry stayed in

Dadizeele.

Just at the junction of the main road we came across a German infantryman on sentry-go, getting within 100 yards of him before we saw him or he saw us. We opened fire and dropped him. At the same moment we came under a hot fire from the north, and discovered that there were some trenches manned by German infantry about 500 yards from us, and about 200 yards to the west of the road. We gave those infantry something to think of, as Warner with the 3-pounder could enfilade them; they couldn't stand this, and came out of their trenches, running towards St. Pieter. The Maxims brought down four or five as they ran. Altogether we considered we had killed eight or nine and wounded some more.

I then sent the 3-pounder lorry back to Dadizeele, and remained with the two armoured cars at the crossroads well sheltered by some cottages.

We remained in this position for some time, until we got intelligence of a large body of German Infantry coming along the road from Menin. As the surrounding country was very bad for motorcar fighting it would have been fatal to stay where we were, because they could have surrounded us in no time. We gave the advance party a few rounds and then bolted for Dadizeele, where we discovered that the Royals and Northumberland Hussars had fallen back from Dadizeele to Terhand. Following them to the latter place, I found that our infantry of the 7th Division had arrived, and that they had started to dig a line of rifle pits from Terhand to the south-west, covering Becelaere.

The Royals having received orders to rejoin their regiment, I was left with a roving commission, and as we all wanted to have a go at the German infantry, I determined to try to work down, to the Roulers-Menin road from another route, striking south towards Pannemolen and then east. I found the road very bad for the heavy lorry, and our progress was slow. Just as we were approaching Pannemolen, one of the men saw a handkerchief being waved from a window, and the sails of a windmill towards Gheluwe immediately started to revolve.

I ordered Warner to take a shot at the windmill, as it was certain that it was occupied by either Germans or spies. The range was 2,000 yards. Warner hit the building with his first shot. I told him to lay his gun for the ladder which went up to the entrance, and wait in case anybody came out. Sure enough, out popped a German. Warner fired and scored a bull's-eye; it was a splendid bit of shooting. Warner fired half a dozen more shells at the windmill; but no one else came out, so we assumed that either there was no one else there, or we had killed them.

A very excited Belgian civilian then arrived on the scene, who informed us that a large body of German infantry were coming through the wood on our right flank; this wood was within 10 yards of the road, and we were therefore in a bad position. I sent the 3-pounder lorry back beyond the wood to a safe distance from it, out of rifle range, but easily within range of the 3-pounder. Laycock and Carrington with six men went into the wood to stalk the Germans, whilst Osmond and I stayed outside with two cars.

After a time, our party returned reporting the wood clear; evidently the Germans had fallen back or the civilian had been mistaken. Going back to the lorry, we saw some men by a farm; we could not tell whether they were English or German, so Laycock and I did a scout towards them. We found they were a patrol of the Northumberland Hussars. This finished our day, as it was getting late, so we returned to Poperinghe; our return journey was punctuated by subdued chuckles from Warner, thinking of the German who had come out of the mill. On our way we passed a Squadron of Life Guards, who greeted us with shouts of, "Hallo, Jack, you've still got your ——— ladder?"

Chapter 15

Co-Operation on the Roulers-Menin Road

On October 19th we had some very tough fighting, and the 3-pounder proved its worth. Reporting to General Byng, he sent me on to General Kavanagh, one of the Brigadier's 3rd Cavalry Division, and from him I received orders to split up my party. One section, consisting of two armoured cars, was to attack Ledeghem in support of some cavalry, whilst the other section, which comprised two armoured cars and the 3-pounder lorry, was to support a squadron of the 2nd Life Guards, who were to deal with some *Uhlans* at Rolleghemcappelle. I sent Osmond in command of the first section, and went myself with the second, taking Marix, Warner, and Lathbury. Staff-Surgeon Wells, with an ambulance and a touring-car, was in attendance on both parties.

We crossed the main Roulers-Menin road, and leaving the 3-pounder about 400 yards to the east of the road, by a windmill within 2,200 yards of Rolleghemcappelle, I went on to the cavalry, the majority of whom were close to the railway crossing about midway between the lorry and the village. They had already driven off the *Uhlans*, and were dealing with one or two snipers in the field close by, who were making the road rather unhealthy.

As this road was impracticable for the 3-pounder, I went back to it, meaning to take it farther to the east. I had just got back to the lorry, when I heard heavy rifle fire, and looking towards the village saw large numbers of German infantry pouring out of it and spreading over the fields.

They were giving the Life Guards a very bad time, and I could see the horse-holders suffering severely from the fire; the dismounted troopers were running for their horses. We immediately opened fire with the 3-pounder and the two Maxims. Warner got his gun firing at full speed, getting off more than sixteen rounds a minute at the Infantry, who suffered severely from his direct fire at 1,500 yards. Marix, with his car, moved about 20 yards farther up the road, where he got a good enfilade fire to bear on another big body of Germans debouching from a wood on our side of the village. This fire stopped them from advancing, and they fell back. Meanwhile, the Germans who could not stand the 3-pounder fire retreated to the village.

Whilst they were doing this the Life Guards got a chance to get away, and they came streaming past us, many of them two on the same horse. As they came up to us, they shouted out that our gun had saved them, and it was certain that it had.

We had fired forty shells, and I could see over twenty German corpses lying on the ground.

Funnily enough, in 1925 I was stopped in the street by a man who came up to me and said:

"I am glad to see you again, sir. You wouldn't remember me; but I was a trooper in the Life Guards, and you saved us with your gun outside Moorslede. If it hadn't been for you, we would have had a very bad time of it."

Where we were we had a splendid position with an excellent field of fire practically all round; the windmill provided a good lookout post, and nobody could get within effective rifle range of us without being seen. The two armoured cars, which I placed about 200 yards in front of the lorry, could cover the ground with their machine-guns, and I determined to stay where I was as long as possible. The cavalry were supporting us on the main road behind; thus there was no chance of being surrounded unless we were attacked from the Roulers direction.

We soon got into action again, as from the windmill we saw bodies of German infantry to the west. They were well within range of the 3-pounder, and every time we saw some Germans in close order, we put three or four shells into them at ranges of between 2,500-3,000 yards. We were now joined by two horse artillery guns, and the situation was ideal from our point of view, as we combined with the R.H.A. guns in the following manner. If we saw the Germans get into the shelter of a house, we used to put two or three shells into it, and about fifteen seconds after we fired the R.H.A. would send over a couple of shrapnel. Our shells always made the *Huns* move, and then they got caught by the shrapnel. This went on for about an hour, and we enjoyed ourselves immensely. Old Warner was in his element, but like all good things in this world it had to come to an end.

I received a message that large bodies of German infantry were coming down the main road from Roulers, and that the cavalry were falling back. This meant that there was every chance of our being cut off and surrounded, so we ceased fire, and retired to the junction of the Roulers to Menin and the Moorslede roads. Osmond and his cars joined me here; as he was short of ammunition and petrol, I sent them back to Ypres, and at the same time Lord Annesley was dispatched to bring out some more 3-pounder ammunition. Wells also arrived on the scene with his ambulance and car full of wounded, and went off to Zonnebeke to unload them. Osmond had experienced some fairly heavy fighting round Ledeghem, and the cars had accounted for a fair number of Germans.

The cavalry and artillery returned to Moorslede through Snosekot, passing south of the Moorslede road, which I was on. The only troops left near us were a machine-gun section of Life Guards, who were in the fields close behind where we were. Looking round for a good position for the 3-pounder lorry, I found an excellent spot about 50 yards up the Moorslede road. A handy haystack provided a spotting position. Our dispositions were soon made. Lathbury was stationed with one armoured car about 50 yards up the Roulers-Menin road. The ladder was placed against the haystack, and I mounted to my observation-post.

As nothing was in sight, Warner delved into his larder and produced lunch, which we commenced to eat. It would have been difficult to find a better situation than the one we were in, providing as it did a practically clear field of fire along the Roulers road and across the fields between this road and Moorslede, which stood on hilly ground about 2½ miles distant. We had hardly started our meal when I perceived a patrol of German infantry coming through Veldmolen village, 1,700 yards from where we were. Four 3-pounder shells not only sent them back in a hurry, less one or two, but provided us with excellent registration on the junction of a big wood with the Rouler-Menin road.

Within five minutes a large body of Infantry came into sight marching in column of fours along the outside of this wood.

Their numbers seemed endless: probably there were two battalions; unfortunately, I couldn't open fire until they reached the road, as a clump of trees prevented the gun from bearing on them. Warner was therefore told to lay on the road at the point where the end of the wood adjoined it, and stand by to fire ten shots rapid. Having fired these, he was to shift his point of aim to a convenient tree standing 100 yards on the Moorslede side of the road and then to stand by to fire six rounds rapid. It was most tantalising to see this splendid target without being able to fire at it, and I couldn't understand why Lathbury was not firing. I found out afterwards that he couldn't see them. I nearly fell off the haystack trying to attract his attention.

To my delight the Life Guards machine-gun section moved their guns up and opened fire at a range of about 1,000 yards. I had never up to date seen such effective shooting. The Germans were literally mown down like corn with a scythe; their casualties must have been at least sixty or seventy. I will say one thing; they did not break their ranks, but went steadily marching on. I waited until the first ten or twelve parties of fours had crossed the road and then told Warner to fire. The result was beyond my wildest expectations. Our little shells, filled with lyddite, burst right amongst them, and those that escaped the first tornado of shells ran into the second one. I could see them dropping like ninepins, and the road was strewn with bodies.

The Life Guards machine-guns now fell back at the trot, passed behind us, and went on to Moorslede. Lathbury followed them. It was apparent that we would have to move, and do it quickly, so I ordered "Stand by," and came down the ladder. Within ten seconds we were ready to move, the ladder in position, and the gun secured. Fortunately, along the Moorslede road there were about half a dozen cottages, fairly equally spaced apart, and all on the Germans' side of the road. I realised that we could make good use of them, and fight a very effective retiring action from cottage to cottage, as we could fire the gun whilst practically the whole of the lorry was sheltered by the cottage.

We spent nearly forty minutes fighting like this, until we reached Moorslede. We used to stop behind a cottage, and wait until we got a good target, then fire half a dozen rounds and bolt to the next cottage. The *Hun* field guns which turned on to us never had a chance, as they couldn't do anything against us behind a house, and they never knew when we were about to make a dash for the next one.

They made very bad shooting at the moving lorry, and only once did they burst shrapnel in close proximity to us. We enjoyed ourselves immensely at this game; our only regret was that we were very short of ammunition.

Our horse artillery meanwhile were firing from the crest of

Moorslede Hill, and there was no doubt that the *Hun* infantry was suffering heavily from their fire, and was also held back every now and then by our 3-pounder enfilading them.

Arriving at Moorslede, I found General Julian Byng standing on the sky-line surrounded by his staff. I went up to report to him, and he asked me how much ammunition I had left. I told him thirteen rounds. He then said that he was evacuating Moorslede, and was going to retire to Passchendaele. He would leave one Squadron in Moorslede, which would remain until I was ready to go. I was to wait for fifteen minutes after the cavalry had retired, and then I was to expend my last thirteen rounds on the first good target I could see; having done this I was to retire through Moorslede to Passchendaele and then to Zonnebeke; to fill up with ammunition there, and finally report to him, if I could do so before dark.

Whilst he was giving me these orders the Germans started to shell us; but he went on quite unperturbed, although he was as I said standing on the sky-line. Practically every time I had to report to him, I got mixed up in a "hate," and I used to want to avoid him as much as possible, as he seemed a magnet for shells of all shapes and sizes.

He then moved off, after expressing his pleasure at our work.

The R.N.A.S. was now in the proud but lonely position of covering the retirement of the 3rd Cavalry Division, and also remaining with their guns in action after the R.H.A. had been withdrawn. The site we were told to stay on was rather exposed, and the time period felt extraordinarily lengthy. Luckily, we had not long to wait after it elapsed, as the Germans were collecting behind some trees. We soon got a fine target, range 1,200 yards, on a big body of Infantry coming out of a copse, and we gave them our last twelve rounds, keeping one for eventualities.

It didn't take long for us to get from our site to Moorslede village. Passing through it, followed by the squadron of cavalry, we were nearly clear of the village when the German field guns opened on it with shrapnel. Warner saw the hands of the clock on the church tower go back fifteen minutes, showing that there was a spy at work. Unfortunately, no one could stay behind to deal with him, as the Germans were coming on fairly quickly.

We got to Zonnebeke, and waited for our ammunition to arrive; but it did not come until nearly dark; therefore, we had to return to Poperinghe.

I was very pleased with the behaviour of the gun mounting and lorry, which had stood up to the strain of rapid fire without a sign of giving way. Warner was in the seventh heaven of delight, although he was bruised all over and possessed a black eye through the jump of the gun.

Marix arrived back at Poperinghe late that night, having had a most interesting time. He had, after leaving me at the windmill, gone back to Moorslede, and then got into Roulers, where he found the French cavalry about to retire. On the way back from there he found the Duke of Roxburghe, who was severely wounded, lying in a farmhouse with his servant standing by him. Marix got him into the car, and thus saved him from certain capture. Coming along to Moorslede *via* Passchendaele, he arrived at the former place, where he found some cavalry outposts outside the village. I had just left, he was told; at the request of a staff officer, he did some covering work with his Maxim on the Germans, who were apparently about to advance through the town. In this work he was assisted by a Belgian armoured car driven by M. Charbon, a most gallant gentleman, who well earned a great reputation for his armoured-car work.

Chapter 16

Hollebeke and Ypres

Unfortunately, next day, when close to Zonnebeke, we got bogged, and one of the springs of the lorry broke. This put it out of action for two days, but the spring was repaired by a local Poperinghe blacksmith, who made an excellent job of it.

The aeroplanes were doing good work during this period; but we were very much handicapped by a shortage of them. I made frequent applications for additional machines; but unfortunately, there were hardly any available in England at this period; therefore, we had to get on as well as we could with what we had. The result was that our flying was not on as big a scale as we wished.

On the 20th and 21st October armoured cars were in reserve during the fighting at Zonnebeke, and were not engaged, although they encountered a fair amount of shell-fire. Reconnaissance work was also carried out on the Menin road.

Felix Samson, who was, with one section of cars, being sent out ahead on a motorcycle, suddenly came across a patrol of *Uhlans*, nearly running into one of them coming round a corner; turning round his engine stopped, and he had to run with it until it started, being chased back by them for a short distance; and though a motorcycle can soon run away from cavalry on a road it was touch and go.

On the 22nd I reported to General Byng, and he sent me to operate under the Brigadier who was holding Zandvoorde. I had the 3-pounder lorry and three armoured cars with me, and on getting to the foot of the hill on which Zandvoorde stood we found that we couldn't get the lorry any farther owing to the shocking state of the road. I therefore went up to Zandvoorde in a car. On finding the brigadier, he ordered me to send some cars to support a squadron of cavalry which was going down to a *château* on the north side of the railway line close to Hollebeke. This *château* was occupied by the enemy, and they were to be driven out.

I sent Osmond with two cars to carry out this job. With the lorry and the other car, I waited midway between Klein Zillebeke and Zandvoorde in case anything turned up, and as nothing did except some big German shells, I went off to see how Osmond was getting on. Taking a wrong turning, we found ourselves right on top of the *château*. Fortunately for us the Germans had been ejected, and a troop of dragoons were in occupation of it, with a picket on the railway embankment crossing the canal, which was parallel to the railway line.

I found Osmond close to the canal behind some cottages; he had been firing at some German infantry who were between him and Houthem. The situation was that the 4th Hussars were in trenches at Hollebeke, that a troop of dragoons were in the *château* on our left flank, with a picket on the railway embankment abreast of us, while we were 700 yards in front of the hussars.

The position seemed ideal for us; the only danger was the enemy getting to close quarters from the direction of Houthem, as the country between us and that village was covered with small copses of trees, and there were also one or two houses which provided cover for an advance. I determined to stay where we were, as we might be of value.

One armoured car along the path to our right provided a flank guard; Osmond scaled a tree and provided a lookout on the country in front of us; I got on to the roof of a cottage, from which I could see along the railway line and the canal, and I was also in verbal communication with the dragoon picket on the embankment.

The 3-pounder lorry was alongside the cottage, and had a clear field of fire down the canal towards Houthem, which was distant 2,500 yards from us. Two bridges across the canal were at ranges of 800 yards and 2,000 yards respectively; we therefore commanded the approach to Houthem from Commines and from the east, and also covered the ground in front of Hollebeke. We soon got into action as parties of Germans began to cross the two bridges. Three or four rounds from the 3-pounder at each party caused many casualties amongst them; and there was little doubt that we were annoying them. Unfortunately, Osmond came down from the tree, as he was getting cramped, and sent a man up it to replace him who had not got such a sharp pair of eyes as Osmond.

This resulted in a party of Germans getting into a house within 200 yards of us, and we were suddenly subjected to a heavy rifle fire at this close range. I was at the moment talking to Osmond alongside one of the armoured cars, and we both had some narrow squeaks, although most of the fire was directed at the lorry. Fortunately, the gun shield was bullet-proof. The fire was coming from two directions: from a house about 200 yards in our front, and from some trees about 400 yards to our right front. Osmond turned his machine gun on to the trees, whilst I ran to the lorry and told Warner to shell the house.

Warner and Hughes worked the gun whilst the rest took cover. The 3-pounder shells soon caused the rifle fire to cease except from one window, where I could see that a steel plate had been placed, behind which a stubborn fellow kept up his fire. At this short-range Warner soon got a direct hit on the plate, and this finished the fire from the house. Warner then turned his gun on to the trees, and half a dozen shells into them made the Germans run for home. The dragoons who were on the embankment dropped one or two of the survivors as they came into sight. The whole episode only lasted about a couple of minutes; but while it was happening it was a pretty hot engagement. Extraordinary to relate, we did not suffer a single casualty, although the lorry and cars had many marks on them.

This made us keep a better lookout, and a post of two men was stationed behind a wood pile about 50 yards in front of the armoured car, providing a clear view of the approach in that direction.

We remained where we were for about another hour, when I received a message from Major Howell, in command of the Hussars in Hollebeke, asking me to come up there, as they could see Germans in Houthem providing good targets for my gun. I took the lorry into the village, leaving the armoured cars at our old position.

We remained in Hollebeke until dark, shooting at various targets close to Houthem, being provided with excellent observation by two hussar officers in an attic, who had a splendid view. One target we fired at was the lock house on the canal bank close to Houthem, the range being 2,300 yards. Twelve Germans were seen to go into the house. We fired ten rounds at it, scoring eight hits; one shell scored a direct bull's-eye on a German who was looking out of the window. The IV Corps *gazette* reported on this incident as follows: "Neither head nor shell has since been seen." The house was badly knocked about, and only five Germans were counted as they left it; therefore, it was safe for us to claim seven.

The next day, October 23rd, we were again sent to Hollebeke. On this occasion we were not the only artillery on our side, as a battery of R.H.A. were in action about 1,000 yards from Hollebeke in the direction of St. Eloi. These guns were shelling the enemy, who were digging a line of trenches in front of Houthem. We took part in this whenever we could get a suitable target. The only ones worth shooting at with our gun were bodies of men in close order, or houses occupied by the enemy. We got two lucky shots at some transport wagons, who were, as they thought, concealed behind a hedge; three wagons were put out of action, and some horses killed. On the whole the day was a very quiet one, as up to date the Germans had not shelled Hollebeke to any extent.

I had started an anti-aircraft patrol, consisting of one aeroplane, which used to fly over our artillery positions with the object of preventing hostile aeroplanes from discovering them. In conjunction with this we were working a ground signal above Hollebeke. Marix was in charge of this, and he always said he disliked the job, as they seemed always to select a spot that was inevitably subjected to a severe "hate."

Our anti-aircraft patrol was of little utility, because the only aeroplane available was too slow and a bad climber, the only efficient aeroplanes being used for reconnaissance. In the one or two encounters our aeroplanes had with the enemy, the *Huns* always ran away and didn't wait to be shot.

Practically all the armoured cars were now sent to Dunkirk to be re-armoured in accordance with our designs, General Sir H. Rawlinson considering that at present during the trench warfare the cars were of little use, and that if open warfare were restarted the cars would be of greater value if properly armoured than they were before. I was of the same opinion. We had our design ready, and Felix Samson was sent to Dunkirk to supervise the work, which was carried out by our old friends the "*Forges et Chantres de France.*"

We now had additional aeroplane reconnaissance to carry out, having been ordered by the Admiralty to keep a patrol over the coast between Zeebrugge, Ostend, and Middelkerke; this made it harder work still for the few aeroplanes I possessed. Two new Bristols were allocated to me, one of which Rainey successfully brought over; the other one was shot down over Dixmude.

Two splendid officers were lost in this aeroplane. Beevor, who was one of the original members of the squadron, and an old Eastchurch man, and Lord Annesley, who came over as his passenger. They were both sterling good fellows, and we all felt their loss very much indeed. It appeared that they lost their way in the mist, and coming out of it found themselves at a low altitude over the German lines. Curiously enough, both of them had fought for the Turks in the Balkan War. As well as being fine officers, they were both very cheery messmates.

An addition to our squadron was old No. 3, whose age I would be sorry to state; but an aeroplane had to be in a pretty bad way before we sent it home. A modern pilot would have had a shock if he had been asked to take any of our aeroplanes on a flight; we were pretty well hardened to things, however, and if the machine flew, we were grateful.

German aeroplanes started to pay a little attention to Poperinghe, dropping bombs nearly every day, but as they kept at a very high altitude and the bombs were only about 12 lb. weight, they didn't worry us very much. We did a little in retaliation, and one day Davies let go a bomb on Poperinghe by mistake owing to the bomb gear, which was of home-made type, functioning when it shouldn't have done. Funnily enough, it fell in the garden of his own billet; we had to assure the owner of the house that it had been dropped by a *Hun*.

On October 24th I took the 3-pounder lorry to Hollebeke again; the village was now held by the 129th Baluchi Infantry, who had relieved the 4th Hussars. This was the first time Indian troops had been put in the line, and it was rather interesting—talking to them. One or two I found could speak English, and with the few words of Hindustani I could remember I found I could get on with them.

The 3-pounder was used every time we could get a suitable target; but the latter were not plentiful that day.

During the afternoon Hollebeke became the centre of attraction, as firstly the naval armoured train arrived, and taking up its position close behind the village began to unload its 6-inch and 4.7-inch shells into Commines. After this had been going on for some little time a Taube came over to see what was happening. Having seen the armoured train, it fired some lights, and the Germans started to get busy with 8-inch howitzers and 5.9-inch guns. The train cleared out, luckily, as the second shell exploded on the railway line exactly where the engine had been. The train having departed, the Germans turned their attention solely on Hollebeke. The first shell they fired fell just short of the village close alongside Marix and myself, who were sitting by the roadside selecting a target for the 3-pounder. The Germans soon got the proper range, and shell after shell burst in the village, which soon began to lose its orderly appearance.

The Baluchis came out of the trenches, but were sent back to them, as they were far safer, it was explained, where they were than in the village.

The 3-pounder had one or two narrow shaves, and as the streets were soon rendered impassable for it by debris, I had to send it back clear of Hollebeke. We remained in the village with an armoured car until dusk in case of an infantry attack, and then left for home.

This finished our active operations at Hollebeke, as on arrival next day we found the road impassable for the lorry, and we had to give up any further idea of using it there.

The 3-pounder had no further fighting at Ypres, although we made two or three attempts to get it into action. This was due to the terrible condition of the roads, which were torn up by shells and covered with mud. The only roads passable for us were the main roads. The side-roads were impossible, and we had some bad times getting the heavy lorry out of ditches.

Every day, in accordance with the general's orders, it was taken to Hooge to stand by at Corps H.Q. in case it was required. One day Warner got it into Gheluvelt and got off a few rounds; but he was too close to the enemy to render it possible to remain where he was, and he had to beat a hasty retreat.

On the 24th, as Corps H.Q. had moved to Hooge, I moved my H.Q. to Ypres, where O'Caffrey had found us an excellent residence, possessing one of the few bathrooms in the town.

A welcome addition to my force arrived in the person of Anthony Wilding, the Lawn Tennis champion, who held a temporary commission in the marines; he soon proved himself a most excellent messmate, and was full of energy and fighting spirit.

One day, whilst I was waiting outside Hooge *château*, Colonel Seely came along in a car, and recognising me asked me to come with him up to the front line. Leaving word where I had gone, I got into his car, and we went on towards Gheluvelt. Arriving in the outskirts, I said we had better get out of the car and proceed on foot, as Warner had been badly sniped there about an hour before, and a good many Germans were evidently still in the outskirts on the Ypres side.

The gallant ex-Minister of War was loath to leave his car until I said if he wanted to see anything he could see far more on foot than he would in the car, for we were certain to draw shell-fire as well as provide a target for snipers at the slow pace we were forced to go; in addition, I pointed out that the lunch that he carried in the car might suffer if the car got hit by a shell.

Taking my advice, he left the car in a side-road, and we went on afoot. We hadn't far to go when we proved Warner's statement to be true, and a late Cabinet Minister was nearly in the Roll of Honour. We got to a good position, where we could see everything; in fact, we were right up as far as any of our troops, and after he was satisfied with what he could see, which was really very little, and long after I had had enough, he proposed a return to the car and lunch.

Getting back to the car, we found the site had been chosen as a target for the German artillery; but Colonel Seely insisted on having lunch where we were. Although the meal was very good, I would have much preferred to eat it farther back. I noticed his driver was of my opinion, because he took his food farther away; in fact, he must have gone nearly a quarter of a mile back. I was extremely glad when at last the colonel said we had better go back. This trait of appearing to enjoy shell-fire seems a failing of Cabinet Ministers, as Mr. Winston Churchill suffered from the same complaint at Antwerp. The crew of the armoured car I had detailed for his use said that he always got them into the very hottest corners and then stopped apparently to look at the view.

I had a couple of expeditions with General Montgomery, Chief of the Staff to the IV Corps, who kindly took me out with him along our line. He always used to take Sergeant-Major Jenkins, who was the Chief Clerk of the IV Corps, as Jenkins said that a breath of fresh air was good for him, and he seemed to enjoy these excursions.

The Corps Office was in the Town Hall at Ypres, and Mr. Smeeth and Mansell were provided with desks in the General Staff Clerks' room. I was allowed to do my work in the General Staff room next door to General Rawlinson's office. Sir Henry always insisted on the aeroplane pilot and observer bringing their reports in to him personally, and I felt certain that this was an excellent scheme in those days of few aeroplanes; it provided that personal feeling of confidence in your general that is so important in war.

There couldn't have been a happier family than the staff of the IV Corps, and tea-time was always a function I attended. Even in the worst times Sir Henry and General Montgomery were always cheerful; so were Colonel Dallas, Major Amery, M.P., Major Baird, M.P., the Duke of Westminster, and Lieutenant Borrett, who used to drive Sir Henry. Luncheon with Sir Henry was always a meal to be looked forward to.

From October 26th our principal duty was to observe the coast-line to see if guns were being mounted. It was certain that we would soon be unable to do the work required for the army and that wanted by the navy unless reinforcement of aeroplanes were sent to me. Ypres was itself shelled for the first time on the 28th. The shells were of small calibre, and appeared to come from a naval gun, about 12-pounder. I have never understood where the gun was, as the German lines were still too far away for it to be possible for a gun of this size to reach Ypres.

On the 30th I moved my headquarters back to Poperinghe in order to be close to the aerodrome, as armoured-car work was of little further use.

CHAPTER 17

The Last of Our Armoured Cars

The Duke of Westminster joined up with my squadron on November 2nd, as the IV Corps was being broken up, and Sir Henry Rawlinson was going home to bring out a new division. The 7th Division and 3rd Cavalry Division were practically reduced to the size of brigades. The casualties they had suffered were tremendous, and there is no question that the IV Corps saved the situation. I had the honour in this war to fight with the three finest bodies of the old Regular Army, the former two in Flanders, and the 29th Division in the Dardanelles, and if any troops were better than these three divisions, they must have been superhuman.

We soon found that along the Belgian coast the antiaircraft guns were becoming a factor in our lives soon to develop into a perfect nuisance. Anti-aircraft gunnery always seemed a more perfect art on the German side than on ours, and on the coast, guns appeared to be more plentiful and to shoot more accurately than elsewhere.

On November 6th Field-Marshal French sent for me, and I had the honour of having breakfast with General Sir Henry Wilson before I was taken in to see the field-marshal. I will always remember that day, firstly because of the varied menu at breakfast, rather a different meal from what I had been accustomed to at our mess, and secondly for the interview of over half an hour which I had alone with the great commander. He struck me as looking so very fit and confident.

He was much interested in armoured cars and their capabilities, and he decided that a section of the cars which had been re-armoured by me should when ready be sent to General Sir H. Smith-Dorrien in the La Bassée zone to test their utility. He proposed that the whole of my command should be attached to G.H.Q., and both aeroplanes and armoured cars used directly under general orders. I was all for this, as I was finding it very difficult to work satisfactorily under two masters at the same time, *i.e.,* the 1 Corps and the Admiralty. He then decided to send me to England immediately, carrying a letter from him to Mr. Winston Churchill, stating that he wanted me put directly under his command, and that I should be given some more aeroplanes.

I went off at once in my car, taking the Duke of Westminster and Bill Samson with me. At Boulogne my car was placed on board, the field-marshal's letter being a very potent password. I arrived in London the same night, and found the metropolis looking exactly the same; you could hardly tell a war was on, in fact, and hardly anybody I met seemed to realise the situation in France.

I stayed with my father and mother, who were very much surprised to see me, and naturally anxious to hear all my news. Luckily enough my youngest brother, Philip, who was unfortunately killed in the last fortnight of the war, happened to have come up for a night's leave from his regiment, in which he was a second lieutenant under training.

We all had a great night, going to a theatre. I will never forget my mother's delight in the fact that all her four sons were serving and that three of them were with her again.

She was doing great work herself, as she had organised a fund to send out clothing and comforts to the R.N.A.S. This organisation grew by leaps and bounds, and although her name never appeared, she was not only the instigator, but the chief worker during the whole war. Few realised what a debt of gratitude they owed to her.

She was a wonderful mother to us four, and even when we were together, she always used to write to each of us separately, two letters a week.

Next morning, I went to the Admiralty and saw Mr. Winston Churchill, to whom I gave the field-marshal's letter. I explained the whole situation to him, and how we were handicapped by the lack of aeroplanes. Lord Fisher, who had just taken over the post of First Sea Lord, was in the room at the time. Mr. Churchill said that it was extremely likely that we would have to concentrate our energies on the Belgian coast, and make every effort to attack Zeppelin bases in case they opened some in Belgium.

I returned to France on November 8th and found my squadron back in its old quarters at Dunkirk. The marines had been sent home to England, as it had been decided that armoured cars were of little use for trench warfare. We had, in fact, no further experience of this type of warfare, although as will be seen we were enabled to make good use of the 3-pounder from time to time until we left France.

I had by now six cars armoured according to our own ideas. They certainly provided more efficient protection for the crews, and we all wished that we had had them from the start, as we could have caused the Germans a great deal of trouble with them. I had a name painted on each car and selected the names of places where we had fought with success, like "Cassel," "Orchies," "Aniche," and "Douai." The cars were well camouflaged by being painted in various colours and patterns, and they really looked a very workmanlike unit.

Warner, Felix Samson, and I were constantly working at new designs, and we produced and had built three novel war machines. One was the forerunner in a way of the tank. A 5-ton Mercédès lorry was armoured completely, and provided with an armoured battery, mounting six machine-guns. A conning tower was added for the commanding officer, and an additional steering-wheel was placed to enable the lorry to be steered with ease when going backwards.

The chassis took the weight with ease, and it would have been a tough nut to tackle in open warfare. Its only drawback was the necessity of keeping to the roads.

The second weapon was a travelling mounting to carry a 3-pounder provided with a shield; this was towed by a Rolls Royce car, armoured all over. This mounting proved excellent. We took it to the Dardanelles with us, and funnily enough in 1916 I found the gun and mounting on board H.M.S. *Hannibal* at Alexandria. The captain kindly let me have it, and I placed it on board my ship, H.M.S. *Ben-my Chree*, where it got into action twice, finally going down with the ship when she was sunk. This type of mounting was used in North Russia in 1918-19.

The third invention was an anti-aircraft mounting on a lorry. This proved first-class, and was of extremely simple and straightforward design.

We never received any acknowledgment for our designs, except from the French, who were very much interested in them.

General Foch, hearing of them, sent his chief of staff to look at all three, and he expressed his admiration for them and considered they would all prove of utility.

Part 2: The "Iron Coast" (November 1914–February 1915)

Chapter 1

Dunkirk Again

I now set about reorganising the squadron. Owing to lack of accommodation at the aerodrome two houses were taken in Malo-les-Bains, the northern suburb of Dunkirk. In one house H.Q. was installed, containing the office and the H.Q. officers, consisting of myself, Staff-Surgeon Wells, Surgeon Anderson; Felix Samson, in charge of transport and armoured cars; Bill Samson, Intelligence; Lieutenant Warner, Armament Officer; Lieutenant Wilding, Transport Officer; and Lieutenant Aspinall, Transport Officer.

The other house was occupied by Lieutenant Davies, my second-in-command; Surgeons Williams and Scott, Lieutenant Bernard Isaac, observer officer, and the pilots.

One duty officer and a doctor in rotation slept at the aerodrome. A garage was obtained in a big shed at the docks, and Felix Samson soon organised an efficient repair shop for our armoured cars and motor transport.

The French gave me every assistance, and turned over to me the one permanent hangar at the aerodrome. This hangar was used as an engine and aeroplane repair shop. The aeroplanes in flying trim were kept in the open, until some hangars were put up; but they were not completed until February.

Cavrois O'Caffrey was installed at Folkestone, where he organised his intelligence service, with agents in Belgium. He kept in communication with these agents through Holland, and he soon had a splendid service going. I think there is little doubt that our intelligence at this time was quite the most reliable. The Admiralty gave me a very generous allowance for O'Caffrey's work, resulting in a good class of man being employed. O'Caffrey himself used to come over to Dunkirk twice a week to report. The English Mission with the Belgians was now under the command of Colonel Tom Bridges, shortly to be made a general.

His office was at Furnes until Belgian G.H.Q. was shifted to La Panne, when he moved to the latter town. On his staff he had Prince Alexander of Teck, Major Baird, M.P., and Lieutenant Shoppee, R.N.

I soon got into touch with Colonel Bridges, and he was always a great friend to the R.N.A.S., doing everything in his power to help me, and arranging for our 3-pounder to operate with the Belgians and French when required in the coastal zone. He and his staff were kindness personified, and it was difficult to escape from staying to lunch or dinner if you went there for anything.

Colonel Bridges or Prince Alexander made a daily tour of the front line, and the example they showed did wonders in keeping up the Belgian appreciation of the British officers' disregard of shell-fire. I accompanied Colonel Bridges on two of his outings, and he certainly took one where you could see things happening. On one occasion I drove him in my car to Nieuport. He took me by way of Wulpen and along the canal to the east of Nieuport. Arriving at a corner about 200 yards from the first houses of Nieuport, he asked me to stop; we remained stationary for about fifteen minutes in full view of the enemy; the road at this spot was well above the level of the surrounding country, and we were only just out of rifle range.

When he had finished looking at the view, and we had started off to enter Nieuport, I asked him why we had stopped such a long time in that exposed position, as I had expected some shelling. "Oh, I did it because Field-Marshal French is coming out to Belgian G.H.Q. tomorrow, and I wanted to test if this road was a dangerous one to bring him on."

He then took me to an advanced observation-post in a house, on the far side of the Yser, from the attic window of which we had a splendid view of the German trenches at quite close quarters. To reach this house we had about 60 yards to go in full view, and within easy rifle range of the Hun, before getting behind some houses.

Lady Dorothy Fielding showed a splendid example of an Englishwoman's pluck and nerve. I lent her one of my drivers for a week or so; when he came back, he told me that he had lived in shell-fire the whole time, as she had taken the car all over the place picking up wounded. He appeared quite glad his job was over, remarking that he was a married man, and that the girl would have got him killed if he had had to stay with her any longer, and adding, "It's a shame to take

PEIRSE, MISS MAXINE ELLIOTT, LADY DROGHEDA, AND ANTHONY WILDING, DUNKIRK, 1914.

a Rolls Royce amongst them big shells; why don't she have a Ford?"

Among other interesting people I came in contact with whilst I was at Dunkirk was Maxime Elliott, who had a barge full of food and clothing for the relief of Belgian civilians. She lived on the barge on the canal close to Furnes, well within shell range. Lady Drogheda was with her for some time, and they certainly showed a splendid example of grit and hard work, and did an enormous amount of real good. I found Maxime Elliott too good a poker expert for me, but I had many a cheery time on board their barge when duty called me to Furnes or La Panne.

Lady Bagot was another who did sterling work. She arrived with a portable hospital, and three men to transport it from Dunkirk to La Panne and then erect it. Of course, the job was impossible with her resources, but she was going to do it somehow. I lent her Felix Samson, some men, and two lorries, and they erected the hospital. They came back full of admiration for her, saying that she used to work like a slave, paddling about all day knee-deep in the good solid Belgian mud helping to put the sections together. I gave her the first proper meal she had eaten for nearly a week. It certainly was a welcome relief from our work to have a visit occasionally from these splendid women, especially as they were so appreciative of any assistance, we could give them.

Other excellent institutions started at Dunkirk were the Duchess of Sutherland's Hospital and the Scotch Women's Hospital, both first-class affairs, which were practically solely run by ladies. The Duchess on one occasion was the direct cause of some English wounded who had been forgotten being picked up.

Hardy, Wells, and the other doctors assisted in the Sutherland Hospital whenever they could.

Our work now was:

(1) To do our utmost to prevent Zeppelins being stationed in Belgium.

(2) To prevent submarines being put together at Bruges.

(3) To attack Zeppelins on their way to and from England.

(4) Reconnoitre Ostend and Zeebrugge daily, watching for submarine activity.

(5) To reconnoitre the coast for guns and batteries.

(6) To make bomb attacks on batteries, submarines, workshops, etc.

This entailed a tremendous amount of flying over a very hot anti-aircraft defence. The German anti-aircraft batteries in the coastal zone were by far the most efficient, and they daily increased in numbers. Our aeroplanes were under constant shell-fire from the instant they crossed the Yser until they recrossed it on the return journey. With the slow speed and bad climbing powers of the aeroplanes I had, anti-aircraft fire was a serious annoyance. A 70-mile-an-hour aeroplane flying at 4,500- 5,000 feet, as we did, was not a very difficult target to hit. The aeroplanes were hit by shell fragments and shrapnel on practically every trip, and we had some very narrow escapes. It was extraordinary how one got used to "Archie," as anti-aircraft guns were soon named; but I always experienced a great feeling of relief when I had safely recrossed the Yser on the homeward journey.

I had my old No. 50 to fly once more—Mr. Brownridge had refitted her in fine style, and she flew as well as she had done when new. Some new pilots arrived shortly after we were installed at Dunkirk, and although at first they were treated with suspicion by the old hands, we soon found them to be real stout-hearted fellows: Hayland-Wilson, G. L. Thomson, and Butler were the newcomers, each of whom has written his name in large letters in the annals of the R.N.A.S. Butler shot down more Gothas who attacked London than anybody else; Thomson became the great expert on Handley-Pages; and Wilson had a crash in the Dardanelles which put an end to his flying career. All three served in the Dardanelles with me.

Davies, Rainey, Courtney, Peirse, Osmond, Marix, and Collet were still with me of the old crowd, all Eastchurch men, and pilots of the first water: Briggs and Sippe left early in November for a special mission, which soon turned out to be the Friedrichshafen attack.

The men worked like slaves, and I never had a case for disciplinary action the whole time I was in France. Any of the carpenters were capable of building an aeroplane, and we did practically do that at Dunkirk. The engineers were equally good; and there is no doubt that it was simply through the hard work and skill of our men that we were enabled to keep up any flying at all with our aeroplanes; no words of mine can adequately express my appreciation of their work, and I venture to say that in addition they were proud to belong to the old squadron.

CHAPTER 2

More Work with the 3-Pounder

On November 10th Colonel Bridges, at the request of the Belgians, asked me to send the 3-pounder lorry out to Kerckmolenburg, midway between Pervyse and Ramscappelle, to try to dislodge about 500 Germans who were in a lot of farm buildings close to Schoorbatthe, as they could not do anything with their field guns.

I took the lorry and a touring-car to see what we could do; Wilding, Warner, and Aspinall came along with me, with Redmond, who was the driver of the lorry in all its fights, while Corporal Brewe and Armourer Hughes completed the party. Great credit is due to Redmond for the way he had driven the heavy lorry over appalling roads and through seas of mud; he had undergone a good deal of shell-fire and rifle fire; but always kept cool and collected, and the skilful way in which he handled the lorry contributed in a great measure to the success it achieved in all its fights.

After a reconnaissance in the touring-car, the only possible route for the lorry was found to be through Pervyse, or what remained of the village, which had suffered very severely and was practically all ruins. From Pervyse to Kerckmolenburg we had to go along the main road, which ran parallel to the Canal de Beverdijk in full view of the enemy. The Belgians in Pervyse told me that we would be certain to be seen, and that the Germans would shell us; they strongly advised us to wait until dark before we went along.

They stated the road was passable if we drove with care, although it was covered with shell craters. I didn't like to keep the Belgians waiting, and in addition I preferred the risk of a bad shelling to the chances of wrecking the lorry in a crater, which was most likely to happen if we tried the road in the dark.

We set off therefore with the touring-car leading to give warning of bad craters. Redmond brought the lorry along in fine style at its top speed, with Warner and company bouncing about like peas inside it, and we safely reached the shelter of a ruined house about 30 yards behind the Belgian trenches. Leaving the motors in shelter, I went to the trench, where I found awaiting me a Belgian staff officer. Wilding and I accompanied him across a field to their advanced picket, from where he pointed out the houses occupied by the Germans, and the suspected position of a couple of field guns.

I found a position in the road about 50 yards from the house, which gave a clear field of fire for the 3-pounder, but at the same time exposed the lorry to full view of the enemy, without any protection. We were out of rifle range, however, and if they started shelling, we would probably be able to get into shelter before they got the range. I took our range-finder about Io yards ahead of the lorry, and found the range to be 2,700 yards. At 11 p.m. we opened fire on the farm buildings. I was controlling the fire, using the range-finder; at the third shot we scored a hit, and we went on hitting, firing thirty rounds during ten minutes.

The Germans were evidently annoyed, as they opened fire with their field battery at 2,200 yards range, using shrapnel. The only thing to do was to cease fire and get back to the shelter of the house, but as luck would have it the engine had stopped and refused to start. I therefore ordered everybody to get to cover in the ditch at the side of the road, until the Germans ceased fire. Fortunately, we all got to cover untouched, and we spent about ten minutes in the ditch watching our ewe-lamb being strafed. Old Warner was in a terrible state, fearing his pet would get damaged. The Germans, however, did not shoot well that day, and they also seemed to have been short of high explosives, as they only used shrapnel.

When a pause occurred, I told Warner to make a dash for it. Warner, Redmond, and company were out of the ditch and into the lorry like a streak, Redmond getting the lorry started first pull of the handle, and off they went for Pervyse. The lorry looked a funny sight bumping along at full speed, and I expected every second to see them disappear in a shell crater; but Redmond dodged them in a marvellous way. The Germans chased them with shrapnel the whole way; but they got into Pervyse without being hit. The rest of us went back in the car *via* Ramscappelle, where we came across the 6th Territorial Regiment of French infantry, our old Douai friends. They recognised us at once, and we went through them to the accompaniment of shouts of "*A Douai,*" "*Vive les Anglais,*" etc.

Osmond, on the 10th, went by car to Dixmude to see Admiral Ronarch, who was asking for aeroplane assistance, and came back greatly impressed by the grand defence the French sailors were putting up; unfortunately, the weather for the next few days was too bad for any aeroplane reconnaissance to be carried out.

The bad weather, however, gave us an opportunity to overhaul our aeroplanes and motor transport, both of which had suffered severely from the last month's work.

Brownridge and Felix Samson soon got a good move on in their respective jobs, and as they both had first-class men, the results of their labours were soon apparent. Nothing seemed too big a job for them to take on, and the transport section, with the aid of blow-lamps and a vice, completed work that appeared impossible to do without a properly equipped workshop.

An armoured car that we had lent to the Oxfordshire Hussars was found lying outside the Motte au Bois, near Hazebrouck, and was brought in by one of Felix Samson's parties, who used to scour the country, picking up cars and lorries which were found abandoned through breakdowns by the roadside. Some were English, others Belgian or French. We got one or two quite good vehicles in this way, which helped to swell our transport column.

The 3-pounder had outings on the 14th and 15th at Nieuport, where it was sent at the request of the French, and under Davies it had the gratification of turning some Germans out of a house in Lombartzyde, and smashing a machine-gun that they brought out to fire on the lorry. The Germans ran to shelter, leaving the wreckage of their gun.

Surgeon Graeme Anderson, who was in attendance with the ambulance, had an unpleasant experience, as he came in for a heavy strafe, no less than twenty 5.9-inch shells bursting close to them in three minutes. The only casualty, however, was Sergeant-Major Bishop, who was firing the gun in place of Warner; he came back with a very bad black eye caused by the jump of the telescopic sight. They were all pleased at the result of their duel with the machine-gun. Captain Courtney, Peirse, and Bill Samson were other officers engaged with the lorry on these two days and again on the 19th.

The 21st saw practically the end of our active operations with the 3-pounder lorry, although on occasions it and armoured cars were sent out to Nieuport to stand by to assist when attacks were planned. I doubt, however, if we would have done any good, as the roads and streets were by this time practically impassable for us.

The weather for the rest of November was appalling, and we found it hard work flying against the strong wind; it was also very unpleasant crawling back in a 70-mile-an-hour aeroplane against a 50-mile-an-hour wind past Zeebrugge and Ostend. They used to give one a fairly heavy dose of anti-aircraft fire, and our aeroplanes got badly shot about. On one occasion I was nearly an hour getting from Zeebrugge to Nieuport, continually altering course and altitude to escape being hit. I distinctly saw one big shell which must have been an 11-inch from one of their naval guns coming at me. It burst about 100 yards in front and slightly to the left of me.

This was the first occasion that I had seen a shell in the air whilst in flight, and I remember that the other pilots doubted my statement; but Peirse soon confirmed it. It was a fatal policy to keep over the sea, as if you did that you were fired at by all the big naval guns.

We used to drop bombs on every flight, and we so improved our accuracy in this art that we were really quite good shots later on in France and the Dardanelles. We used to depend solely on our eye, and did not use the very kindergarten type of bomb sights then available. In fact, I personally relied upon my eye alone in 1915 and 1916, with, I think, fairly satisfactory results.

On the 21st we heard of the splendid attack made on the Zeppelin factory at Friedrichshafen. Two of these pilots were old members of our squadron, Briggs and Sippe, and it made us feel that we were really a very fine crowd and second to none.

On the 24th Courtney, Peirse, and myself set out to try the experiment of bombing the minefield off Ostend with the hopes. of setting off the mines. We ran into a bad patch of fog, and I couldn't find the buoy off the Kursaal, which was supposed to mark the end of the field, so I expended my bombs at the Middelkerke batteries. Courtney found the buoy, and although he didn't explode any mines with his bombs, he destroyed the buoy.

One of the armoured-car drivers had picked up in Nieuport a little dog of no particular breed. He was, except for some nuns, the last civilian inhabitant in the town. He soon became the pet of the Squadron, and was christened Nieuport. He always used to accompany his master in the car, and his favourite position was standing on the bonnet. He went all through the Dardanelles with the squadron, and was successfully smuggled past the Customs on our return to England.

CHAPTER 3

The First Night-Bombing Flight

On November 25th we started off to do an attack in force on Zeebrugge and Ostend. We could only raise three aeroplanes, however—old No. 50, which I took; a Bristol, which Courtney flew; and a new Maurice Farman, with a 100-h.p. Renault engine, piloted by Rainey, who took Commander Groves as observer. This officer was on the staff of the Director of the Air Department, and was over having a look at us.

The clouds were very thick over Ostend and Zeebrugge, and no bomb-dropping could be done there, so we went for the batteries at Middelkerke, getting fairly good results. We encountered a very hot antiaircraft fire, the hottest we had yet met. Rainey gave Groves a good view of the enemy, as he throttled down and dived to about 1,500 feet before letting go his bombs. They nearly got into trouble, as his throttle jammed, and he had some difficulty in opening out his engine again; altogether Commander Groves was provided with a good sample of what war as carried out by aeroplanes was like.

We were very pleased with the 100-h.p. Maurice Farman, as she showed a good turn of speed, and carried quite a heavy bomb load; after new petrol tanks were fitted, she used to fly with 4½ hours' fuel and three 100-pound bombs.

On the 27th Peirse again went to Ostend, and to illustrate what the weather conditions were like, it took him forty-five minutes to do the 10 miles from Ostend to Nieuport, which showed that there was a 55-mile-an-hour wind blowing. He had to endure "Archie" for more than an hour, and his aeroplane was hit many times. This flight was really a splendid performance, and so I reported on it to the Admiralty.

My pilots were constantly carrying out this type of work, real sound reconnaissance flights against the hottest anti-aircraft fire on slow aeroplanes in very bad weather conditions. The cold was intense, as in these days our flying kit was not of the elaborate nature that was devised later on. In fact, I was incapacitated at that time through getting frost-bitten.

We got another new Maurice Farman this day; also, an Avro. The Maurice Farman was flown to us from Paris by M. Maurice Farman himself, and it was very interesting to meet this famous aviator, one of the pioneers of the air, who still continued to test every aeroplane constructed by his firm. I had a long talk with him, and we discussed the types of aeroplanes that war had shown were required. An aeroplane that could carry a heavy bomb load was at the moment my principal desire.

We had great excitement one day at the aerodrome, due to Rainey returning from a bombing flight in one of the Maurice Farmans. In those days all our bomb gears were home-made affairs, and although they generally functioned splendidly, on occasions bombs were likely to hang up on the rack. Rainey approached the aerodrome flying very low, and proceeded to give us an exhibition of his skill in handling the big aeroplane; most of us were out on the aerodrome watching him, as although he was a very determined pilot, he was not always very skilful in his landings. Our interest in his manoeuvres was quickly spoilt, however, by Mr. Brownridge saying: "Good lord, sir, he has got a bomb hanging on to his chassis wires."

Sure enough this was so, and we all bolted for cover, expecting every minute that the bomb would drop off. We signalled to him to try to attract his attention to this bomb, which might have dropped off every minute; but he didn't understand our frantic wavings, and kept on circling round over our heads, and over the hangar, which was our only shelter. At last, he landed, and even then, despite our attempts to make him stop, he came taxiing towards the hangar at full speed. The bomb hung on, although we found it was only caught up by one of its fan blades. Rainey didn't get a good reception.

An interesting experiment was carried out in armouring an aeroplane, the idea being to see if it was possible to protect the pilot, passenger, and engine from shrapnel, and from rifle and machine-gun fire from the ground, in the case of a Zeppelin-shed attack. We realised that at present it would be impossible to carry the weight of armour which would be required if protection was to be provided from every direction; therefore, we concentrated on providing armour against fire from below. We had some armour-plate, which was surplus to our armoured motorcar requirements, and Brownridge soon worked out a design. The *"Forges et Chantres de France"* cut the plates to his requirements, and they were fixed to the two Maurice Farmans by Brownridge and his staff.

A good number of flights were successfully carried out by these aeroplanes with their armour; the extra weight did not prevent them from carrying their usual bomb-load. We were, I believe, the first to fly over the lines with armoured aeroplanes, although the French soon produced an armoured Bregnet Biplane. It was not until practically the end of the war that we went in for armoured aeroplanes, which were produced for ground strafing at low altitudes.

A new addition to our force now arrived. It was a motor-launch, about 80 feet long, belonging to the two brothers Guiness, the well-known amateur motorcar racing drivers. One was captain with the rank of Lieutenant R.N.V.R., the other was second-in-command, and held a temporary commission as a Sub-Lieutenant R.N.V.R.

They were both very keen to do anything or go anywhere. Their duty was to patrol between Nieuport and La Panne whilst we were flying, in case an aeroplane or seaplane was forced to alight in the sea, when they would tow it back if a seaplane, or pick up the pilot if it was an aeroplane. As they were very anxious to have some armament in case they came across any enemy craft, I decided to give them one of our 3-pounder guns and a Maxim. They were delighted with this armament, and I believe they would have taken on anything with it.

Warner took charge of the work of mounting the guns, and as usual made an excellent job, strengthening their deck to take the weight and withstand the strain of firing. The 3-pounder they were given was our old original one, which by this time was practically smooth-bored; but it would still shoot fairly accurately at short ranges.

The great event was when the time came for gun trials, Warner and Felix Samson with Platford setting out to sea, with as much pomp and seriousness as if they had been going to carry out the gun trials of the latest Dreadnought. They had quite an adventurous cruise, as they ran ashore, and also had the unpleasant experience of nearly hitting a mine, which bobbed up about a fathom ahead of them. Warner nearly lost his reputation as the great gunnery expert, owing to the Maxim jamming, and he being unable to make it function for nearly an hour. Warner never heard the last of this, and it was always dragged up against him in the mess whenever he was lecturing some of the younger members.

On December 1st I sent the following letter to the Admiralty, which is interesting only in view of the famous attack on Zeebrugge in 1918:

> "I have the honour to submit the following scheme for the attack on Zeebrugge. According to information received, there are three lock-gates or caissons on the canal at Zeebrugge. Damage to the seaward one will, I am led to understand, seriously interfere with traffic owing to the difficulties of locking the water in the lock.
>
> A Belgian volunteer, M. Cloquet, whom I know well, spoke to me about this. His plan is as follows:
>
> (1) A fast silent motor-boat, or hydroplane drawing very little water.
>
> (2) A foggy night.
>
> (3) Attach a charge to the gate and blow it up.
>
> From his plan I have elaborated a more advanced one, as for success I think it is absolutely necessary that the lock-gate should be struck under-water by something that will completely wreck it.
>
> I propose the following:
>
> (1) A special boat should be built, the boat to carry dropping gear holding a 14-inch torpedo. It is essential that the draft of the boat should be as small as possible, as there is every possibility of a minefield.
>
> It should have plenty of engine power, and also strength to get through a boom.
>
> The engine should be silent; therefore, I consider either a very-much-silenced petrol engine or electric propulsion should be used.
>
> The crew consisting of one man with good local knowledge, a naval officer in command, a torpedo rating and an engineer.
>
> Some protection for the crew and engines should be provided by means of plating; but only of sufficient strength to keep out rifle bullets.
>
> (2) This boat should be lowered from a ship on a suitable night well out of searchlight range of Zeebrugge. As soon as the boat is in the straight part of the harbour in line with the lock, the torpedo will be released, set to run at between 5 and 10 feet.
>
> If the torpedo strikes the lock-gate under water, it should be completely wrecked. "Continuous bomb-dropping from aero-

planes could not achieve this. It is evidently a job for a torpedo. A point that will have to be considered is the provision of protection for the torpedo, before it is launched, against rifle bullets....

I got hold of the Zeebrugge engineer, who was serving in the Belgian Army, the Belgians lending him to me for as long as I required, and sent him with M. Cloquet over to England under the care of Lieutenant Hayland-Wilson to report to Commodore Sueter, the Director of Air Service. The Admiralty turned down the scheme, however.

On December 5th I sent in the following programme of work which I proposed to carry out as soon as the weather improved:

(1) To attack the reported submarine depot South of Bruges, using the two Maurice Farmans and one Avro; or

(2) To attack the Zeppelins at Brussels or Antwerp, using the same aeroplanes. Whichever attack is first carried out to depend on whether Zeppelins are at Brussels or Antwerp, as an attack on an empty shed will achieve nothing, and probably prevent a successful attack when the shed is actually occupied.

(3) To drop bombs by night on coast between Ostend and Middelkerke, using the Maurice Farman, carrying twelve 16-pound bombs. This should cause some good moral effect and, it is hoped, damage. This will be carried out independently of attacks (1) and (2). Secrecy will be observed, and French and Belgians will only be warned at the last minute. Alighting will be effected on the sands at Dunkirk. I will do the flight myself, as I have considerable experience of night flying. (In fact, I believe at the date I was the only pilot who had flown an aeroplane at night without an illuminated aerodrome or lights on his aeroplane. The only other night flights that had been made were by Mr. Gates at Hendon, when the aerodrome was illuminated; certainly, I was the only one who had made any cross-country flights.)

(4) Scouting flights every possible day by one suitable aeroplane along coast to Zeebrugge.

(5) Preparation for special flight to bomb Essen.

As regards the latter flight, Reggie Marix had heard of an aeroplane under construction by M. Breguet in Paris. This aeroplane was being fitted with a 200-h.p. engine. Marix was sent to Paris to look at it, and to try it when ready; meanwhile, the Admiralty bought it for us. Marix, whose scheme it was, was wild to fly over Essen, and if the aeroplane could have been got ready, he would have made the attempt all right; luckily for him the Breguet was only ready in time for our departure to the Dardanelles, and it came with us. It was not a nice machine, and it nearly finished Reggie and myself one night; but that is another story.

On December 14th I sent off three aeroplanes to bomb the submarine depot at Bruges. Davies went on a Maurice Farman, carrying nine 16-lb. bombs, and Rainey in the other Maurice Farman, carrying six 16-lb. bombs; both these aeroplanes were armoured.

Collet was in an Avro, carrying four 16-lb. bombs.

Rather a pathetic little party in comparison with raids in the later years of the War; but it was the best we could do, and anyhow, it was the beginning of organised bomb-raids on the enemy.

The weather was very unsuitable for the attack; but the Admiralty were urgently asking for Bruges submarine depot to be bombed, so I sent off the aeroplanes at the first chance. Home authorities of course constantly bombarded me with demands for impossible jobs, but one must expect this sort of thing; still, it was rather trying at times.

Davies got to Bruges and saw the shed, but could not see any signs of submarines. He dropped eight bombs, but could not see the explosions, as he got enveloped in fog. He was practically certain that some must have hit the target, as he was stationary owing to the high wind, and his altitude was only 1,700 feet—a very fine effort, considering the anti-aircraft fire.

Collet couldn't find Bruges in the fog, so he dropped his bombs on the Ostend-Bruges railway line. Rainey did not return.

I was not too downcast over his absence, as I felt certain that he would turn up sooner or later, as he was such a redoubtable fellow, competent to get out of any trouble. We soon got news that he had suffered from engine trouble, and got into Holland, where he was interned.

He had got to Bruges, and had hit the shed with two of his bombs. The Dutch had a terrible time with him, and they must have been glad when he escaped again, as he did in a coal bunker of a ship.

Two of Collet's bombs, we heard afterwards from our agents, had hit a train carrying German marines, and about twenty were killed, with several wounded.

THE AUTHOR STARTING ON A FLIGHT IN NO. 50, FRANCE, 1915.

On December 21st I made the first night flight of the war which was carried out by either side. For this job I selected one of the Maurice Farmans which was fitted with a 130-h.p. Canton Unné engine. It was of the "Pusher" type, which means that the engine is behind the pilot with the propeller mounted at the rear end of the engine. Brownridge had made a bomb carrier holding eighteen 16-lb. bombs, which were arranged so that I could either drop them singly, or in threes, or all together.

This gear was most ingenious, and worked splendidly. My sole equipment consisted of an electric torch, which I carried in my pocket, and a Verey-light pistol. I had no lights on the aeroplane at all. Arrangements were made that a petrol flare was to be ignited if I fired a Verey light. I determined, however, to alight on the sands of Malo-les-Bains in front of my H.Q., as I considered it safer than trying to get into our aerodrome, to reach which I would have to glide over some high telegraph wires and over the big hangar. The wind, fortunately, was blowing along the coast-line, which provided me with a long stretch of sand to alight upon.

I arranged that warning was to be given to the French and Belgians at Dunkirk, La Panne, and Nieuport only about ten minutes before I started, as I did not want spies to have any chance of giving warning to the enemy. I made a good start at about 10 p.m., headed out to sea for about 4 miles, and then kept parallel to the coast about this distance away in order that my approach should not be betrayed by the sound of my engine. I hoped to find some submarines lying at Ostend. Climbing steadily, I soon reached 6,000 feet, and when I had got close to Ostend I turned towards it, gliding down with the engine throttled right down, thus giving no audible warning of my approach.

When I got over the harbour, I could see no signs of any submarine; I therefore determined to bomb the batteries just to the south of the town, where there would be little risk of killing civilians. The lights of the town were all lit, and the view was splendid. The flash of guns and the glare of bursting shells was a wonderful sight all along our line through Dixmude to Ypres. By the time I had reached 1,000 feet I opened out my engine and turned south, passing along the sea front of Ostend. As soon as the noise of my engine was heard pandemonium started. Star shells, rockets, and searchlights played into the sky, and the lights of the town went out in about two minutes, but they stayed long enough for me to pick out my objective.

I let go my eighteen bombs in salvos of threes, and the flash of their explosions was a most satisfying sight. Having unloaded my cargo, I set out directly to seaward. By this time the air was alive with shrapnel, but all well away from me; the searchlights were sweeping the sky, but all the beams were well above me. Getting out about 4 miles to seaward, I headed for home, turning round every now and then to look at the view. The air behind me was a mass of bursting shells, rockets, and star shells, and it was certain that the *Hun* had been badly shaken. The performance was still going on when I had got within gliding distance of Dunkirk, showing that they had really panicked. I made a satisfactory landing on the sands, coming to rest directly in front of my residence.

We had quite a little celebration in our mess, the opposition household from the Villa Albatross coming over. We decided next time that I should take three 100-lb. bombs if we could get the gear ready in time. Everybody was keen to come as my passenger, Collet especially so, as he had a hatred of the Germans. The first that they had seen of the aeroplane from the house was when I touched the ground, although they could hear me coming from a long way off. This seemed very satisfactory.

CHAPTER 4

Two Fine Flights by Davies

From now until the beginning of January, nothing much of interest occurred; we kept up our scouting flights daily, whenever the weather permitted, to Zeebrugge and Ostend, dropping bombs on practically every flight.

On the 28th a very heavy squall came on, doing a lot of damage to the aeroplanes that were pegged down in the open. The Belgians had practically all their few remaining aeroplanes wrecked. We were luckier, or our aeroplanes were more securely tied down, as we only suffered damage to one, which was a Bristol biplane. On the 30th the Germans made their first bomb-raid in force on Dunkirk, three or four aeroplanes of biplane type coming over at a great height and letting go their bombs indiscriminately over the civilian portion of the town.

They were in a great hurry over the job, which appeared to be needless, as there were no anti-aircraft guns in Dunkirk to worry them. From now onwards they periodically repeated the operation; but whilst we remained in France they did no material military damage, although the docks and railway offered splendid targets. They seemed to be solely bombing with the object of killing civilian inhabitants, at which operation they were fully successful from their point of view, as a good many women and children were killed and wounded.

After the first raid we kept as many aeroplanes as we could spare standing by to fight the raiders, and on occasions we kept an aeroplane on patrol over the town, unfortunately without bringing down a Hun, as they were all superior in speed to my machines.

Surgeon Anderson was very interested in the material effects of bombs, and on every occasion on which the Germans carried out a raid he used to visit each spot where a bomb had fallen to note the results—the sizes of craters, zone of dispersion of fragments, etc. One day a *Boche* came over Malo and started unloading his cargo. The first bomb fell on the sands in front of H.Q., and out dashed Anderson; when half-way to the crater *"wump"* fell a second bomb between him and his objective. Anderson turned right-about and made for home, and crash went a bomb midway between him and home. This completely finished Anderson's scientific inquiry into bomb effects, causing him to lie down until the German was well away on his way home. Meanwhile, Warner and Felix Samson were cheering him on from a window.

It took Anderson a long time to outlive this incident, and reference to it was always resorted to when arguments concerning Halma became acrimonious.

Warner once more got into his element, as we had got ready three 3-pounders as anti-aircraft guns. One was mounted at the aerodrome on a platform, one was fitted to a lorry, and the third was fitted up by digging a pit and sinking the trail of the 3-pounder travelling mounting. He now had a battery of two in front of our H.Q., and nobly assisted by the fierce-looking Platford, they were the heroes of the small boys of Malo-les-Bains as they strutted up and down with martial strides in front of their ordnance. Warner was always missing a German by inches, according to his own statements; but it was difficult to prove their accuracy, owing to the fact that the tracer shells only provided a stream of smoke for about 1,000 feet; after that the passage of the shell through space was unseen by any human eyes except those of Warner and his staunch adherent Platford.

The pilots and other officers were always pulling Warner's leg on the subject of his shooting; but he used to take it in very good part, and was always full of life and fun. He loved getting his own back, and when I started him on to drilling the officers in rifle exercises and machine-gun work, he reverted to the old sergeant-major manner, and his word of command could be heard from one side of the aerodrome to the other.

Platford never seemed to be far away when Warner was about, and he stuck to Warner all through our time in France and the whole of the Dardanelles campaign. They were sterling good fellows, and who is better than a good Royal Marine?

One day, early in January, about 10 a.m. we received an urgent message from Bergues, which is about 5 miles from Dunkirk, that a Zeppelin was flying over the town. We all rushed out to see if we could see it; but couldn't see anything. Two of us went up at once, and arriving over Bergues no traces of it were visible. We returned, and hadn't been down more than five minutes when Bergues telephoned again. I am afraid I told them they had most wonderful eyesight, as a 700-foot Zeppelin flying in broad daylight is not the sort of thing you could miss seeing.

Davies carried out two splendid flights early in January. The first was an attack on the airship shed at Brussels, as I had received reports that an airship was in the shed. Davies took a Maurice Farman with twelve 20-lb. bombs. Starting off at dawn on his long journey of 83 miles to his objective, he arrived there, and quickly located the shed. He came down to a low altitude and let go his bombs, two of which hit the shed. He encountered a heavy fire from two anti-aircraft guns and many machine-guns; but his aeroplane was not hit. He saw some smoke coming out of the shed, and hoped that he had destroyed the airship. His return journey was uneventful, the engine running beautifully, and he landed after a flight of just over four hours.

O'Caffrey came over and reported that an agent of his who was employed at the airship shed was actually close to the shed when the attack took place. He reported that a Parseval airship was in the hangar at the time, and that it was damaged by the explosion, although it was not set on fire. The whole attack caught the Germans unawares, and until the bombs dropped, they thought it was one of their own aeroplanes. Three soldiers had been killed and three or four wounded. Although the material results of this attack were not very great, it caused the Germans some annoyance, with consequent moral effects.

Davies's next effort was in a flight to Zeebrugge with Bernard Isaac as passenger. When passing Ostend on the outward journey they encountered some heavy shelling, and Davies was wounded in the leg by a piece of shrapnel. Undeterred by this, he continued on his mission, a really splendid example of pluck and determination. When he got back, he was so weak through loss of blood that he could not get out of his seat, and had to be lifted out. He spent the next three weeks in the hospital ship *Liberty*, which was attached to my command. For this flight he was awarded the D.S.O., an honour he had already earned three or four times.

He was a splendid fellow, Davies, and had been my First Lieutenant at Eastchurch since 1912 and in the war. He went all through the Dardanelles campaign with me, where he gained the highest award, it is possible to earn—the Victoria Cross. No one could have had a more loyal second-in-command than I had, and to a large extent the happiness of the squadron was due to his tact and popularity, a man without any conceit or selfishness, a brilliant pilot, and a doughty man of war if there ever was one. For nearly four years we were together, and never once did we have a row.

With him, Collet, Marix, Osmond, and Peirse I had stalwart assistants, and it was truly a band of brothers that set out to make war on the Germans and afterwards the Turks. They could all fly anything that would fly, and would make anything fly that didn't want to fly.

About this time Hayland-Wilson, who for some reason was always called "Old Bill," developed a great keenness to be taken up as passenger with his pet rifle to shoot a Hun. He was popularly supposed to be a great big-game shot, and many was the flight we did with him and his rifle patrolling over Dunkirk waiting for a German to come. It was a cold job in winter flying at about 7,000 feet insufficiently clad, and the pain on alighting whilst the blood started to circulate once more to one's frozen extremities was intense. One day we did come across a *Hun*, but Old Bill was too frozen to shoot.

The cold was really awful, and whatever clothing you put on you began to get frozen after half an hour or so. I used to put on so many clothes that I could hardly walk, and then get into the aeroplane feeling warm; but after half an hour one's feet and hands used to start to get numb and gradually you got frozen all over. Once we got so cold that I told Wilson I was going to land outside our house at Malo, as I couldn't stand it any longer, so down we came. By the time we had landed I could hardly feel the controls, and had lost practically all power of movement. Whilst the blood was returning to my feet, I was suffering agonies, and I am afraid I was rather brusque to two pretty nurses that arrived and asked me when I was going up again.

It was a cold-blooded business seeing the snow being scraped off the aeroplane before you started; this frequently had to be done owing to the aeroplanes having to be kept in the open all the time.

On January 10th, at 9.20 a.m., Collet as pilot with Butler as passenger ascended on the 130-h.p. Maurice Farman, as a German aeroplane had been reported crossing the lines. Collet met the German close to Furnes, and chased him for an hour, keeping him away from Dunkirk; Collet twice succeeded in getting to close range, and Butler got in a good many rounds with his rifle. Owing to the German's superior speed and quicker manoeuvring powers, the *Boche* eventually got past Collet, and over Dunkirk; but Collet, who displayed great skill and persistence, again got close to him, and chased him over the lines.

The Maurice Farman was then refilled with petrol, and as other German aeroplanes were reported to be crossing the lines, I ascended as soon as possible, carrying Hayland-Wilson armed with a rifle. I sighted seven *Huns*, and after engaging one which was already over Dunkirk and considerably above me, I got across the bows of two more, and gave chase, engaging each in turn. Their superior speed enabled them to get past me. I then climbed and took up a position to intercept two more who were over Dunkirk.

I could not get very close to one of them; but I got directly over the other at very close range, and we had a rifle duel. We were certain that we had hit the observer, as he ceased to take any further interest in affairs. The *Boche* pilot put his nose down and dived for the lines; I followed; but a Maurice Farman is not a rapid aeroplane at that type of work, and the Hun got away. During the whole time the French and Belgian guns had been shelling us both indiscriminately, and, in fact, continued to shell me the whole way home, and as a grand finale, a Pom-Pom belonging to the R.N.A.S. kite balloon station had a go at me too.

The Germans had only hit our aeroplane three times. As soon as I landed the old Farman was got ready again with bombs put on it; and Collet with Wilson as passenger went to Ostend to pay a return compliment to the Germans with eighteen 16-lb. bombs and some rifle grenades. They unloaded their cargo on the docks and railway stations at Ostend. I was always a great believer in quick retaliation. Collet came down fairly low, and had a hot time with "Archie."

In the afternoon six more *Huns* came over Dunkirk. Davies and Thomson went up, but could not get close to any of them; again, the *Hun's* extra 10-miles-an-hour speed made a big difference.

CHAPTER 5

Extension of Night Bombing

Towards the middle of January, a R.F.C. flight came to Dunkirk to assist us in fighting the *Boche* aeroplanes. The flight was under the command of Major Raleigh. He had been at Eastchurch with his squadron from the first week of the war. This flight had very bad luck, as although they had faster aeroplanes than ours, they only bagged one *Hun*, and two of the pilots were killed, Raleigh himself, unfortunately, being one of them. He was an excellent pilot, and used to fly a tremendous amount himself, thus giving a good example to his squadron.

In my mind every squadron-commander and wing-commander ought to lead his pilots in the air, as it is certain that if he does so the work of the unit is greatly increased in efficiency; by this I don't mean that he should always be up in the air; but that he should frequently go up. I feel certain that the practice that grew up of the squadron-commander and wing-commander living in an office and directing their aeroplanes from there was bad, and that *esprit de corps* suffered from this. There is little doubt that a leader who flies himself and frequently crosses the lines realises far better the difficulties of his pilots, and understands the strain that war flying produces. He can also form a better opinion of the capabilities of his aeroplanes and pilots.

Poor Raleigh was killed in an accident, falling into the sea just close to the aerodrome. After about a week the flight returned to St. Omer. They were all very impressed by the volume of anti-aircraft fire put up by the "Iron Coast."

On January 22nd Peirse, with Thomson as observer, found two submarines lying alongside the Mole in Zeebrugge harbour; he let go twelve bombs at them, and reported that one bomb had hit.

Unfortunately, the weather was too bad for any further flights to be made until the 27th. I received intelligence from O'Caffrey's organisation that one of Peirse's bombs had hit a gun on the Mole, damaging it badly, and killing three soldiers. On the night of the 27th, as the weather was getting better, I decided to make a night-raid. Whilst we were going to the aerodrome in a car a German aeroplane flew over and started bombing. Neither Marix nor I could see it, although it passed close overhead. Half an hour afterwards I was in the air in the Maurice Farman, with Marix as passenger and carrying twelve bombs, which we let go at the Middelkerke batteries.

Unfortunately, one bomb failed to release, a fact I discovered when on my way home. Not liking the idea of landing with it on, I kept jerking at the handle and rocking the aeroplane to make it drop off, which it finally did. As I was over the sea, I am afraid I did not pay much attention to where it fell; to my horror it exploded in the water quite close to H.M.S. *Excellent*, an old-fashioned gunboat that used to lie off Nieuport each night. They were very upset about it, but we explained that it must have been a *Boche* bomb. I didn't think they believed me.

On February 1st we again bombed a submarine at Zeebrugge. Collet was the pilot, with Leading-Seaman Close as his observer. They dropped twelve bombs at the submarine; but unfortunately missed the target with all of them; anyhow, it must have made the German very nervous.

That night I went up, with Collet as my observer, to try to bag this submarine. We took the usual aeroplane, the Maurice Farman, and got over Zeebrugge at 11.30 p.m. We found the submarine lying alongside the Mole in the same position. I came down to 1,200 feet; and Collet let go the bombs in salvos of three; whilst I steered a diagonal course across the target. Collet was certain that one bomb exploded on the deck of the submarine; but I doubt if it did her much damage, as the bomb was only a 16-pounder, fitted with a direct-action fuse. We got back to our aerodrome at 12.40 a.m., having been two hours in the air.

Mr. Brownridge and Warner were working away at producing a mounting for a Lewis gun, fixed in the upper plane of the Avro's and Sopwith Tabloids. They finally got out quite a good design.

About this time the celebrated Garros, one of the very finest French pilots, arrived at Dunkirk with a Morane Saulnier monoplane of parasol type. He had a most ingenious method of using a machine-gun—shooting through the propeller. This consisted of metal plates being fitted to the propeller in line with the gun. Any round that hit the propeller was caught by these plates and deflected. This was an excellent method; but it caused a loss of efficiency for the propeller of about 10 *per cent*.

Our method suffered from the fact that only one charger could be used, because the pilot could not reach the gun to replace the empty charger; this restricted us to forty-seven rounds. For a long period, tractor aeroplanes were handicapped as fighters until the various types of synchronised and interrupter gears were invented, which permitted of the guns being fired through the arc swept by the propeller blades without risk of hitting them. As soon as the invention was produced, the tractor aeroplane was pre-eminent as a fighter.

We made a mounting for a Lewis gun in the Maurice Farman, and whenever possible it was sent up on patrol, lying in wait for the German aeroplanes. It certainly kept them away from Dunkirk on many occasions; but was too slow to catch them.

This Maurice Farman flew 120 hours in France from the date we received it, November 30th, 1914, until we left France on February 26th, 1915, practically forty hours a month. I took it out to the Dardanelles, where it did yeoman service. Without doubt it was the most reliable machine I have ever flown; it never once let its pilot down, and I doubt if any aeroplane has dropped so many bombs on the Germans as did this old warrior. We all loved it, and I think if anybody had crashed it, we would have lynched him. I never used to let anybody fly it except the old hands.

On February 3rd we received a reinforcement, as the Admiralty reopened the Dunkirk seaplane base, putting it this time under my command.

Rathborne was in charge of the station, with Nanson, Bone, and Penney as the other pilots. The seaplanes were at first in very poor condition, and suffered from a bad attack of *Anno Domi*ni. One of them would probably have flown splendidly, except for the fact that some bright lad in the Air Department had sent it over with a note attached to the engine, which stated: "Engine correct except two pistons lacking."

I had recently received from England a lorry fitted with a dynamo and searchlight. As the Belgians were very short of searchlights, I lent the lorry to them, and it proved most useful. Two of my men went with it, and they had a pretty tough time of it, on occasions taking the searchlight close up to the front line; they used to draw a good deal of shell-fire; but came out without a scratch on themselves or the lorry.

On February 3rd I made another night flight to Zeebrugge, hoping to find a submarine there. I took Collet as my passenger, with a view to training him in night flying, and also because he was a good bomb dropper. On arrival no submarines were found either there or at Ostend. We therefore dropped our bombs at the railway sheds at Zeebrugge; three bombs hit. We got back after being up two hours. There was the usual display of rockets, star shells, and searchlights.

The following letter, which I sent to the Admiralty on February 6th, will explain our operations and requirements:

> As night flying has given very good results, as shown by the last two flights over Zeebrugge, more good aeroplanes are required. The requirements essential for night work are:
>
> (1) Very reliable engine.
> (2) Speed of 70 miles per hour or more.
> (3) Capability to carry 300 pounds weight of bombs.
> (4) Pusher Biplanes.
> (5) Silenced engine as an extra is very desirable. "I submit that aeroplanes like this should be easy to produce. I believe in England at present there are a certain number of 100-h.p. Renault engines and 100-h.p. Mercédès engines. The French have an excellent aeroplane in the 'Voisin' with 130-h.p. Canton Unné engine.
>
> War experience has shown the following:
>
> (1) Small bombs are not much use.
> (2) Aeroplanes that carry a limited weight of bombs, like Avro, Sopwith, etc., are of little value for bomb dropping.
> (3) From Ostend neighbourhood you are often fired at by between thirty to forty guns.
>
> What is wanted are the following aeroplanes at Dunkirk:
>
> A certain number of high-speed aeroplanes—these are less likely to be hit. They are used simply to see if submarines are in harbour and to report their positions.
>
> A large number of the special type I have recommended. These will carry (*a*) eighteen 20-lb. bombs, or (*b*) three 100-lb. bombs. They will carry on dropping bombs, during the night for preference, sometimes by day.
>
> The ideal aeroplane, of course, would be one that could combine all: *viz.* speed of about 90 miles per hour or more, and carrying 300 lb. weight of bombs.
>
> The neighbourhood of the towns of Middelkerke, Ostend,

Zeebrugge is the best-defended country against aeroplanes in the whole of the war zone. People without practical experience of what this means can hardly realise the accuracy and volume of fire that are concentrated on an aeroplane from this neighbourhood.

I am certain that if the following programme could be carried out submarines would not care to make use of Zeebrugge and Ostend. The programme is as follows:

4 p.m. Sopwith scout reconnoitres and reports submarines on Ostend.

9 p.m. No. 1 bomb-carrier starts.

10.30 p.m. No. 2 bomb-carrier starts.

12 midnight. No. 3 bomb-carrier starts.

1.30 a.m. No. 4 bomb-carrier starts, or No. 1 again starts.

Up to date we have had only two bomb-carriers; one is now interned in Holland, the other we use constantly.

Practical experience in warfare has shown me that bomb-dropping is only successful at the present moment when carried out by aeroplanes carrying a number of bombs. 100-lb. bombs are wanted against submarines.

I am quite confident of being able to use 200-h.p. Short Seaplanes adapted as aeroplanes for this work. They should carry four 100-lb. bombs, and would be used at night. "Between 1,500 and 1,800 feet is a very good height for night bombing. The ideal machine is, of course, the 'Pusher' type, as then the accuracy is much better.

I submit that sending a number of Avro aeroplanes to drop bombs and to expect good results will be a waste of aeroplanes. Steady persistent work will have a much greater effect.

If an example is wanted, I would point out the German raids on Dunkirk: effect nil, except loss of life to people in the streets. The present condition of my squadron is as follows:

130-h.p. Maurice Farman being overhauled, ready at one hour's notice. I am making a bomb-carrier for three 100-lb. bombs for this machine. When she is ready, she will carry out the night work.

Two Sopwith Tabloids under repair, new strut fittings being made for them.

Two Avro Biplanes; Lewis guns are being fitted to these for

patrol work fighting German aeroplanes.

One B.E. Biplane, fitted with rifle using incendiary bullets for Zeppelin work.

One Sopwith Gun aeroplane, requires a lot of work on it to make it safe to fly.

Provided I had six more Maurice Farman or similar type aeroplanes of 70-miles-an-hour speed, I would then have a very fine force, able to make Ostend and Zeebrugge extremely uncomfortable for submarines.

When it is remembered that one small bomb was seen to explode on the submarine on Monday night, it is a great pity to consider what would have happened if this had been a 100-lb. bomb.

I submit that orders should be given at once for aeroplanes to be made to carry twelve 100-lb. bombs, and then the aeroplane will prove a valuable weapon.

Every day that is wasted by not having good aeroplanes is another day gained by the German defence. They will find improved methods of dealing with aircraft by night, and by the time the aeroplanes are ready the defence will be ready. At present they are uncertain how to deal with it, and also, which is very important, rather scared.

I submit that every effort should be made to get these Maurice Farmans with 100-h.p. Renaults from the French, and also that some more long-distance Breguet and Voisins should be ordered.

C. R. Samson.

CHAPTER 6

Our First Organised Air-Raids

Our bomb attacks on Zeebrugge and Ostend had impressed the Admiralty Air Department with their value, and early in February it was decided to make a bomb raid on the German coast ports with as many aeroplanes and seaplanes as could be collected.

My opinion was asked for on the subject, and I was provided with a copy of the Air Department's plan. I was very keen on the project; but was in opposition to the plan of attack, which did not provide detailed objectives for each aeroplane. I was also adverse to the employment of seaplanes, except against those parts of the coast that were not well provided with anti-aircraft guns.

I sent in a detailed plan, allocating targets for each unit, and also proposing that night bomb attacks should be carried out during the night preceding the raid, with the object of giving a disturbed night's rest to the anti-aircraft gunners, and generally shaking the morale of the defence. My programme was adopted, except that the raid was directed from Dover, which I considered was a mistake. As it turned out, the first attack failed through Dover being selected as the port of command.

Aeroplanes and seaplanes which were to take part in the attack were provided by my Squadron and my Seaplane flight at Dunkirk, Dover aeroplanes, Dover Seaplanes, Hendon aeroplanes, H.M.S. *Empress* seaplanes, and flying-boats from Felixstowe.

These made a number of twenty-two aeroplanes and twelve seaplanes, by far the biggest number of aircraft ever yet employed in one operation in war up to date. Commodore Murray F. Sueter, C.B., the Director of the Air Department, came to Dover to control the operations. All the English aeroplane units were collected at Dover in readiness for the attack. The *Empress* was at Dunkirk, under the command of Lieutenant Bowhill.

The objectives were apportioned as follows:

Dover Aeroplanes.—East side of Ostend harbour; guns close to the lighthouse, and shed opposite the railway station.
Dunkirk Aeroplanes.—Guns on the western side of Ostend, and tramway lines between Ostend and Middelkerke.
Eastchurch and Hendon Aeroplanes.—Ostend harbour railway station, and sheds close to it. Any vessels in Ostend harbour.
Dunkirk and Dover Seaplanes.—Zeebrugge buildings and railway lines on the Mole.
"Empress" Seaplanes.—Zeebrugge. Store sheds on the Mole.

The night of the 10th was very stormy, and it was impossible to carry out a night attack. I telephoned to Dover describing the weather. At an early hour of the morning of the 11th the weather was far too bad to start, so I told the aerodrome to take the bombs off the aeroplanes, and gave orders that the pilots should fall out. Hardly had I done this when we descried a number of aeroplanes flying past, heading towards the enemy. I immediately ordered the aeroplanes and seaplanes to carry out the attack; but about five minutes afterwards countermanded it, as some heavy storm-clouds were beating up.

One seaplane and two aeroplanes had started, but the seaplane, with Bone as pilot, was the only one that reached its objective, as the others found the weather far too bad. Two of the English aeroplanes reached their objectives; the rest either turned back or landed at Dunkirk, finding the weather conditions along the coast extremely bad, snow and thunderstorms being encountered.

The pilots that reached their objectives were Sitwell and Haskins. Sitwell's machine was very badly shot about, and it was extraordinary how he got back, as his controls were practically all shot away. He had bombed Zeebrugge at 700 feet.

Bone had carried out a splendid flight. Reaching Blankenberghe unperceived, he hit the railway station there with a 100-lb. bomb, with corresponding good results, killing a number of German soldiers.

Grahame-White, on a Henry Farman, ran into a thunderstorm, and was driven down into the sea off Nieuport, where, after spending nearly an hour in the water, he was picked up. I now had a fine array of aeroplanes on the Dunkirk aerodrome. I telephoned to Dover, and received orders to take command of the operation. I determined to make the attack at the first favourable opportunity, as it was impossible to hide our aeroplanes from the Germans or from the many spies who were present at Dunkirk.

Fortunately, the night proved feasible for a venture, and I set off in the Maurice Farman with three 100-lb. bombs. Getting close to Nieuport, I ran into a thick bank of fog. I just got a fleeting glance of the Mariakerke batteries, and let go my bombs; but it was impossible to see the results. I had a tough journey home, as the fog got worse; but in the end I got safely down to my aerodrome. I refused to let Peirse and Collet go off, as I felt certain they would get into trouble. They were very depressed; but it couldn't be helped. I gave Peirse No. 50 as a compensation to fly in the daylight attack.

We all sat up during the remainder of the night at the aerodrome, praying for a fine morning. The morale of the pilots was splendid, and competition was very high. My old Dunkirk crowd were going to show the newcomers how to bomb, and the newcomers were going to show us how they could behave. It must be remembered that three-fourths of the other pilots were fresh to war, and also only half of them were experienced pilots. This spirit foreboded ill for the *Hun*.

It was quite an interesting sight, and I felt proud to command such a keen lot of fellows. We drank gallons of cocoa, and by the time dawn broke and the weather appeared to be feasible for our job, I felt very sick at having given No. 50 to Peirse, as I felt I ought to go out again. The start was really a wonderful sight, but unfortunately, we began badly, Wing-Commander Longmore having a crash when starting off, through his engine stopping.

The resulting effort was really a fine performance. Out of twenty-one aeroplanes that started, fifteen got to their objectives. The seaplanes had bad luck, only one out of the six that started getting to the enemy. This was Bone, who again proved himself a stubborn, determined pilot. He went to his old Blankenberghe again, and badly messed up the railway line outside the station.

All my four Dunkirk pilots got to their targets, and did good work. Marix, who was flying our ewe-lamb, the old Maurice Farman with the bloodthirsty Collet as passenger, dropped three 100-lb. bombs at the harbour railway station; he got a direct hit with one, which immediately started a fire.

The station burnt for the remainder of the day, and later reconnaissance showed it was badly wrecked. Peirse safely brought back No. 50, having unloaded his bombs on the wharves at Ostend. Wilson and Newton-Clare were the other two of my crowd. Unfortunately, we hadn't aeroplanes enough to go round. The only casualty besides

STARTING FOR ZEEBRUGGE, FEBRUARY 1915, IN NO. 50.
The figure on the extreme right is Mr. Brownridge.

MEN LINED UP AT AN AIR-RAID WARNING, DUNKIRK.

Longmore was Maude, who had an engine failure, and fell into the sea; he was picked up.

The total number of bombs dropped worked out at 61, and the total weight, 1,820 lb. This appears a ridiculous amount when compared to 1917 and 1918; but it was the best we could do with our small engines and old-pattern aeroplanes. The old Maurice Farman out of this total accounted for 600 lb., or very nearly one-third.

Osmond hit a German mine-sweeper, and Rigall hit the power-station at Zeebrugge. All the pilots came back delighted with their experience, all reporting that the anti-aircraft fire was very heavy but inaccurate. The Germans were no doubt put off their aim by the numbers of aeroplanes, all arriving according to my plan from different directions.

As this first attack had given such good results, I asked permission to retain all the aeroplanes at Dunkirk and carry out a second attack; this was approved. Both Commodore Sueter and Mr. Winston Churchill were highly pleased at the results obtained. The latter was always keen on aeroplane work, and the help and encouragement he had given to the R.N.A.S. ever since he took over the post of First Lord of the Admiralty were fully appreciated by all of us who were in a position to know. Without his keenness and driving power the R.N.A.S. would not have reached the state of advancement it had done in 1914. One of these days the nation will understand what a truly great administrator he is.

The weather determined that we were not to have another chance until the 16th, when about 2 p.m. it improved and I gave orders for an attack to be carried out. This time I practically concentrated all our efforts on the gun positions at Mariakerke and Middelkerke, and the harbour works and railway sidings at Ostend. The French had been greatly impressed at our first effort, and asked me if they could join in. I was only too delighted for them to take part, and after a consultation we decided that they should proceed to the German aerodrome at Ghistelles and bomb it whilst we were bombing the coast. They set off with eight Voisin aeroplanes, carrying 50-lb. bombs. The aerodrome was a fine sight, covered as it was with aeroplanes waiting to start; everything went like clockwork, and they all got away without any confusion or mishaps.

As my squadron only had three aeroplanes which were fit to send, there were some heart-burnings amongst the pilots who had to be left behind. I took No. 50 myself, and Collet was given the ewe-lamb.

Butler took the third aeroplane. Wilson wangled a trip as passenger to Courtney, who was now in Longmore's squadron. Sippe was also in this squadron. Unfortunately, this time the German anti-aircraft guns brought down four of our machines, probably benefiting by the experience they had gained during the first raid. The pilots we lost were Flight-Lieutenant Murray, who was flying a seaplane. His engine was hit by shrapnel when over Zeebrugge; but fortunately, he was able to get into neutral waters, and was interned in Holland.

The others, Flight-Sub-Lieutenant Spencer, Flight-Lieutenant Rigall, and Flight-Sub-Lieutenant the Hon. D. O'Brien were shot down and killed. They were all keen fellows, full of a desire to do their bit, and we felt their loss acutely; but losses have to be expected if results are to be achieved, and we felt certain from what information we obtained that they had all dropped their bombs on the enemy before they were shot down.

Altogether eighteen British aeroplanes and seven British seaplanes took part in the attack, dropping five 100-lb. bombs and sixty-two 20-lb. bombs; giving a total of 1,740 lb. In addition, the eight French aeroplanes provided the *Huns* with approximately 800 lb.

The Admiralty later reported that the damage we had done was:

Two workshops containing submarines in progress of assembly damaged; twenty workmen wounded.

One submarine severely damaged at Zeebrugge.

Several batteries on the coast to the south of Zeebrugge damaged, and several guns damaged.

The Cockerill Works badly damaged.

A train containing stores, including submarine parts, wrecked. The harbour railway station at Ostend and the goods yard destroyed by fire.

Transport wagons on the Ghistelles-Ostend road wrecked.

The bridge at Ostend, called the De Smet de Naeyer, damaged.

One officer and thirty-seven soldiers killed at Ostend. Thirteen soldiers killed and thirty-five wounded in a train at Blankenberghe.

Blankenberghe station totally wrecked.

At Knocke, some guns damaged, and one officer and seven men killed.

A seaplane shed on the Mole at Zeebrugge badly wrecked.

Considering the number of bombs dropped, this can be considered as a very satisfactory result, due entirely to the pilots attacking at low altitudes despite the tremendous volume of anti-aircraft fire encountered. I was particularly pleased at the way the young pilots had behaved.

One lesson we learnt, which I already personally suspected, was that seaplanes should not be employed for this type of bombing. The 100-lb. bomb also proved its worth, and it was certain that it was essential to develop aeroplanes that could carry a number of heavy bombs.

Orders were received for all the outside aeroplanes to return to England, which they did in the following days with their reluctant pilots. I would very much have liked to have retained them, and gone on with the good work; but it was not to be, and we were once more left to carry on with our feeble resources.

The French aviators were delighted with the attacks, and it did a lot to cement our already good *entente* with them. The populace of Dunkirk were also pleased at the idea of the *Huns* receiving a good dose of bombs.

CHAPTER 7

Last Days in Flanders

On February 14th I sent in the following report to the Admiralty, dealing with night bombing by aeroplanes. This report may be of interest, when taken in comparison with what happened in 1917-18:

I can claim some experience of this work, having flown by night more often than anybody else. I am certain now that an aeroplane raid on London by night is easy to accomplish, given the following conditions:

(1) Pilot experienced in night flying.
(2) Clear weather.
(3) Moonlight.

The last is by no means an essential. I have frequently flown on nights on which there has been absolutely no moon; in fact, on December 21st I flew when it was so dark that I could see nothing at all of the ground until I had got to within about 300 feet. On a moonlight night cross-country flying depends on the following; either—

(a) The pilot having a very good *air* knowledge of the route; or

(b) The pilot having good landmarks to steer by. The landmarks required are: (1) rivers; (2) sea-coast; (3) well-lighted towns (these are now, I presume, not present); (4) lighthouses.

To get to London by night on a moonlight night is very easy, even without local *air* knowledge of the route. The chart will show this without further comment on my part. Towns are not required as guides.

For the first time in my experience, or as far as I can discover by interrogation, a German aeroplane flew over hostile territory on the night of January 27th. This shows that, although over a month behind, they are beginning to find out that the uses of an aeroplane by night, as I have frequently submitted in the last twelve months, are not to be despised. I imagine that this flight will be the commencement of many more, and that in time they will extend their radius.

An aeroplane by night is a very useful weapon. The following facts will show this:

(1) At 1,200 feet, though I passed within 200 yards of twelve observers, who heard me, not one could see me (the night was quite clear, practically full moon).

(2) Whilst I was going to the aerodrome, I heard and saw bombs drop and explode within 200 yards or less from where I was. I got out of the car, and in the company of two other officers and five or six French soldiers, tried to locate the aeroplane. We could hear him distinctly, but could not see him at all.

(3) If this is possible on a moonlight night, it is much more so on a dark night.

If therefore aeroplanes can fly at night, and cannot be seen, it is very important to consider how such an attack can be dealt with.

Searchlights from the ground are of very little use, as an aeroplane can so quickly dive and escape from the beam. The only use of searchlights would be as follows: a large number of very powerful searchlights lighting up a very big area, continually shifting their area of search. It is very important to take into consideration the following fact: you will be unable to hear the engine of an aeroplane in the midst of the noise of London traffic.

The best defence of all is, of course, the London fog. Increase this fog by means of anthracene or other method furnaces and a powerful shield is present. Place this fog between London and the coast. The aeroplane will come on a certain route.

I submit that methods, however absurd they appear on paper, might well be worth a little cheap experiment. From what I have seen and experienced so far, an aeroplane with a determined pilot has all the chances on its side. It will time its arrival so that it reaches the coast just as darkness has come; after that the rest of the journey is simplicity itself.

It is rather difficult with trained guns' crews and proper-sized anti-aircraft guns to bring down an aeroplane by day; how much more difficult will it be by night?

C. R. samson.

On February 21st we had a good day's work, as we were constantly at it throughout the day and also during the night, both aeroplanes and seaplanes getting over Zeebrugge. This night was rather a memorable one, as it was the first time, we had two aeroplanes up on a night raid. I sent Collet up in the Maurice Farman at Io.20 p.m., taking Butler as his passenger. He carried three 100-lb. bombs, with Zeebrugge as his objective. The bombs were dropped on the breakwater there, as no submarines could be seen. A searchlight was put out by one of the bombs, which was a fairly satisfactory result. I set out twenty minutes after Collet, going in No. 50, my old B.E., with two 20-lb. bombs, to Middelkerke. We both got back safely, Collet making a splendid landing on his first night flight as a pilot. I wished I had half a dozen Maurice Farmans with which to have stirred the *Huns* up.

On February 26th we had a great seaplane day, no less than four seaplanes going out on patrol off Zeebrugge and Ostend looking for submarines—Nanson, Bone, Blackburn, and Petre were the pilots.

The same day I had set out for a run to Ypres in a Rolls Royce with Felix Samson and Surgeon Anderson, the former driving. Approaching Cassel with the speedometer showing 65 miles per hour, the tread came off one of the front tyres and locked the steering. We turned completely round twice, then hit a tree and capsized into a ditch. We were all shot out of the car like bullets, and I can well remember, now, seeing Anderson's form flying past me in mid-air. Fortunately, we all fell soft—and also wet, as the ditch was full of muddy, slimy water; not one of us received a scratch, and the car was practically undamaged except for a broken screen and a lamp or two. Warner got a bit of his own back on Felix Samson when we arrived home.

Our household arrangements at H.Q. were of rather a Spartan order, as the house was fairly small and we were pretty crowded. I shared a bedroom with Felix Samson. Tony Wilding, who was a hardy fellow, slept on the verandah outside, even in the coldest weather. He appeared to flourish on it. Next door Hardy Wells and Bill Samson were in occupation of another bedroom; Aspinall and Anderson lived upstairs in another; Warner was well dug in in a tiny room adjoining.

The opposition party at the Villa Albatross lived in far better style than we did, as they had the services of two French ladies, who owned the house, to cook for them. They used to have most elaborate meals, and we looked forward to invitations to dinner.

On stormy nights we used to sally forth and dine in the big *café* in the Square of Dunkirk, called the *Café des Arcades*. We were always certain of a cheery meal there, as we used to meet many of our old French and Belgian comrades of Douai and Antwerp. Carpentier, who used to drive the commandant of the French Aeroplane *Escadrille*, and Garros until he was captured, were always the centre of attraction at the *café* for the crowds of civilians and others who thronged it.

Orders were received from the Admiralty that we were to be relieved by another squadron, and were to return to England. This came like a bolt from the blue, and was not at all to our liking. We felt quite happy where we were, and hated the idea of returning to England to carry out coast patrols or even, horrid thought, to have to turn ourselves into a training unit to teach new pilots. The last two or three days were spent in closing up our accounts, and settling which aeroplanes we would take home, and which we would leave behind for the new-comers. I received orders to bring the Squadron back to England as a complete unit with its aeroplanes and motor-transport, only leaving behind certain armoured cars and one or two aeroplanes.

Two of the doctors had to be left, and lots were drawn who they should be.

Although Commodore Sueter did not give me definite intelligence, yet from telephone conversations with him I rather gathered that we would not be left in England, and that there was some chance of the old squadron going again to foreign parts.

Our orders were to move to Dover, and wait there for further instructions.

Osmond, who had been recently transferred to another squadron, was at Dover, in charge of the aerodrome.

The last days were very sad ones, and I was quite sorry to say goodbye to all our French friends. The officers on the staff of General Bidon had always been such delightful men to work with, never so busy but that they would attend to our needs. The day before our departure I had lunch with the *commandant* of the French Aviation Squadron, and it was a lunch. After that event I drove back to the aerodrome, followed by the *commandant* in his car, which was driven by Carpentier. I am afraid that we both drove like Jehu; but anyhow, we arrived safely, and the Frenchman made his farewells to my officers.

His second-in-command one day in July suddenly arrived by air at my aerodrome in Imbros to look me up.

A sweep was got up amongst the pilots, the winner to be the one that first arrived in England. On the morning of February 26th, the word was given, and off three of us started, but the fog was so bad that Wilson and I turned back; the other went on, and later reported that he had landed at Calais, finding it too thick to cross. We all then adjourned to lunch at the *Café des Arcades*. Whether it was that the lunch was good or that the liqueurs afterwards made the weather appear perfect, or what, I don't know; but anyhow, I soon found myself back at the aerodrome in old No. 50.

I had the worst trip I think I have ever had; the Channel was covered by a sheer pea-soup of a fog. After I had got well out from land, I felt that I had been a fool to start; but I wanted to win the sweep, and I knew that Marix with his 200-h.p. Breguet had already started from Paris, and he wasn't the sort of fellow to be stopped by a fog.

Suddenly I ran out of the fog, and found myself about a mile off Dover. This rather pleased me, as it had proved my navigation to be good. In those days the regulations ordered that you should land at Folkestone, but I determined to risk it, as I doubted if anybody would see me gliding in out of the fog. I had experienced quite enough of the air for that day, and I wanted to feel *terra firma* again, so I throttled down and alighted on our new aerodrome without anybody seeing me.

I found the usual figure there, Dessoussois, Grosvenor's old mechanic, a great fellow, whose job was looking after No. 1241, the Maurice Farman with the Canton engine. Whenever it was up, he used to stay in the middle of the aerodrome waiting for it to return; rumour had it that he slept under its wings. Anyhow, it never let us down, solely due to his care of it.

As soon as I landed, I said, "Am I the first in, Dessoussois?"

"Yes, *Mon Commandant*; but where is my machine?"

"Oh, that has broken down at Calais," I said.

At that he rushed off to the shed, and came back in half a moment with a bag of tools the size of an American tourist's steamer trunk. I must say this rather confirmed my suspicions that, however short anybody else was of tools, Dessoussois always seemed to be well supplied. I expect he was not very conscientious as regards visiting motorcars arriving at the aerodrome with their owners gazing into the air at the aeroplanes.

He got to No. 50, and was starting to put his outfit in the passenger's seat when I said: "Here, what are you doing?"

"I am ready, *Mon Commandant*; you will fly me to Calais, and I will repair 1241."

I had then to tell him that his pet was only fogbound.

The others arrived during the afternoon and the next morning.

Next day I was called up to the Admiralty, and I will never forget the strained look on everybody's face when I returned and they waited to hear the verdict as to our future. When I said the one word Dardanelles, they were as happy as a crowd of sand-boys, especially Dr. Williams, who had lost the toss, and had to leave France.

We had a great celebration that night. On the way down from London I was caught in a police trap and, naturally not having my driving licence with me, I was informed by the constable that I would be summoned for exceeding the speed limit and failing to produce my licence. I am afraid that I didn't treat it very seriously. Eventually, at the Dardanelles, I received a long document saying that as I could not be traced, the summons had been allowed to lapse; in fact, the Chief Constable of Kent had been kind enough to note on it that Commander Samson would not be proceeded against, as he evidently had been in a hurry.

The original pilots who went over to France with the Squadron now hold the following honours:

Davies: V.C., D.S.O., Legion of Honour France.

Briggs: D.S.O., O.B.E., Legion of Honour France.

Osmond; C.B.E., Crown of Belgium Officer Belgium.

Courtney; C.B.E., Crown Italy, Legion of Honour France, St. Anne and St. Stanislas Russia.

Lord Edward Grosvenor: Crown Italy, St. Maurice and St. Lazarus, Italy.

Sippe: D.S.O., O.B.E., Legion of Honour France, Order of Leopold Belgium.

The observers, doctors, etc.:

W. L. Samson: D.F.C.

F. R. Samson: O.B.E.

H. W. Wells: C.B.E.

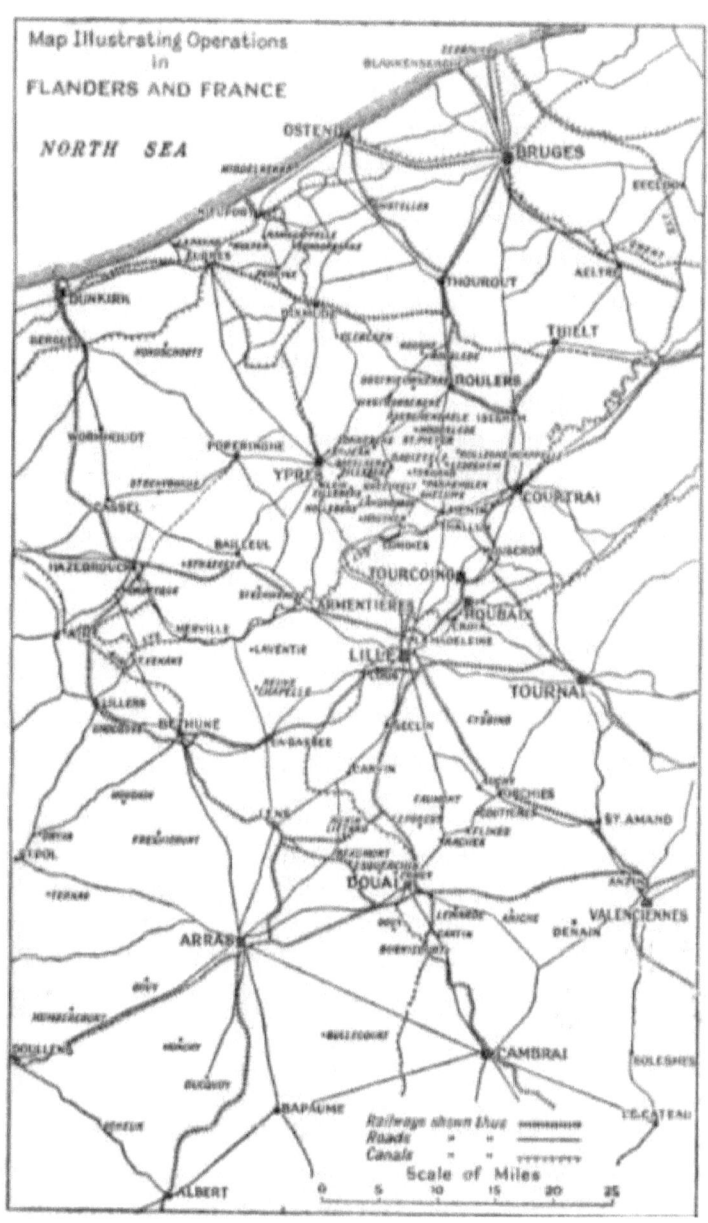

Part 3: The Dardanelles (March to December 1915)

Chapter 1
Tenedos

The work of preparing for service in the Dardanelles now went with a swing. It was decided that we should take as many aeroplanes as we already possessed which were in working order, and that additional aeroplanes should be ordered in France.

As our presence on the scene of action was urgently required, I was ordered to proceed overland across France with an advance party, and embark at Marseilles, where we would pick up the new aeroplanes. I decided that at least I would arrive with one aeroplane that I knew could fly, so I gave orders that No. 50 should be got ready for transport by road within twelve hours. Brownridge reported that she was ready.

The advance party consisted of Collet, Osmond, Butler, Bill Samson, and myself, with twenty-seven men.

We took two lorries, which carried No. 50 and certain stores consisting of a small amount of petrol and oil, a selection of bombs, tools, and spare parts.

In addition to the lorries, I took two touring-cars and two light tenders. Our route was *via* Boulogne and Paris to Marseilles.

The remainder of my squadron under Davies was to embark on board ship at Plymouth, and proceed by sea to the sphere of action.

They had our faithful old Maurice Farman, one B.E.2, two B.E.2 C's, 2 Sopwith Tabloids, and Reggie Marix's Breguet, of which we had great expectations.

Sending on the two heavy lorries at an early hour to Folkestone, I followed on with the remainder of my party.

When I got to the cross-Channel steamer I found that Osmond had encountered difficulties in getting the heavy lorries on board, as the cranes were not powerful enough for the job. Being a very competent person, he had removed the bodies, and thus lightened the load; but he was a bit doubtful as to whether we could replace the body-work in a short time.

Arriving at Boulogne, I told Osmond to be in Paris that night without fail; but I must say that he didn't look any too cheerful, as no doubt he was faced with a pretty tough proposition, having practically to rebuild the body-work of the two lorries, and restow old No. 50, and then to travel a good distance all within about sixteen hours.

Personally, I didn't worry, as I knew that Osmond and Collet with the twenty odd Eastchurch men would get there all right, even if they had to push the lorries.

As regards the men, naturally they were the cream of the Squadron, and could have done anything or got anywhere.

Bill Samson, Butler, and myself then went on to Paris in the Rolls and another car. I went to the Ritz, and found there that everything as regards our new aeroplanes had been fixed up splendidly by Lieutenant Thurstan, and that they had already been dispatched to Marseilles.

After a good dinner I went to bed in the best bedroom at the Ritz, placed at my disposal by my old friend Mr. Ellis, who unfortunately has passed away.

In the morning, on demanding my bill I was informed that my party were considered as guests of the hotel, a fact of which I am afraid I did not inform the accountant people at the Admiralty. In fact, it was the sole occasion during my career that I was able to score off the Admiralty over travelling expenses.

The first thing that I saw when I came downstairs was Osmond looking like nothing on earth. He had just arrived, so I said, "Well, you have half an hour for breakfast, and then off you can go to Marseilles. We will stop the night at Bourg, and I will wait for you there."

Osmond said, "The men are a bit tired."

I said, "They will be a good deal more so before we get to Marseilles. They can sleep in the transport, and take turns driving."

Osmond said, "Commander, do have a look at the lorries and the tenders; there isn't much room to sleep in them with all the stores."

"Osmond," I said, "come in and have breakfast."

I then went out to the men and said, "Next stop Marseilles; you have half an hour to see Paris."

Of course, they weren't tired; you couldn't tire my old crowd.

Anyhow, I thought Osmond had had the worst of it so far, so that when I saw Butler looking extremely spick and span, I said: "Butler, you, as you live in France and like motoring, can go with the lorries, whilst Osmond comes with me."

We had a good run to Marseilles, taking it leisurely myself, and waiting *en route* for the heavy transport to pick us up.

I spent a comfortable night half-way to Marseilles, but the main body had to keep going the whole time. Arriving late at night at Marseilles, I found everything O.K. The aeroplanes had already been embarked on board the *Abda*, and they would embark our transport early in the morning, and sail at 9 a.m.

We stopped the night at the Louvre et Palais, and drove down to the *Abda* at 6 a.m.

I found the last of the cars being hoisted in, and two Maurice Farman and eight Henri Farman aeroplanes' taking up the whole of the upper deck.

The *Abda* was a very fine steamer, which was usually employed in carrying passengers and a certain amount of cargo between France and Morocco.

We were the sole passengers, as she had been especially detailed by our Allies to take us to the Dardanelles. I had a very comfortable voyage, enlivened by the cheery companionship of the captain and doctor, who were full of tales.

The captain said that when war broke out, he was at sea, and a deputation of the crew came to see him and asked permission to put two German commercial travellers who were on board into the furnaces. He said he refused permission.

On March 23rd we arrived at Imbros, a small island in the north Aegean Sea, about 20 miles from the Dardanelles, where I found most of the fleet, except for the commander-in-chief. Admiral Wemyss, however, was there in charge of the base, so I went off to report to him. Everybody looked very glum, and I soon realised that the fleet had suffered a severe set-back.

Later in the day the commander-in-chief, Sir John de Robeck, came into harbour, so I went on board to report. He was delighted to have aeroplanes at his disposal, as the seaplanes which were available had a very poor performance, and were, of course, quite unsuitable in the present stage of their development for reconnaissance over the land. There was little doubt that the seaplane party had done splendid work; but the task was beyond their powers. I saw one or two shell holes in the *Queen Elizabeth*, and met one or two old friends.

I had a long consultation with Sir John and Roger Keyes, his chief of staff, who immediately impressed me as a man of action of the first class.

Sir John said that Clark Hall, one of my old Eastchurch officers, who was in command of the *Ark Royal*, the seaplane-carrier, had got well under way with the construction of an aerodrome for me at Tenedos. Tenedos was a small island about 30 miles south of Imbros, and a few miles farther from the Dardanelles than the latter. Sir John asked how long it would take for me to get ready for action, and I said that I would guarantee an aeroplane in the air within twelve hours after we had landed.

He seemed surprised. I didn't tell him that No. 50 had only to have her planes put on to be ready.

I guaranteed to Sir John that we would be able to keep up a continuous reconnaissance of the Straits, whatever the weather was like; but that we had no wireless installation in our aeroplanes. He said wireless was essential for spotting for the warships' fire, and promised to do his best to get the requisite instruments.

After a long discussion of plans, he told me to return to the *Abda* and proceed to Tenedos, and he detailed the *Vengeance* to assist in landing the aeroplanes. We set off that night, and daylight found us off the south coast of Tenedos.

I landed as soon as possible with the whole of my party, and two collapsible hangars of the Hervieu type, in which we intended to live until we got settled in.

Unfortunately, we could not land the aeroplanes until the 26th, as a howling gale was blowing. Ashore we had a miserable time, lying huddled up in the canvas hangar, which continually threatened to blow down. We had practically no equipment and very little food, being provided with the latter by the navy. The navy is not organised to feed shore parties, and although we were by this time fairly seasoned campaigners, we suffered from both lack of proper food and terrible cold and wet. Our food shortage was not improved by the arrival of Rear-Admiral Thursby, who, accompanied by his flag-captain and flag-lieutenant, landed at the island, and came up to the aerodrome to discuss methods to be used in landing the aeroplanes.

Unfortunately, having been strictly brought up, I asked him to stay to lunch. The extra mouths to be fed out of our scanty ration caused distinct misgivings to Bill and Osmond, who anticipated actual starvation if this sort of thing continued.

Luckily, on the 26th the weather improved, and we started disembarking the aeroplanes. We had to unload them from the *Abda*, transport them in ships' boats, then disembark them on to an open beach,

THE AERODROME AT TENEDOS. THE AUTHOR STARTING IN NO. 50.

and finally haul them up to the aerodrome, about a quarter of a mile distant. When it is realised that the Maurice Farman aeroplanes were stowed in packing-cases 47 feet long, it can be readily understood that we were faced with quite a considerable task. No. 50 was of course easy to handle. She was hoisted out, put in a launch, and run ashore on her own wheels. As soon as we got her to the aerodrome, half a dozen of my best men got her ready for flight, and that evening I made a test flight on her.

Before I describe the work of landing the other aeroplanes, I had better describe the aerodrome. The site which had been selected by Commander Clark Hall consisted of a vineyard about 3½ miles from Tenedos town.

A large gang of Greek labourers were turned loose, all the vines were dug up, and the whole area levelled and smoothed out. The Greek owner was well paid for his vines, and also received a big rent. He, I understood, did very well out of it. The whole area was 600 yards by 300 yards, with an extension of 200 yards by 150 yards at one end. In fact, the area was L-shaped.

A rough road was made from the aerodrome to the beach, and by the time we arrived everything was ready.

The method employed to land the aeroplanes in their cases was that the battleship's launch and sailing pinnace were lashed together and a platform was built over the pair of them. The cases were then placed on the platform, and the boats towed in to the beach. The most difficult part was the actual unloading of the cases from the boats on to the beach. This was a most ticklish operation, as the cases were very heavy, but distinctly fragile; but there is little that the R.N. cannot do, however novel it may be, and we got them all ashore without any damage. One hundred sailors and sixty Greeks made light work of hauling the cases up the rough road to the aerodrome.

The whole job took two days; and by nightfall of March 27th, I had at the aerodrome: No. 50, two Maurice Farmans, each fitted with 100-h.p. Renault engines, and eight Henri Farmans, fitted with 80-h.p. Gnome engines.

These latter were found, as I suspected, to be practically useless for war work, as they soon got out of tune, and could not carry a passenger. They were really only suitable for school work or peace-time flying. Before I left England, I had expressed dissatisfaction at their purchase; but I was told that as these were the only aeroplanes obtainable at that time, I had to take them or nothing. The Maurices were splendid machines for their day, and right nobly they served us.

Next morning, the 28th, I took up one of the Henri Farmans for a test. When it is considered that this was a new aeroplane that had to be removed from its packing-case, rigged, and have the engine installed, it was a pretty smart piece of work on the part of my small body of men to have it ready for flight within twenty-four hours.

The same day I took No. 50 up the Dardanelles as far as Kephez to have a look at the lay of the land. I was very much struck by the beauty of the scene, and extremely interested in seeing the large forts lining the shores.

Next day we started in to work properly. We soon got used to continually having to fly over the sea. For aeroplanes, the only possible landing-place was on Mavro or Rabbit Islands, very nearly midway between us and Helles. The rest of the land of course was enemy territory.

On the 31st I set off in one of the Maurices, taking Osmond as observer, and we made a hunt for mines, amongst other intelligence required.

On April 2nd Osmond and I chased off to Rabbit Island, as an enemy aeroplane had arrived and bombed H.M.S. *Albion*. We didn't find her, though.

The same day I started bombing the Turks, dropping three small bombs from No. 50 on the Soghon Dere Minefield batteries. I didn't hit anything; but it was good practice, and I felt it was time the Turks realised that Eastchurch had arrived on the scene.

April 3rd was memorable, as it was our first attempt at controlling a warship's fire by wireless telegraphy. I took up one of the Maurices, and Osmond came as observer to work the wireless. As the wireless was a rather home-made affair, we decided that I should do the actual spotting while Osmond devoted himself to the signalling part. H.M.S. *London* was the ship selected for our first effort, and she was to engage batteries on the Asiatic side near Achilles Tomb.

They were quite pleased with our first efforts, and I received a signal from the captain to express his thanks for our co-operation.

As Osmond and Collet were the only competent signallers we were rather busily employed, and I was anxiously awaiting the arrival of the rest of our party.

They turned up within a few days on board s.s. *Inkosi*. It was a great pleasure to see the old familiar faces once more, and feel that now I could really get going.

They were all in fine fettle, but rather anxious to know how we had got on, especially Brownridge, who never felt happy at any of us flying a new aeroplane unless he had first vetted its rigging.

They had an assortment of aeroplanes with them, some new, some old, consisting of—

Two B.E.2 C.'s, which were "improved" B.E.2's; but we soon found that they were not half so good; in fact, they wouldn't take up a passenger with any comfort.

One B.E.2, which was really built out of bits of three machines; but she was a real good machine.

Two Sopwith Tabloids, which were single-seaters and not of very much use, as although they were fast and had a gun, they were not efficient as fighters in those days before inventors discovered how to fire through the propeller area. Also, they had a habit of shaking out their engines.

Marix's big Breguet, a most impressive machine for that day, with an engine of 200 h.p. The nacelle was armoured, and it certainly looked a most useful customer. Marix was most enthusiastic about it; but nobody else seemed to be so, as the engine was a doubtful performer.

Last, but by no means least, our old No. 1241, Canton Unné Maurice Farman, the pride of the Squadron. She had already done 120 hours' flying for us in France, and she carried on in the same style at the Dardanelles.

I now had altogether twenty-two aeroplanes; but only five of these were really of practical use.

I got Sir John to wire home for some more Maurice Farmans, as it was obvious that the only aeroplanes that could be used for controlling the ships' fire were the latter and our two B.E.2's. As this work was at present all-important, it was likely we would not be able to keep up with the increasing demand.

We soon settled down at the aerodrome. Some of us lived in the Greek owner's house, the rest in tents, and we used a large marquee we had obtained in some mysterious way as a mess tent. The men made splendid homes for themselves in the aeroplane packing-cases. I had altogether 102 men and 18 officers. When it is considered that we used to do all our own overhauls and repairs, practically rebuilding aeroplanes without the assistance of a repair depot, I think no one can

OFFICERS' TENTS, TENEDOS.

OFFICERS' KITCHEN, IMBROS.
Note pickaxe employed to break up our beef.

deny that my men were very competent and hard-working.

Our main equipment consisted of six canvas hangars, a workshop lorry, and our searchlight lorry, which we had brought from France. Warner immediately set about installing electric light in the camp. I will never forget the moment when in the mess tent at dinner the first night after he had completed his task he strode over to the switch and with majestic mien switched on. Nothing happened, and amid a storm of jeers from the more critical members he sent for Platford.

On Platford's arrival it was discovered that he had omitted to have the plant started up.

Meanwhile, Felix, who was the Transport Officer, had sat quietly waiting for Warner to give himself into his hands.

Warner of course was a godsend, as he was a born organiser, and no one ever had to complain about our armament.

I soon got some more observers, as it was obvious that we couldn't carry on using pilots for this work. Two army officers, Major Hogg, Central India House, and Captain Jenkins, a special reserve officer, arrived to join us; also, the commander-in-chief sent me St. Aubyn, Sissmore, and Chappell, midshipmen.

Other observers who joined up later on, and whose names will appear in this narrative, were Captains Walser and Edwards, the latter of whom is now Managing Director of National Flying Services; Captain Jopp, an Australian who was a great fellow, and usually came with me (I came across him in 1927 at Durban, when I was flying back from Cape Town to Cairo, where he was a big estate owner); the Hon. M. Knatchbull-Hugessen, a Horse Gunner; and Whitaker, who was shortly to have a very strenuous time as my liaison officer at Helles.

All these officers were real good fellows, keen as mustard, and they did splendid work without much recognition. In fact, I don't think any of my squadron ever got adequate award for the work they did; but I don't think that ever worried them very much. As a general rule the man who sits at Headquarters gets more ribbons than the men who do the fighting. Anyhow, Davies got a V.C., and the three Snotties and Butler got D.S.C.'s; but several very fine jobs of work went unrewarded.

Bill and Bernard Isaac were put in charge of intelligence, which soon became a big job, and they had plenty to do, as well as a good bit of flying.

The two doctors were terrors on Camp Sanitation; but they were such persuasive souls that we soon followed out their ideas, with splendid results.

Davies as per usual ran the whole camp like clockwork, as well as flying continuously. He and I had a close race for hours flown, and I just beat him with 305½ hours to his 302.

Marix, Peirse, Osmond, Collet, Butler, Bill Wilson, the two Newton Clares, and Thomson made a pretty useful crew of pilots.

I still had my good old gang of Eastchurch men, some of whose names I must repeat, as, after all, it is the man on the ground who safeguards the life of the pilot. Keogh, Bradford, Leigh, Platford, Russell, Lacey, Dessoussois, Snow, Brewe, were some of them.

New pilots told me that they felt far more fear taking up old No. 1241 in face of the anxious looks of these fellows, who I believe would have lynched anybody who crashed it, than flying at 1,000 feet in a 60-mile-an-hour aeroplane over Ostend.

CHAPTER 2

The "Landing"

We were busily engaged from now onwards in spotting for the battleships engaging shore batteries. We got some quite good results, and several guns were hit owing to our observations. We were doing a fair amount of reconnaissance work in addition, and I made it a rule for each aeroplane, as far as possible, to carry bombs, and to drop them whenever a good target was seen; generally, bomb-dropping was carried out after the spotting had finished. Thus, I made an economical use of my few pilots and aeroplanes, at the same time developing our full effort.

On April 11th a notable flight was made. This was our first attempt to locate all the trenches and light-gun positions at Helles and Anzac. A fairly good result was obtained, and a tracing was forwarded to the military authorities. The great difficulty we encountered in the Dardanelles was the bad maps available; in time we got out our own maps, and towards the end of the campaign an excellent one was produced by the Survey Department from our photographs.

Butler was entrusted with the photographic work, and right nobly he did it. I gave him a Henri Farman, which was quite suitable for this single-seated work. He got badly wounded later on, and during his absence Thomson took on the work.

On April 12th I took up Lieutenant-Commander Brodie, the captain of Submarine *E 15*, taking him at fairly low altitude up the Dardanelles to beyond Kephez Point, so that he should get a good idea of the lay of the land, as he had been detailed to make the first attempt to pass the Narrows in his submarine. I must say I preferred my job to his, and I rather felt as if it would be the last time, I would see him.

About this time, I was told about the proposed landing, so we made every effort to get good photographs and drawings of all the possible beaches, with the positions of any defences. I think that before the

"Landing" we provided a clear report of all that was there, except for the Sedd-el-Bahr trenches, which were impossible to locate from the air, as they were very well sited and hidden. Better results could have been obtained with the improved cameras that were produced later in the War. Our camera was one I had borrowed from the French Aviation, and was excellent for its period.

On April 15th we located the enemy aerodrome at Chanak, the chief town on the Asia Minor side. We had been looking for it for some time without success. Next day I had a narrow squeak from falling into the sea, as a big-end bearing went whilst Osmond and I were spotting, and we had to give it up and make for home. On the 17th Brodie made his gallant effort to get through the Narrows. All my aeroplanes were up to cause a diversion, and we bombed Maidos, Khalid Bahr, etc., but unfortunately poor Brodie ran ashore at Kephez. We kept off the Turks from the submarine for a short time by bombing, but we soon saw that E 15 was hopelessly aground.

The next day we made a couple of flights spotting for H.M.S. *Triumph* firing at E 15 to prevent any possible salvage by the Turks. I am afraid we never hit her. It was left to Commander Robinson, who had already gained the V.C. for a landing exploit, to torpedo her successfully from a picket boat. This was a very daring piece of work, as he was faced with tremendous fire at short range in a slow 56-foot steamboat punching against a six-knot current. On April 18th an enemy aeroplane came over, and had the cheek to bomb my aerodrome. None of his bombs went off, however. So, Davies, Collet, and I set off to repay the visit. We let him have six 100-lb. bombs in place of his three 16-lb. Davies hit the hangar, and from trustworthy reports I received in 1919 he wrecked the aeroplane.

I always made it a rule, whenever possible, that if anybody bombed my aerodrome, we always returned the visit immediately, and gave them worse than they gave us. I certainly found it paid us, as they generally treated my aerodrome as holy ground. Every now and then, when some new Austrian or German arrived, they had a go; but they found it an unpopular pastime. One fellow actually came over on Christmas Day 1915 and dropped a bomb, which broke up our football match, Officers *v*. Men, to celebrate the day. It was just as well, as some of us were feeling we had had quite enough of football on top of Christmas dinner. We all rushed for our aeroplanes, and everybody went to the enemy aerodromes, loaded up with every sort of bomb and frightfulness we had.

Whilst on the same subject I had better relate what Marix did on September 18th. A German came over and dropped some bombs at G.H.Q. about 10 p.m. As we always kept an aeroplane standing by, Marix got away before the German started for home, and arriving at his aerodrome before the enemy, found it splendidly illuminated in expectation that the aeroplane they heard was Herr Fritz; but unfortunately, they discovered their error too late, as Reggie, always a real thorough fellow, came in low and let go three 100-pounders, I have since heard, with adequate results.

I don't think the German when he arrived was altogether popular; anyhow, it caused night flights on their part to cease. I set off myself to their Galata aerodrome in case he had gone there; but they never showed a light, and of course I could not locate it sufficiently accurately in the dark, so I turned back; but luckily, finding a party with plenty of lights and a fire apparently unloading stores at Kilia Liman, I was provided with something substantial at which to release my cargo.

On April 19th I had the great pleasure to score a direct hit on a big howitzer near In Tepe with a 100-lb. bomb.

About this time Sir John de Robeck reported that "the R.N.A.S. has done excellent work of great value to our future operations."

April 23rd saw our first big raid. Five of us went off to attack Maidos, where large numbers of Turkish troops were reported to be quartered. We dropped seven 100-lb. and six 20-lb. bombs with fairly good effect, as twenty Turks were killed, and several fires started. But the after-results were better, as the Turks left the town, and camped in the hills.

Before this we had caused them to leave Jessoi camp, which we ruthlessly bombed, Hogg hitting no less than ten tents.

Little affairs like this all help, as the Turks had to give up comfortable camps and live in burrows in the hills. This continued until the end of the campaign. The moral effect was therefore worth the expenditure of a few bombs.

I received visits at Tenedos from Sir Ian Hamilton, who had been an old visitor to Eastchurch in 1912 and 1913, and had been taken up by us several times, and Sir Aylmer Hunter-Weston. They had a careful look at all our photographs, and thoroughly discussed the part we were to play in the "Landing."

I was greatly impressed by Sir Ian's remark that he expected to lose nearly 50 *per cent.* in casualties before he obtained a footing. Personally, as a result of my constant flights over the peninsula, I thought the landing would be impossible.

I had frequent discussions with the Military and the Naval Staffs over the future, and from my close personal touch with Sir John de Robeck, Sir Ian Hamilton, and Roger Keyes, I feel that nobody could have done the job better than they did with their available resources. The plans were most elaborate and well-thought-out; however, I thought at the time, and still think, that the whole scheme was too cut-and-dried, and no alternative tactics were catered for in case the situation developed contrary to the general idea.

It particularly failed, and I think those who were on the spot will agree with me, because there was no provision made for a rapid exploitation of a local success or for withdrawal of any part of the force and reinforcement therewith of other parties who had succeeded in gaining a footing, with adequate hopes of pushing on if reinforced.

All along I have refrained in this book from expressing opinions gained and information received from official sources, and in the case of the Dardanelles I will not refer in any way to the data I gained from my membership of the Dardanelles Committee. I am merely attempting to recount my experiences and those of my command, and recording incidents out of my private logs and diaries.

Greater brains than mine have written pages about the "Great Landing," and expressed criticisms sometimes merited, generally rather hard. I do not propose to attempt to follow in their steps.

The day before the "Landing" a large fleet of transports gathered on the north side of Tenedos.

As I viewed this *armada*, I felt a distinct feeling of fear and uncertainty, as I realised that very many of the soldiers on board these ships were for certain death. I pictured in my mind hundreds being shot down before they reached the shore, and then mowed down long before they could leave the beaches and reach the Turks' positions. I imagined that they would never be able to take these trenches, and would be driven back to the beaches, where they would find it impossible to reembark.

I cannot truthfully say that I thought the attack would succeed, and I felt that the Empire would read of a great disaster on the morrow.

Being a sailor, I had a sort of feeling that the navy had not, up to date, taken enough risk in trying to force the Straits, and that the Senior Service had stood aside too readily to let the army have a try. I know, and we all know from reports that have been made public in many books published about the Dardanelles, that there were several distinguished sailors on the spot, who wanted to have another try at what the ships could do. I had personal evidence of this. I feel certain that the fleet could have forced the Dardanelles at this time, which was, it must be remembered, before the arrival of the German submarine in these waters. Once the ships had passed Nagara, they could have rendered the landing of the supporting army an easy task.

Returning to my thoughts at the time, I felt that my squadron had done all it could have done in the time, with the constant call for different jobs; it is certain, however, that if we had been allowed to concentrate solely on close reconnaissance of the landing beaches, we would have produced fuller results than we had been able to do.

As it was, we had made no less than forty-two reconnaissance and eighteen photographic flights. My duties for the morrow were to look after all the Helles landings. We were to be up in position over the beaches before the tows left the ships, and were to spot certain ships' fire on to any guns that were firing on the boats; then we were to shift the fire on to any bodies of the enemy who were resisting the landing. After the landing had been effected, we were to spot the ships on to any large bodies moving down to reinforce. In addition, long reconnaissance had to be carried out up to Bulair to watch for possible movements of the Turkish reserves.

We worked hard all day, and most of us made three flights; we practically all found that the ships took little notice of our signals until too late. I started off at an early hour in one of the Maurice Farmans, taking Osmond as my observer; we were to look out for the Lancashire landing, rather appropriately, although I didn't realise it at the time, because I am a Lancashire man.

It was a splendid morning for air work, also for the ships' boats.

The ships were firing at the beaches and beyond on to various positions that were thought to be held by troops or occupied by guns. I saw the tows leave the ships, and then finally break off from the steamboats and row for the shore. Just before the tows were slipped the Turks started firing, and I saw Hell let loose. The sea was literally whipped into foam by the hail of bullets and small shells. It seemed practically impossible that the boats could get in through that tornado of fire; but still they came on, and we saw the troops jump out and reach the beach.

I saw men fall the moment they reached the shore; but others charged on, some going straight ahead up the slope, others making for the cliffs on the left flank. I didn't see much more, as our principal job was to find the Turks in order to signal their position to the ships. They were not easy to find; but we located some Turks and guns quite close to the beach. Osmond signalled their position; but the ships disregarded our message, and kept their fire too far inland. No doubt they did this because they were afraid of hitting our own people. We dropped our bombs at these Turks; but unfortunately missed them.

My next glance at the beach showed it covered with bodies of our dead; but I could see that the landing had been made good. Reinforcements were arriving, and the Naval beach parties could be seen hard at work regardless of the fire.

As our time was up, and we were relieved by another aeroplane, we returned home, passing over Sedd-el-Bahr, where I could see that the landing was held up. The *River Clyde* was fast ashore; but the lighters ahead of her were not in the right position, apparently, and gaps occurred. These lighters were full of corpses; the beach and water close to the shore were strewn with bodies. It was an appalling sight for us to look at from our safe position in the air, and made one think that we were not doing our bit. I could see, however, that some of our men were holding out behind a ridge about 30 yards or so inland. The Turks were keeping up a hot fire on the *River Clyde,* and it seemed impossible for anyone to get ashore from her.

Some shells were arriving from the Asiatic side; but undoubtedly the most serious obstacle was the rifle fire from Sedd-el-Bahr village.

I saw one gallant deed, which impressed itself upon my memory. A naval steamboat came in right close up to the beach in face of a terrible fire and towed off a cutter which was full of dead and wounded; they did the job as neatly as if they had been taking liberty-men off in peace-time. The sea for a distance of about 50 yards from the beach was absolutely red with blood, a horrible sight to see.

After an hour at Tenedos refuelling, I set off once more, this time taking Collet as observer. We were fully occupied in spotting for the warships' fire. I saw that apparently everything was going all right at Lancashire landing; but we were still held up at Sedd-el-Bahr. The *Queen Elizabeth* had arrived, and was firing salvo after salvo of 6-inch at Sedd-el-Bahr fort and village. I could actually see the shells passing through about six walls before they burst.

The Turks must have been tough fellows to have stuck the continuous bombardment; but as a matter of fact, as I saw afterwards, having been shown by a Turkish officer the actual positions they held, they were practically untouched by the shells, as their trenches were sited

LANCASHIRE LANDING, CAPE HELLES.

just below the sky-line and perfectly invisible from either the air or sea. Our journey this time was curtailed, owing to my throttle-control wire parting, thus making the engine run full out, so we had to return earlier than we wanted.

On my last flight, again accompanied by Collet, we had to spot H.M.S. *Goliath* and *Swiftsure*, who were firing at Krithia and Achi Baba.

I saw a real V.C. feat this time, if anybody could award V.C.'s to anyone, where all equally deserved them. I saw four men advance across the open, on the plateau between Lancashire landing and Sedd-el-Bahr, go up to the wire entanglements, and obviously attempt to cut them; they seemed to bear charmed lives, as they were at work for what seemed hours to me, but really, I suppose, were only a few minutes. They failed, however, as I saw two of them hanging over the wire, evidently killed and the others were lying prone, probably also out of action. Hundreds of deeds like this were undoubtedly done this day by the glorious 29th Division; but this was, I suppose, one of the few instances where such a noble endeavour was viewed from the air at close range.

Our propeller got hit by a rifle bullet during this flight; but we got safely back to Tenedos, although the vibration set up made us rather worried. I felt the old Squadron had done its bit that day, as we all had made two if not three flights apiece.

Everybody had been up, of course, and Bill Wilson, who was quite our heaviest pilot, had gone up on a long reconnaissance over Helles at necessarily low altitude with the thirteen-stone Bill Samson as his observer on one of the Henri Farmans. This was a fine performance, as the Henri was very reluctant to leave the ground with two people. They came back very pleased with themselves, with several holes in the planes, and said everybody seemed to have had a shot at them.

All my pilots were full of admiration at the behaviour of our troops; but we all felt rather depressed, as it was obvious that the landing was a failure, and we were held up and unable to advance. We fully expected that our men would be driven off again, once the Turk moved down their reserves, as we seemed to have suffered tremendous casualties, and as far as we knew no reinforcements were at hand. It seemed to me beyond the powers of human endurance for the 29th to advance and take Achi Baba after their tremendous efforts of the day.

I must here place on record my humble opinion that the Dardanelles landings have rather tended to be mainly spoken about as an

Anzac show, with not enough credit given to the 29th Division. I mean no disparagement to the Australians and New Zealanders, for whom I am proud to say I flew many thousands of miles; but I do think that the landings at Helles were feats of arms showing, if I may so vulgarly put it, sheer guts and fighting powers totally unsurpassed.

Anyhow, all were heroes that day, and although the campaign ended in our withdrawal and terrible loss of life, yet our naval beach parties, boats' crews, Anzacs, and the 29th Division proved that the British Empire cannot be licked in fair fight.

I always think that if my squadron had been given a freer hand, and allowed to devote itself to low bombing, we might have been able to assist the landing to a greater extent than we did. As it was, we were practically reduced to spotting for the ships' fire the whole time, and in those early days of aeroplane wireless and general lack of experience on both sides in aerial fire control, the ships generally paid little attention to our signals.

Of course, we were greatly handicapped by having only six effective aeroplanes at that time; but shortage of aeroplanes and pilots was always our lot.

Next day we were hard at work keeping up a constant reconnaissance looking for movements of Turkish troops and spotting for the warships' fire.

This sort of work went on for a long time, and we reported practically every movement of the Turks. We also located the Asiatic guns, which were firing at the Helles beaches. This day and the next we could see the Turks digging in all across the Peninsula. Trenches used to spring up like magic. On the 28th and 29th we sighted no less than 4,000 Turks on their way to Helles; also, several batteries of Field Artillery.

On the 29th, spotting for our favourite ship, the veteran *Prince George*, we had the pleasure of hitting one of the Asiatic batteries. There was little doubt that with certain ships we always seemed to get better results. Our favourites were the *Prince George* and the *Agamemnon*.

On this occasion the *Prince George* got direct hits on to the battery; the aeroplane saw the guns' crews run from their guns. She immediately signalled "up 200 yards shrapnel," and the old P.G., ever keen to respond to us, fired two salvos of 6-inch shrapnel, which blew half the crews to *Allah*.

Two days after the landing I went ashore at Helles to find a landing-ground. It was a wonderful sight, as everybody seemed to have settled down quite completely, and the beach parties especially didn't seem to worry the slightest bit about shells. I had landed with Admiral Phillimore, whom I had often met previously on the hunting-field. He was principal Beach Master, and there is little doubt that his utter disregard of shells assisted the others to treat them with apparent indifference. I found a suitable place just alongside "Hunter'" Weston redoubt, which was about half a mile from Lancashire landing. It wasn't much of a place, and when I visited it in 1919, I thought: "Well, we were some aviators to have been able to land and get off again from that little patch."

From now onwards we used to keep one or two aeroplanes working from there during the daytime. It was a hectic spot, as of course it was within full view of the Turks, and well within field-gun range. Every time you landed you got shelled. Fortunately, there was some shelter behind the hill to which you could taxi and then hide the aeroplane; but you got it pretty hot whenever you emerged. I lost five aeroplanes there, hit by shells, and at last it got too expensive, and we gave up the use of it, except for special purposes.

In addition, Corps H.Q. began to dislike us being there, as we drew a hate to their locality. Towards the end of the campaign, at General Davies's suggestion, we one night rigged up a dummy aeroplane. It succeeded admirably, as next day the Turks fired 127 shells at it, which all helped towards making them waste ammunition. At this aerodrome I kept Captain Whittaker, one of my observers, and two men. They had a very tough time, as they had to come out each time an aeroplane landed and help it taxi into shelter, and of course got a good dose of shelling on each occasion. I frequently proposed to relieve these men by others, as I thought they must have had enough of it; but they said they would rather stop there. On closely questioning them, they said that they got more and better food at Helles than we got at Tenedos. This was really true.

On the 30th a very good flight was made to beyond Bulair to locate the enemy's reserves and movements of his troops. The aeroplane brought back an excellent report, having sighted no less than 7,000 Turks in various places. To my delight they said that no less than 3,000 Turks had camped near Boghali. I immediately set off with as many aeroplanes as I could muster, and we let go six 100-lb. and nine 20-lb. bombs on this camp with, as far as we could see, excellent results.

Shortly afterwards a Turkish prisoner reported that aeroplane bombs had caused more casualties than ships' shells.

On May 2nd we had our first successful air fight, as an enemy seaplane came towards Tenedos. Marix set off in chase of him, and caught him up near Kephez point; he forced the seaplane to land on the water, and killed the observer. Marix came down to about 50 feet to do this, and of course got a hot time, as he ended up only about 300 yards from Chanak.

One fact stands out as a result of our work during the period from the landing to about the middle of May, and that is that the Asiatic fire always died down whenever an aeroplane was up.

The Turks now began to develop plenty of antiaircraft fire; but rarely at first were any of my aeroplanes hit by shell fragments, although we were constantly hit by rifle bullets.

Later on in the campaign, if I wanted to pay particular attention to a certain zone, I used to keep all my aeroplanes out of it for about a week, and order everyone to fly over a certain fixed route whenever possible. The Turks always fell for it, and collected their guns in the vicinity in which I wanted them, thus leaving practically unprotected the place I had decided to attack in force.

Chapter 3

Bombing Over the Peninsula

The most popular job among the pilots was the early-morning reconnaissance. This was much sought after, as the aeroplane could always rely upon finding transport on the move and Turks out of their holes sitting round fires. Many were the peaceful parties upset by our bombs, and practically every morning some big convoy of camels was dispersed over the countryside. Looking back to those days, I can imagine what destruction we could have done if we had had the 1929 single-seater fighter. I really believe we could have starved out the Turks, given a modern Fighter Squadron and a modern Day Bomber Squadron, which we could have used by night as well as day.

The Turks at first used to land all their supplies at Kilia Liman; but the ships' fire, controlled by aeroplane, seaplane, or kite balloon, soon made this uncomfortable. So they turned to Ak Bashi Liman, about five miles farther up the Straits. Both places were ideal bombing targets, and if more aeroplanes had been available, we could have made landing stores and provisions a most unpopular pursuit.

On May 17th Marix had his big Breguet ready for action. As our principal objective with this aeroplane was an attack on Constantinople, we had to test it out well before allowing the attempt to be made, so in order to see what it could do I made one of my infrequent trips as passenger.

We carried no less than one 100-lb. and fourteen 20-lb. bombs, and also a Lewis gun, a pretty formidable amount for those days. Off we set with the idea of giving Ak Bashi Liman a look-over. Arriving there, we found the place a scene of great activity. We let go all our bombs and created complete panic, and also did a lot of damage.

I have since talked with Turks who were actually on the spot at the time, and they all said that we put a complete stop to work for two days, as the labourers fled to the hills. The loss of life was severe,

AK BASHI LIMAN, 1915. STEAMERS MOVING TO AVOID BOMBS.

thirteen killed and forty-four wounded.

Marix and I came back delighted with the Breguet; but rather doubtful if the engine was reliable enough, as it was missing fire most of the time. However, we both had great faith in Dessoussois, who said he would get it right.

We now had a very welcome reinforcement at Tenedos, as a French Escadrille of aeroplanes arrived. They were equipped with 80-h.p. Maurice Farmans, which were splendid aeroplanes for the job; but not as good as our bigger Maurices. Their whole equipment was most complete, and they looked a most workmanlike party. The only thing they lacked were proper bombs.

The *commandant* was Capitaine Césari, one of the very best, and an aviator of the finest type. He flew a tremendous amount, and we soon had a splendid liaison between the two units.

Many were the impromptu raids we fixed up together, and I look back upon my many happy days with them, with regret that they are past. There was of course a healthy rivalry between the two squadrons, but we helped each other all the time.

In fact, Césari gave me a Maurice Farman later on, as I wanted a good duck-shooting machine. I in return gave him two Nieuport scouts. Of course, we did these things unofficially. My men used to help his and his fellows always came over and lent a hand to us.

Whilst talking about Césari I would like to relate what happened to him one day. As I have said before, he had no bombs, so he got some shells from the French Navy and fitted them up with a makeshift fuse arrangement. Unfortunately, one of his pilots got blown up by one; but Césari was not the type to be deterred by that sort of thing. He set off one day to Helles by himself to bomb Soghanli Dere, carrying one bomb, which was fitted with a time-fuse. The bomb release was worked by his observer, whom he was going to pick up at Helles.

On the way there he suddenly realised that the time-fuse had started to function. He knew the only thing to do was to release the bomb, and he had only a few seconds before the bomb would explode. He couldn't reach the release lever. He had to let the aeroplane fly itself whilst he got out of his seat to get to the back of the nacelle. He had a job to do it, as Maurice Farmans, when you let go the control lever, didn't exactly fly themselves. He did it, however, and released the bomb, which exploded about 200 feet below him. He went on to Helles, landed, shipped another bomb of the same type, and paid his visit to Soghanli Dere. I heard rumours of the occurrence, and went to ask him about it. I said: "You must have been scared stiff." He replied, not being much of an English scholar, "*Mon Commandant*, I was all muckoo sweato."

I know what he must have felt like, as one day with three bombs on board I released all three; but I could only see two burst. I thought therefore that one was still on the machine, hung up on the undercarriage. I was alone. I rocked the aeroplane; but still no bomb fell off. I knew if it was hung up on the under-carriage that the safety fan would unwind, and the moment I landed I would be blown up. I got out my knife and cut a hole in the bottom of the nacelle to try if I could see the bomb; but I couldn't.

So, after screwing up my courage I came into land expecting the moment I touched, to go up with a bang. I made the very softest landing I have ever made in my life. The moment I touched I was out of the seat, and jumped from the aeroplane, just missing the propeller by rolling away as the plane passed over me, still going about 10 miles an hour. They all thought, as Warner remarked, that the commander had gone mad at last.

The bomb wasn't there; it had dropped all right a long time ago, but hadn't exploded.

Peirse once had a bomb hang up on the under-carriage, and his passenger climbed out and lowered himself on to the skids, where he perilously clung, gradually working the bomb loose with his feet. After ten minutes' strenuous labour of the most unpleasant type, he got the bomb off. They were both quite pleased with themselves.

Whilst on the subject of bombs I will complete it by my experiences one day later on in the campaign. When we were at Imbros, I had a single-seater Nieuport scout. I started off one day with my usual equipment of three 20-lb. bombs. The moment I left the ground a most awful bang went off, and my machine was tossed about like a feather, bits of metal flew all over the place, and a 6-inch hole appeared in my petrol tank. Petrol streamed all over me. Luckily the machine held together, and my aerodrome being within 200 yards of the sea I flew on and pulling all the bomb releases heard two explosions. I turned round and landed, expecting every minute for the aeroplane to catch fire before I could get down. I had no choice, of course, as I either had to land in the water or the aerodrome, no other bit of ground being possible.

When I landed the tail plane and rudder fell off. We discovered that the holding bolt of one of the bombs had got rusted through and broken off, thus allowing the bomb to drop the moment the bumping of the take-off commenced.

Captain Jenkins, whom I had taken up as observer on a spotting trip for a ship firing at guns near Gaba Tepe, provided me with some unpleasantness. We were in No. 50, and the engine kept on practically stopping, then going on again. I made for home, and we went dot and carry one the whole way. Every minute I expected to have to take the ocean; but we got home at last. When I landed, we tried the engine and found it was O.K., and after some investigation discovered that Jenkins had, every now and then, got foul of the air control cable, thus giving the engine full petrol and no air.

We had a lot of work to do for Helles, and soon commenced fire-control flights for the Artillery in addition to close reconnaissance work.

Knatchbull-Hugessen as a gunner was most useful at artillery work of course. He and Edwards, who joined us later on, were generally detailed for this work.

Osmond did a great performance on May 29th, as, finding an old Turkish battleship, the Barbarossa, lying off Ak Bashi Liman, he bombed her and scored a direct hit. We heard afterwards that he had put the centre turret out of action and killed eight men. Anyhow, she cleared off to Constantinople and never returned.

Towards the end of May I received a reinforcement of two Voisin aeroplanes. They were not half bad machines, fitted with 130-h.p. Canton engines, but they were not so good as the big Maurices. June 4th was a hard day, as the 29th Division, assisted by the French and the Naval Division, made the first big attack. Great things were hoped for this day; but the actual results were not much. The narrowness of the peninsula made it a case of frontal attack, and as experience has shown frontal attacks against a determined opponent well dug in, unless the attacker has great artillery strength, cannot hope to succeed.

Armoured cars were used; but of course, were of little use against the trenches. Personally, I always think it was a great mistake that they were not landed on landing day, as I feel certain that then they would have achieved splendid results; in fact, might have turned the tide.

Naturally, I was intensely interested in the possibilities of the armoured cars, and it was rather surprising that no advantage of my experience was taken by the Army. Certainly, taking into consideration that these cars were of fine design with gun turrets, I would have urgently pressed for their immediate landing.

We had four aeroplanes working from Helles aerodrome that day, and we kept going the whole time. I could follow the whole course of the proceedings, as not only was I constantly up in the air, but when on the ground I was with the Corps Staff. General Hunter Weston was full of optimism; but gradually he realised that we had insufficient strength to gain decisive results. If adequate reinforcements had been at hand there is no doubt that we would have rolled the Turks back and taken Krithia and Achi Baba. The Turks, as history has proved, were greatly shaken, and were on the point of retirement. One final punch would have completely defeated them; but alas, we had no fresh troops to put into the line, and human nature has its limits. Great feats of arms were done that day; but the actual results were practically negligible.

About this time there had been many reports of the arrival of German submarines in the vicinity, and in addition to our usual work I had kept an anti-submarine patrol going. Some days previously I had sighted a submarine off Gaba Tepe. She was submerged, and although I dropped a 100-lb. bomb in close proximity no results could be hoped for, as unfortunately all our bombs had direct impact fuses. Anyhow, they would feel the explosion, and know they had been sighted.

On June 4th during the attack Osmond, who was carrying out the submarine patrol, landed at Helles, and told me that he had seen a submarine close to Rabbit Island. I immediately set off in No. 50 to try to locate it. Sure enough I sighted it at a good depth below the surface proceeding up the Dardanelles close to Morto Bay. The French battleship *Henri IV* was directly in its path. I came down low over the submarine and let go my bomb, which exploded on the surface about 50 yards away. The submarine proceeded absolutely undisturbed, and passed directly under the French battleship.

I then lost sight of the submarine, which obviously had dived deeper to go under the minefields. Another aeroplane was sent up to try to find it; but no further trace was seen until late in the afternoon, when I was on a long reconnaissance up the peninsula. I then sighted my old friend on the surface off Ak Bashi Liman, proceeding towards the Marmara, escorted by a torpedo-boat.

I had no bombs, and the nearest supply was at Tenedos, which double journey would have taken me over two hours, and it would have been dark by the time I could get back to her expected position. I have rarely felt so disappointed and angry at my lack of sense in not having had some bombs at Helles. This was the first real chance I had got of bagging a submarine, as my other attacks had been at night. I felt certain I could have bagged her. The only thing to do was to go down low over her to tell her she had been seen, and pretend I had a bomb. I did so, and fired a few shots at her with my rifle, which was clamped to the side of my fuselage. The submarine didn't seem to mind much; but the torpedo boat let off a few rounds from a small gun.

I returned to Tenedos, feeling that I had missed the chance of a lifetime; as it proved I never had such a golden opportunity again.

This was the same submarine that subsequently bagged H.M.S. *Majestic* and *Triumph*. I would have probably saved Admiral Nicholson a jaunt ashore in his pyjamas.

Talking of admirals, we had some good ones out there to work for. Sir John himself, Nicholson, and Thursby were all keen to help the R.N.A.S.; but I had a ticklish time keeping popular with the admirals under whose direct orders I was, and at the same time working for the generals. Each of course naturally thought his own requirements were the most important. I would receive orders to spot for the ships, and then urgent demands for increased co-operation with the army.

Both jobs had to be done somehow, with a limited number of aeroplanes and pilots both gradually beginning to feel the strain; but somehow, I kept on the right side of both the admirals and the generals. I was once told by a distinguished air-officer that I lacked tact. If I may be permitted to boast, I think I must have had some in 1915. I made it a golden rule always to have a personal talk with the great men whenever things were getting slightly strained, and tell them the real situation; I never found these good fellows unreasonable if you explained things.

By June I had lost a number of aeroplanes, some being hit at Helles, others having crashed. I kept on pressing for some more aeroplanes and pilots, and we soon got a reinforcement of eight Henri Farmans—perfectly useless, of course. I went to Sir John, who well understood, and he said, "What must we do with them?"

I said, "If we keep them the Admiralty will credit me with eight new aeroplanes, and we won't get any good ones; therefore, I would suggest, sir, you send them off home again somehow."

He gave orders to this effect. These eight aeroplanes absolutely vanished into the blue; they certainly never arrived home. The Admiralty Air Department kept on asking me about them; but I always denied all knowledge of them. Although at times the letters and telegrams got rather sultry, in time the questions simmered down, and at last I got some good aeroplanes. The eight Henri Farmans may develop into a sort of lost tribe. I suppose some accountant at the Admiralty still regards me with evil intent.

I always looked forward with pleasure to H.M.S. *Triad* arriving off Tenedos, as Sir John always came ashore to look at us, and inevitably asked me to lunch. I am afraid I was greatly attracted by the chance of a real meal.

On one occasion M. Venizelos arrived at Tenedos, and I was detailed to meet him. I found him a most charming man, and it was intensely interesting listening to his talk. Another visitor we had was Compton Mackenzie, who was a Lieutenant in the marines at that time. He strolled into our mess and introduced himself to—I think it was—Bill Wilson, also remarking that he had written *Sinister Street*. I fear Bill Wilson wasn't much of a reader; anyhow, he said, "You have come to the right place then, as this island is about the —— limit."

Warner, who was, as anybody who has waded thus far will have realised, distinctly lost without a gun of sorts, had wangled a 12-pounder from one of the ships. This he proceeded to mount on top of a large mooring buoy, which had drifted down to us from the Turks. He now had his desired anti-aircraft gun. Unfortunately, the first time he fired it, the gun fell down inside the buoy.

During the first fortnight in June Marix was hard at work with the Breguet, making frequent flights to get it ready for the Constantinople trip. I went up three times with him, and on one occasion we got the bag of our life, as we found about 400 Turks in a gulley behind Anzac. They were in a dense mass, being paid or drawing rations or something like that. We dropped a 100-lb. bomb at them, and following its flight the whole way with our eyes saw it burst immediately in the centre of them. We could see that the loss of life was tremendous.

As well as Helles and the Fleet, we now had Anzac to look after; and we did a lot of artillery co-operation for the Australians, registering their heavy batteries on to the Turks' guns. Some of the latter wanted a lot of locating, as did some guns that fired from about a mile inland from Gaba Tepe. Jopp, who was an Australian, was the observer whom I detailed to specialise on Anzac; he had an eye like a hawk, and it wasn't long before he had discovered most of the guns that were causing trouble. The chief difficulty in dealing with the enemy guns, however, was the great shortage of ammunition for our own guns. Many was the time, when we had got them on to the target, our guns had to cease fire owing to having used up their allowance.

The enemy aeroplanes never put up much of a show until practically the end of the campaign, as every time we sighted one, we naturally made for it; but they always ran away, and generally escaped by scuttling home at low altitude. Collet forced one to land after twenty minutes' fight within half a mile of the French front line, and the 75's soon reduced it to matchwood.

We kept up bombing the whole time, and it is interesting to note what Major Prigge, adjutant to General Liman von Sanders, says in his book *The Fight in the Dardanelles*:

"Hitherto the enemy airmen had contented themselves with reconnaissance flights; but they now began to take an active part in the fighting by dropping bombs. Terrible was the effect of these missiles on the transport columns and disembarkation places."

On June 21st Reggie Marix, with myself as passenger, set off at 1.30 a.m. for Constantinople. The engine started to misfire as soon as we left; but Reggie, a most persistent fellow, carried on. We got as far as Anafarta Saghir, which is beyond Anzac, when we both decided that it was hopeless to go on, so reluctantly we turned for home. On the way back we bombed every camp-fire we could see, and I hope disturbed the Turks a bit with the fourteen bombs we gave them. We neither of us thought we would reach Tenedos, as the engine went weaker and weaker, and we came down gradually towards the water: we succeeded, however.

Immediately we landed Dessoussois rushed up and started taking the plugs out. He got three out, then flung down his tools, and said, "*Commandant*, what this pig of an engine wants is not a mechanician but one 'ammer." He then burst into tears, and had to be led away. Poor soul, he had worked like a slave on the engine, although suffering from dysentery.

Marix was terribly disappointed, as there was little doubt that the engine was a bad one; certainly, if Dessoussois couldn't make it go nobody else could.

Constantinople had to be given up. None of my other aeroplanes could carry sufficient fuel as well as bombs for this long journey.

I now decided to give the Turks a dose of night bombing, so on June 28th four of us went off and bombed the bivouacs along Soghan Dere. Osmond did a real good flight, as he came down to about 500 feet and got two bombs into a large party round a big fire. On July 6th Hugessen did great work by locating 3,000 Turks in a *nullah* northwest of Krithia; also, an enemy field battery. He got our 60-pounders on to both lots with excellent results.

We had two main recreations at Tenedos: one was to start off from a spot about a quarter of a mile from our camp and run across-country up the big hill and back to the starting-post. Bill Samson and Hogg were the star performers. Doctor Williams used to lay good odds that certain times would not be beaten. He always got fellows to take the odds; and always won, but Hogg, who had been "pulling" unknown to Williams, got Williams, who had timed him many times, to bet him 10 to 1 he wouldn't do it in thirty-two minutes. Williams fell for it, and Hogg then proceeded to do it in twenty-six minutes. Felix Samson, not to be outdone, said he would do it on a motor-bicycle. He got nearly to the top over the awful going, then took a toss, and bicycle and himself came down in record time.

The other pastime was to walk into Tenedos town. The social excitements there were to watch a wedding, which seemed to consist of the bridegroom and his friends sitting at a table drinking with the bride and her girlfriends solemnly walking round them in a circle with joined hands. It seemed a poor sort of honeymoon. Coffee at the *café* was the only other alternative. Reggie Marix once bet me he could run to Tenedos, if I gave him five minutes' start, faster than I could ride on the horse I had captured in France.

Unknown to Marix I sent off one of my most expert marines to clear away some of the principal obstacles, and to mark out the best bits of going, by whitewashed stones; then I accepted Reggie's challenge. He never had a dog's chance; I came close up to him before halfway. Pretending I was in difficulties, he was deceived into making fresh efforts; after a bit I had compassion and passed him, and we called the bet off. I am certain he would have broken a blood-vessel if I hadn't stopped him, as he was a most determined fellow.

Chapter 4

Imbros: The Death of a Friend

At the beginning of July, I lost Flight-Lieutenant Peirse, as he was ordered home to act as Instructor. His departure was a great loss, as he had been with the squadron a long time, and was a wonderful pilot with a splendid record. Osmond was also ordered home. I missed him dreadfully, as he was a proper old Eastchurch man, and we had been together all along in all sorts of shows. We also lost Bill Wilson and Bill Samson, whom I had detached to Mytylene with a small party and a Henri Farman to carry out patrols over Smyrna.

They had a most adventurous time for a period, which was brought to an end by an involuntary fall into the sea owing to engine failure. They had four hours in the water with the wreckage only able to support one. Bill Wilson, being a good swimmer, made my brother, whose leg was damaged in the crash, take his Gieve waistcoat and hold on to the wreckage, whilst he kept swimming. Fortunately, one of our patrol trawlers came up and picked them up just as my brother was practically all in.

One of the trawler's crew got hold of a bomb which was on the aeroplane—you could always trust one of the squadron aeroplanes to have a bomb somewhere—and started to unwind the safety fan. Brother Bill just stopped him in time, and flung the bomb overboard, or it would have gone off any minute.

They both were invalided home. Wilson never rejoined again; but my brother came out in September. Bill Wilson richly deserved the Royal Humane Society's Medal he was awarded.

Butler, on a photographic flight, got badly wounded by shrapnel; up to date he had borne a charmed life, as although his aeroplane was frequently hit, owing to the low altitude at which he had to fly to obtain good photographs, he had escaped serious damage. He had to go home; but we expected him back in about three months or so, and sure enough he turned up again.

Dawson, Kerby, and Ball came out from England to join up with the Squadron; their arrival was welcomed, as there was no doubt that we were all beginning to feel the effects of our constant flying, and the strain was beginning to tell on our health. The doctors were getting worried. Personally, I felt quite played out; although not ill, I was tired. I had flown for 180 hours since April 1st, and this amount in three and a half months is a good deal, especially on top of my experiences in France and Flanders.

Collet also was by no means the man he was. He was ready for any work, the stickier the better; but he wasn't sleeping at night. Davies was marvellous. He had done nearly as much as I; but he looked and was unchanged. He only weighed about 9 stone, and looked as if a puff of wind would blow him over. Looks deceived, though; it would take a 100-lb. bomb to knock him out.

The commander-in-chief decided that we should all have a short rest in Egypt, as the situation on the Peninsula had reached a stage of waiting for something to happen. Meanwhile, it was decided to move the Squadron to Imbros, where we would be in close touch with the General Headquarters in readiness for the next big move in the campaign, which would take place in August.

I arranged for the repair section to remain at Tenedos, whilst an advance party and most of the aeroplanes proceeded to Imbros, where an aerodrome had been roughly made on the Kephalo side of the harbour.

On July 23rd I was asked to carry out a low reconnaissance over the Suvla area to see what Turks were in that part. I took No. 50, and came down pretty low; I couldn't see a sign of life, and only a few trenches. I didn't spend much time over there, as it was important that no attention should be attracted to that area. Next day I set off to Egypt, accompanied by Collet.

The commander-in-chief gave me a passage down to Mudros in the *Triad*, and I arrived on board the S.S. *Aragon*, of unholy memory. They say she was aground on the empty bottles ejected from her. I don't like being unpleasant; but I must say, and many will say the same, that people from the Peninsula never seemed to be *personae gratae* with the *Aragon* people. I suppose all base staffs suffer from the same sort of bias. I certainly had the feeling that I was considered a beastly nuisance, rather untidy in appearance, and generally undesirable.

I am afraid that I resented my treatment, especially when I found that no one would give me a boat to go to the transport on board which I was to sail. I then informed the powers that be that I had come on board in the commander-in-chief's barge, and that I would immediately signal to the commander-in-chief and ask for his barge again to take me to the transport, as they refused to provide a boat. At once everything was *couleur de rose*, and I was the important person to be treated with civility; boats arrived like magic, and Collet and myself were wafted to the *Argyllshire* in luxury.

Some of my people were made most uncomfortable on occasions like this, and I resented it.

On arrival on board the *Argyllshire* I was greeted by a harassed major, who said, "Thank the Lord you are Senior Military Authority; there are forty Canadian auxiliary nurses on board."

I am afraid that I didn't mind that. Anyhow, we had a most cheery trip to Port Said with the Major, Collet, and myself, and a bevy of forty beautiful girls.

I had great fun in Egypt, as Felix Samson was now there with all my transport. It was quite like old times seeing the Rolls, which had been well tuned up. The men were very fit, and rumour had it that they were the only fellows who could hold their own against the Anzacs. It was here I first met Percy Woodland, the famous cross-country jockey and trainer. He was in the armoured cars, and shared a tent with Felix. I was a godsend to the pair of them, because I was temporarily well provided with money. Money was of little use at Tenedos.

Collet never seemed to cheer up much though, and I was getting anxious about him.

I returned to the Dardanelles like a new man, and found my crowd on a narrow little beast of an aerodrome on the edge of a cliff. I immediately hunted around for a new aerodrome, and found a possible site about half a mile away. It was covered with scrub and rocks, and on first sight it looked a long job to clear it; but I had seen from the air how Turks dug trenches, so I went off to G.H.Q. and persuaded them to let me have some Turkish prisoners. They gave me seventy. At first, they were closely guarded; but after we got to know them and gave them cigarettes each day, they used to work like Trojans. I told off one of my sailors to be in charge, and they worshipped him. They used to troop off each night to their cage as happy as tinkers, generally carrying the guards' rifles.

I had some of these Turks as working party for the rest of the campaign. They took a great interest in the aeroplanes, and seemed delighted to watch the bombs being placed on the carriages. In fact, in time I really believe they considered themselves members of the squadron.

We had additional work now with Suvla.

I don't intend to talk about the Suvla landings; but visiting the place two days after they had landed, I didn't find the same spirit as was evident with the 29th Division under the same circumstances. This was natural in a way, I suppose. We certainly had missed a glorious chance of gaining the Peninsula, and now we seemed to be stuck.

No doubt several mistakes were made; some were very obvious to us onlookers, and I have heard many arguments on the subject. There is no doubt, however, that for a job like Suvla you want well-trained regular soldiers, and a Byng or Rawlinson on the spot.

We had a welcome addition to our strength by the arrival of two 130-h.p. Henri Farmans; they were good weight-lifters, but unfortunately, after about forty hours' flying, they began to lose performance owing to various weaknesses in construction. This was a pity, and we were terribly disappointed; but later on in the campaign, I took the first 500-lb. bomb up in one.

Davies went off on leave as soon as I could spare him, followed later on by Reggie Marix and others.

Hogg had left, and Captain Walser had arrived in his place. I made it a rule that whenever possible on bomb-raids one of the men should be taken; practically the whole lot went up, some of them two or three times. They were fearfully keen, and thoroughly appreciated the chance of being shot at by "Archies."

In August two new pilots arrived to reinforce, and badly they were needed, when it is remembered that the maximum number, I ever had was eleven, counting myself, with an average of seven, and we now had to work:

(1) For the ships firing at shore targets.

(2) In co-operation with Helles, Anzac, and Suvla.

(3) On constant anti-submarine patrols.

(4) On frequent anti-aircraft patrols, to keep enemy aircraft from observing our positions.

(5) On reconnaissance.

Really, at least three squadrons were required. The situation would have been improved if I had had more aeroplanes, also of more suitable type for the work in hand. Another difficulty I always had was in our complete lack of spare parts. It was only due to Mr. Brownridge and my splendid men that we kept going at all.

The new pilots who arrived were Keeley, who didn't stay very long, and Morrison, who after a little training soon became a most hard-working competent pilot.

August 19th was a black day.

I set off with Jopp on a Henri Farman to carry out a reconnaissance over the Suvla area. We hadn't been over there for more than half an hour when we got hit in the engine by a piece of shrapnel, which stopped it completely. I had to make a landing on the only patch of good ground I could discover, just south of the Salt Lake, and well within our lines. The ground was fairly steep, and as soon as we came to rest the aeroplane ran backwards downhill again; but finally came to rest quite undamaged. On examination I found that the magneto was completely smashed up.

Within two minutes of our landing the enemy guns started on us, and Jopp and I had to make for cover in a small gulley.

After about ten minutes' bombardment they ceased fire, and we went back to see what the damage was. It was surprisingly little considering the number of shells that had burst all round her; but she was certainly out of action for some time, especially the engine, which had two cylinders hit by fragments.

I obtained a couple of horses from Major Hawker, whom funnily enough I used to know when hunting in Devonshire, and we rode round to the landing pier at Kura Chesme. We had quite an eventful ride, as we seemed to be constantly under shell-fire, and I for one was very glad to get into the shelter of a stone sangar well lined with sandbags.

After signalling to Imbros telling them to get a new engine ready, and also the requisite material for repairing the aeroplane, Jopp and I squatted under protection awaiting the arrival of the Mail Trawler. It was quite a thrilling sight watching the beach parties unloading lighters absolutely unperturbed by the spasms of shelling they had to undergo about every quarter of an hour. There were a number of Indian transport drivers with small carts and mules. Their officer told me that they were mostly Pathans, and the North-West Frontier tribesmen, none of them regular soldiers, but only enlisted for transport work behind the lines. They certainly might have had reason to complain that they were far more exposed to danger than the men in the trenches at that period. They didn't seem to worry the slightest bit about the shelling.

The beach-master told me that the Australian Naval Bridging detachment were his star-turn performers, as after working practically all day, they used to go up on their own to the front line at night, and into No Man's Land, frequently returning with a Turkish prisoner or absolute evidence that they had sent one or two to Paradise. The ones I saw certainly looked nasty customers to bump up against on a dark night.

A good tale, probably quite a chestnut, was also related to me of an old Turk who used to hang up his washing (personally, I never knew a Turk had any) each day on the parapet of his bit of trench. In time everybody got to know about him, and let him climb out and spread it out without firing at him.

When the trawler arrived at last Jopp and I were the only passengers. Before we had gone half-way it began to blow, and as it was very wet on deck, and the air of the after-cabin was like an old-time gun-room after three days at sea, we ensconced ourselves in the dinghy, which was lying in crutches right aft amidships. Fortunately, as it proved, the slings were hooked on to the derrick purchase, which was hauled taut.

Night fell, and we got damper and damper, and the sea got rougher and rougher, and Jopp got sicker and sicker, until he turned from a six-foot Australian into a mere helpless invalid.

All of a sudden, the trawler shipped a real snorter, and the dinghy was torn from its crutches, and with us inside swung out over the raging sea. The next few minutes we spent swinging from side to side of the trawler as she rolled, with every now and then a good crash into the after-companionway, which threatened soon to reduce us to splinters. Luckily the crew, proper North Sea fishermen, were equal to the occasion, and timing the evolution to a split second, they let go the purchase with a run and landed us, dinghy and all, safely inboard.

Thank the Lord for the British deep-sea fishermen. I don't think anybody else could have done it.

Jopp and I spent the rest of the voyage below.

Arriving at the aerodrome, I received the terrible news that Collet had been killed in a flying accident. His death was an awful blow to me, as he had been a companion of mine for what seemed ages. He had always been such a courageous fighting man, with such remarkable powers of observation, that I felt that things would never be so easy in future. There is no doubt at all that his death was a real loss to the R.N.A.S.

I had had, as I have said before, for some time a feeling that he wanted a long rest. It was evident that he was by no means so fit as he had been, although he was so fearfully keen; but I couldn't put him on the easy list without breaking his heart.

The accident occurred in the following way:

Our aerodrome was right on the edge of a cliff, below which lay the sea. As he took off his engine began to fail. He tried to turn back to the aerodrome, and as so many great aviators have done before and since, lost flying speed and crashed. The aeroplane got on fire, and he was burnt to death before the gallant rescuers could drag him clear of the wreckage.

Eastchurch could always produce heroes, and that day into the raging inferno went Keogh, Jones, and Robins. They got Collet out; but, alas, too late. Keogh was dreadfully burnt, and he nobly deserved the Albert Medal which was awarded to him.

We had two fights about this time with German aeroplanes, and drove both of them down to the ground.

In company with Césari's aeroplanes we carried out a big bomb attack on the German aerodrome close to Galata. We later heard we had done a good deal of damage.

On August 20th I took up the 80-h.p. Maurice Farman that Césari had given me; having St. Aubyn as observer, we did a good registration for the Helles counter-batteries. I liked the aeroplane immensely; it hadn't the load-carrying capacity or speed of its bigger brothers; but it was much handier. I decided that it would make a great duck-shooting machine, for which job I later detailed it. Many were the trips we had in November and December shooting ducks over the lagoon at Imbros. Before that time came, however, we made a lot of Service use of it.

I now moved camp to our new aerodrome, which had been made by the Turkish prisoners. It was quite a good spot; too narrow to land across, but as the wind was generally up and down we never found that a great drawback. It had a length of 500 yards; but as the end of the run finished at the cliff-edge, I had a steep bank built up, as we preferred the chances of running into the bank to going over the cliff.

We soon got quite a good camp going with four Bessonneau hangars for the aeroplanes, and tents for the men.

The officers lived in aeroplane packing-cases, and some had quite cosy quarters, especially Brownridge and Warner. Some more packing-cases were turned into workshops and stores.

Our supplies were transported by two big four-wheel-drive Jeffrey lorries and two light tenders. In addition, I started to collect animals, and got from the army two horses, eight mules, and eight donkeys, for all of which we built splendid stables in a gulley. The horses had seen better days; but they provided us with exercise, as did some of the mules, as Jopp found to his misery when he tried to ride one over to G.H.Q. It absolutely refused to answer either to its helm or telegraphs. The donkeys were perfectly splendid, and every now and then we used to make trips on them over the hills to Panagia, the capital.

I had my old friend for my own equestrian exercise, and he was looked after by Barratt, who had made him a fine stable in the gulley. He had a trick, however, of breaking loose and poking his head into the mess or my packing-case for sugar. He was most helpful one day. I had ridden him over to the beach, where I came across a certain Captain, R.N., who had a grievance against us; I forget what about, but he was distinctly peeved with the aeroplanes for something.

Seeing me, he started telling me off. My horse evidently didn't like this, as he suddenly backed into him and knocked him down.

Towards the end of August, a welcome reinforcement arrived in the shape of another squadron of aeroplanes under the command of Wing-Commander Gerrard. They had Morane Monoplanes and B.E.2 C aeroplanes. They were allotted an aerodrome on the opposite side of the harbour.

At first, we thought them a bit of a nuisance, as they were all young pilots except for Smyth-Piggot and two others, and many was the time we had requests from Helles to do their work over again; but after they got used to the job they did very well indeed, though of course my men still regarded them as amateurs.

The Moranes were brutes to fly, and two good fellows were killed on them. Gerrard soon stopped them flying, and replaced them with some Voisins I gave him.

Colonel Sykes came out from England, and was installed as Chief of the Air Force. My squadron was called No. 3 Wing and Gerrard's No. 2 Wing, grand-sounding titles which no doubt looked fine on paper, but we didn't get expanded either by pilots or aeroplanes; in fact, in October, after two months of the wing business, I find that between us we had only twenty-five pilots and forty-four aeroplanes of all sorts; about eight of these were useless for war.

In addition to the aeroplanes an s.s. airship arrived and did some really good anti-submarine patrols.

Colonel Sykes and his staff didn't worry me at all, but left me to go on in my own routine as usual, the only thing being that we had to send in reports to him as well as to the usual people; in fact, as far as my wing was concerned, they might not have been there at all.

His staff started to try to build up an aeroplane repair section; but no one ever saw any result, although they had quite a large party who were reported to be carrying out mystic rites over a Voisin they had in a hangar.

For some time, I had been very keen on trying to get the commander-in-chief to let us spot for a ship and register her fire upon Ak Bashi Liman with the hopes of hitting some of the Turkish transport ships. At last, he agreed, and with Monitor No. 15 we got two splendid shoots, sinking two ships. As several ranges of hills intervened, and the range was about 18,000 yards, it caught the Turks completely by surprise. The result was that no big ship ever afterwards came into Ak Bashi again by day.

CHAPTER 5

Kemal Pasha's Escape

New pilots and new aeroplanes now arrived, and I am afraid I rather neglected old No. 50 for a Nieuport Scout. It was a really fine type of single-seater fitted with a most reliable engine, 80-h.p. Le Rhone. It was capable of about 93 miles an hour, fast for its day, and climbed like a witch.

Davies and I each had one, and many was the low reconnaissance and bomb attack I did with mine. I had two fights with Germans in it; but didn't down them, as I could only shoot upwards at an angle of 45 degrees with my gun, and although I hit one fellow a good many times, he went down to ground level and I couldn't get at him.

Newton-Clare had a forced landing on the Salt Lake at Suvla, and had a sticky time getting to dry land with the Turks shelling him. The aeroplane was smashed up; but we got the engine back at night.

St. Aubyn and I had a most exciting time on September 8th, as we spotted for H.M.S. *Abercrombie* on Chanak, and then sighted a gunboat and a destroyer, on to both of whom we put the *Abercrombie*; we failed to hit either, but some of the big shells went very close until they escaped to the northwards.

Butler rejoined on September 8th, to our great delight; his arrival was worth five aeroplanes.

I now had of the old gang Davies, Thomson, Marix, Newton-Clare Junior, and Butler, and Morrison and Young of the new, only eight of us all told from the end of August until the middle of October, when Smylie, who became a star-turn performer, and Nicholson arrived.

My three midshipmen were still going great guns as observers, each of them worth their weight in gold.

Old Man Isaac, with the aid of four Greeks he had scrounged from the Military, was actively engaged in building a stone mess-house; Garwood, my steward, was advising on the matter. Brownridge and

Warner were rather critical; but the Old Man serenely went on. I may say in 1919 I visited the old spot, and found the house still standing, worthy memorial to the architect. The place was a godsend when the winter blizzards arrived.

September 18th was rather a red-letter day, as General Birdwood came over to the aerodrome and said he would like a trip in the air. I took him up in a Maurice Farman, intending to do a local flight; but he told me to go over the Turks at Anzac. Off we went, and he made me go as far as Maidos, and fairly low down, so that he could see well. We got a proper reception from "Archie," and I felt very anxious carrying such a distinguished passenger. He was the only big noise that went up. I think it rather a pity that some more didn't.

I had quite a busy day that day, as not only did I take him up, but I went up in the Nieuport and bombed German G.H.Q. with three 20-lb. bombs, and then took No. 50 and bombed ships in Berghaz Liman with a 100-lb. bomb.

That night to complete the programme I took up another Maurice with Edwards as passenger, and we bombed Turkish transport ships with four 20-lb. bombs in Berghaz Liman, which is on the Asiatic side opposite Ak Bashi Liman: a total of four different aeroplanes and 5½ hours' flying. On the next night, after having a narrow squeak of falling into the sea with my passenger, Bernard Isaac, through engine trouble, I set off in No. 50 again and stirred up the night-workers at Kilia Liman.

The very next night I went up as passenger to Davies in a Henri to show him the spot to bomb, and we had touch-and-go getting back with a misfiring engine. We had the usual round of work now for some time, except for a very fine reconnaissance beyond Bulair, carried out by Davies and Edwards.

I had an amusing experience with a motorcar, which is interesting when the possibilities are realised. I was up one day in my Nieuport carrying three 20-lb. bombs looking for transport columns, when I saw a motorcar going along a road near Selvili. As we rarely saw motorcars, I naturally expected this was some important general, so I came down fairly low and let go two bombs. They both missed; but not by much. The motorcar stopped, and the three occupants got out and lay down in the ditch. I thought, "If I stay here, they will remain in the ditch and I cannot get them; if I clear out, they will think either I have no more bombs or have given up."

I therefore went off about 3 miles and patrolled up and down,

THE AUTHOR, A MAJOR IN THE R.E., EDWARDS, AND W. L. SAMSON

EDWARDS, TOPP, DAVIES, W. L. SAMSON, AND THOMSON, DARDANELLES, 1915.

keeping a sharp eye on them with my binoculars, which I always carried slung round my neck. Sure enough, after twenty minutes or so they got tired of the ditch, and set off once more. I dived down with engine full out and let go my last bomb, praying for results; but unfortunately, it hit the road close in front of the car. Now for the sequel; in 1919 I met a Turkish officer, and in talking about the war, I asked which was his worst experience.

He said:

> At the Dardanelles, when I was on the Staff of Kemal Pasha; we were in a motorcar and an aeroplane bombed us; we got out and lay in a ditch. After a time, we decided the aeroplane had given up, so we got on board once more and set off; but we had made a mistake, as suddenly the aeroplane reappeared and dropped another bomb which nearly hit us; as it was, the screen was broken by a fragment.

We compared diaries, and it was my car adventure. I leave it to the imagination if I had killed Kemal; the history of the Near East would have been entirely different. Probably Asia Minor would be still in the hands of the Greeks.

We had a certain amount of shooting at Kephalo, at which Captain Edwards was the most successful. At first the navy got in the habit of poaching on our preserves; but after I had posted a sentry at the landing-place to say that no guns were allowed on our side owing to the dangers of hitting aeroplanes, a bluff which worked like magic, we had the whole area to ourselves. I have the game-book still, and we bagged snipe, duck, red-leg partridge, woodcock, hares, teal, plover, and some doubtful birds marked as various; we got 105 head altogether. I issued strict orders that all shooting was for the pot, and sitting shots were allowed. We badly needed some change in diet, as practically our only food were bare rations, and we had bully beef for breakfast, dinner, and supper.

After some time, we improved a bit, owing to Isaac getting very friendly with the officer in charge of the base canteen, whom we unanimously elected honorary member of the mess; but all along we fared very badly, and many were the times I used to lie in bed imagining the dinner I would order when, if ever, I got back to England.

One of the chief events in October was a big bomb attack we made on Chanak. I went with Smylie, Thomson, Newton-Clare, Morrison, and Butler, and we bombed the batteries there with a total of three

100-lb. and nineteen 20-lb. bombs in order to attract attention away from one of our submarines, which was passing through the Narrows.

We were constantly worrying the transport on the roads, and the shipping, which was landing stores at. Ak Bashi Liman and Kilia Liman. Several times we could see adequate results of our bombs.

Davies in his Nieuport had an unpleasant experience, as through engine failure he had to come down into the sea about 5 miles from Imbros. Fortunately, a trawler was close at hand, and after picking him up tried to tow the half-submerged aeroplane to the shore; after about ten minutes the aeroplane broke up and sank. The trawler skipper then turned round to Davies and said, "Bain't nobody else in the machine, Mister, be there?" Davies thought this was a bit late in the day to ask.

I had a forced landing on Rabbit Island one day, due to staying up too long and running out of petrol. I just got to the land, and had no time to pick out the best spot. However, I landed safely; but spent a most boring day before somebody sighted me, and arranged for petrol to be brought to me.

We lost several aeroplanes in the sea, of course; through engine trouble and other causes; but luckily without loss of life.

We paid several visits to Césari and his squadron, and they returned the compliment, and we frequently had combined raids on Galata aerodrome or some other popular target.

One day Césari came over to Imbros and asked me to lunch. As they lived like fighting-cocks I of course accepted, and went over as his passenger. He had one of the Maurices, and scared me stiff, as he smoked the whole time, and dropped the old stubs of his cigarettes still Smouldering in the nacelle.

At the end of October, I got two new observers, Lieutenants Boles and Annesley; also Busk, Heriot, and Barnato arrived from England to swell the number of my pilots. They were all real good boys, keen as mustard, and soon picked up the routine.

Busk was unfortunately shot down by a German aeroplane in January 1916. He would certainly have made a great reputation and risen to high rank. Barnato was also a splendid youngster, and although not the finished pilot that Busk became, he amply made up for that in daring, courage, and determination.

Marix was recalled to England in October. His departure was a great loss to the squadron. Not only was he one of the finest pilots that there ever was; but he combined this skill with the most conspicuous gallantry and grim determination.

If I told him off for a job, I knew the work would be done like clockwork. He never failed me once. I always considered Davies and Marix as the two most skilful pilots Eastchurch ever turned out. Reggie's departure made me feel that the old squadron was beginning to break up. The terrible flying accident he had in Paris cut short his flying career; and at the present time he is only a squadron leader. I consider that he has been most shabbily treated.

Doc. Williams and I used to go for a walk most evenings, and, cheery optimist that he always was, we both felt most depressed the day Reggie went. I have hardly mentioned Williams; but he used to look after our well-being in his own quiet way without our knowing we were being mothered. We all owe Williams and Patterson, who looked after the sanitation and the men, a great debt of gratitude.

I suffered a severe personal loss by Garwood being killed by a bomb which a German dropped on our camp; he was a simple soul who had looked after me for many years in peace, and who absolutely refused to leave me when I went to war. I buried him at Kephalo, reading the service myself, as I had done for Collet. Brownridge's cross still stood in 1919 when I visited Kephalo.

Chapter 6

The Maritza Bridge

I must pass on, however, to more cheerful things. I had been suggesting for some time to the commander-in-chief that we should have a try at damaging the main railway line to Constantinople. The best target seemed to be the bridge across the Maritza River near Adrianople. I thought we could do it, although it meant a journey of 200 miles, carrying a heavy load. It seems nowadays a ridiculously short journey; but in those days it was quite a trip.

The commander-in-chief approved of the plan, so I immediately got under way with the previously thought-out arrangements. I selected, of course, one of the big Maurice Farmans. An extra tank was placed in, so that we had six hours' fuel, which was essential, in case we had head-winds. On November 8th I set off, taking Captain Edwards as observer and two 100-lb. bombs with which to attack the bridge.

We decided beforehand that we would drop both bombs simultaneously, as thereby we hoped for decisive results. We had a fairly good flight to the objective, flying at 4,600 feet with some interference from clouds at 2,500 feet. The Farman took the heavy load like a bird, and I found I could throttle down to 100 revolutions below full power.

The country was quite a change from the Peninsula, and had rather the appearance of Salisbury Plain. We sighted several large camps, and I determined that No. 3 would soon pay a visit to them and give them a taste of what they could expect when they got to the Peninsula. Edwards accurately noted their positions. When I got about 10 miles from the bridge, I started losing altitude, intending to arrive over the target at about 700 feet, which I thought was a safe height, not being absolutely certain at what height we would be affected by our own bombs when they detonated. I knew about 200-300 feet was safe for a single one, so I doubled it and added 100 feet for luck.

I flew directly along the bridge from east to west, the Turks meanwhile blazing away with everything they had. Arriving near the centre of the bridge, I signalled "Stand-by." to Edwards, and then signalled "Let go." We each pulled a toggle, and to our delight heard and felt the detonations of our bombs practically simultaneously.

I banked round steeply and peered over the side to see the result. I could see they had exploded immediately alongside one of the piers. I hoped that this would weaken the bridge. As a matter of fact, I have heard since that our attack put the bridge out of action for four days. After a good look round we turned for home, gradually climbing until we were about 5,000 feet. When still about fifteen miles inland the engine stopped dead, and then went on at reduced revolutions, and with a terrible amount of vibration. I turned round to Edwards and said that we might be for a Turkish prison with its vermin, but I thought I could make the coast, and take the ditch alongside a destroyer which was patrolling about three miles out to sea.

I suspected what the trouble was. The Renault engine was a 12-cylinder V-type, with a separate magneto to each lot of six cylinders. One of the magnetos had given up the ghost; therefore, we were only running on one side of the engine. I expected every moment that either the engine would tear itself out of the machine or that the old Maurice would begin to disintegrate; but she hung together. We actually maintained our height, and sighting the destroyer I determined to keep on and hope we would get home before we broke up.

We arrived all right over Imbros, and I think Edwards and I were really glad when I could throttle down to land.

My already great admiration for the Maurice and the Renault was now amply rewarded. May their bones rest in peace, a real good aeroplane and a fine engine.

On November 10th I sent off Davies with Walser as his observer in the same aeroplane as I had taken to have another go at the bridge.

They carried two 20-lb. bombs as well as two 112-lb. and a machine-gun, in case they were interfered with by hostile aeroplanes. As the pair of them were lighter than Edwards and I, they could take up the extra weight. They had rather adverse weather conditions, and as the hours sped by, and they didn't return, I began to think they were down. In fact, I commenced to write a letter to send to their relations, saying how their loss would affect us and how I sympathised with them.

But they turned up all right. They had encountered heavy rainstorms and low cloud; but had got to the objective and bombed from

1,700 feet; they hadn't hit the bridge, but had hit the railway line between some goods trains at Uzun Kepri station and caused considerable damage. They encountered heavier fire than we had done, and had four holes in the planes close to the nacelle.

At the same time as I sent off Davies, I dispatched Thomson with Jopp as his observer to see what they could do to the large camp I had located at Kara Bunar; right thoroughly they stirred things up with two 112-lb. and four 20-lb. bombs. As they approached, the Turks began to stream out of the tents; but some were too late. One 112-lb. fell amongst the tents and demolished three of them, the second one fell amongst a large body of men running to seek shelter in a gulley. Jopp observed that the explosion killed a great many.

I have always been a believer in the idea that once you start a job you should keep on at it, until you succeed or circumstances arise which make it desirable to shift to something else. Therefore, on November 13th I dispatched Busk with Bill Samson as his passenger to have another go at the Maritza bridge.

Bill had only just come out again to us. They took the same Maurice, and had a very rough trip, as the weather was foul. They got within 10 and 20 yards respectively with their two big bombs. The Turks and Bulgars had by this time realised that we were in earnest in our attempts to damage the bridge, and demonstrated this by having collected a large number of anti-aircraft and machine-guns in the neighbourhood. Busk and my brother experienced a very hot reception, and were hit several times. Bill's written report was most thorough; in private life he was a barrister, and amongst other things he mentioned seeing a dog in one of the coastal villages; but added that he regretted he couldn't be certain of its breed.

I sent off Heriot, with St. Aubyn in the passenger's seat, at the same time as the bridge party, with orders to bomb the Kara Bunar Camp. Arriving at the camp, they found it evacuated, which showed that No. 3 Squadron had made it too hot for them. They then scouted round to find where the Turks had gone to, and located a large camp at Saraili. They caused considerable loss of life to a body of troops they found in a field close to the camp, and destroyed several tents in addition.

The third aeroplane, piloted by Nicholson, with Bernard Isaac as observer, I dispatched to Keshan Camp, which they bombed with two 112-lb. and two 20-lb. bombs.

After the three big aeroplanes had left, Davies and I in our little Nieuports set off to see what we could do against the Bulgars, who had just come into the war. We made for Ferejik junction station. Davies got there about two minutes before I did and I saw his bombs explode, one hitting the railway line just outside the station. I made three very bad shots myself, missing both station and line; but three cavalrymen happened to be in the wrong place, unfortunately for them. I saw quite a lot of soldiers running in all directions, and we got a good deal of rifle and machine-gun fire; but 93-mile-an-hour Nieuports are far harder to hit than 65-mile-an-hour Maurice Farmans, although we were pretty low down.

On the way back I overtook Davies, and thus proved, what I had always maintained, that mine was the faster aeroplane, although he stoutly denied it. I had an unpleasant flight back, as being without a compass I had to keep below the thick layer of clouds, and fly at about 500 feet for the whole 35 miles or so of sea in heavy rain.

I was immensely pleased with the day's work, and especially delighted to find that my three young pilots, Busk, Heriot, and Nicholson, were able to follow in the footsteps of their experienced ancestors. The results were really excellent.

We suffered a serious setback now, which handicapped me for some time, as a fire broke out in our jerry-built workshop, and completely burnt it out, together with the adjoining storerooms. I lost a number of engines, valuable spare parts, and stores which were irreplaceable for some time.

A Court of Inquiry was held, and I found it difficult to convey to the court that a battleship was an entirely different thing from a collection of buildings roughly constructed out of aeroplane packing-cases. Some months afterwards I received a letter stating that I had incurred Their Lordships' displeasure, because somebody had lit a match to look for a ball out of a ball-race, and had ignited a basin of petrol in which the aforesaid ball-race was soaking. How I was to ensure that nobody did such a thing I was unable to imagine.

The censure was, I felt, unfair; but on complaining to Sir John de Robeck he said, "Don't worry, Samson; in my time I have incurred Their Lordships' displeasure three times, and their severe displeasure once, and I have survived it to become a vice-admiral." Anyhow, this was my award for the Dardanelles, and as I look back nowadays it is as good a memento as a decoration or promotion.

Keeping up the good work, on November 15th Thomson, carrying Annesley, took the Maurice on her fourth trip to the Maritza bridge. They were received with a very heavy fire from ten anti-aircraft guns.

They made a very gallant effort under the difficult wind conditions—it was blowing across the bridge. Thomson made three runs before he could get a good line; he then let go his bombs, but didn't hit the bridge; they struck the line just beyond it, however.

The number of guns collected to defend the bridge clearly demonstrated that we were causing damage; also, the Turks were seriously perturbed at our constant attacks. Even if we were doing no actual material harm, we were making them withdraw a large number of guns and personnel from other spheres of action. I now decided to cease the bridge attacks, as the Maurice required overhaul, and let the Turks' guns remain there practically out of action, whilst we devoted ourselves with our limited resources to other fields.

A promising field for action which, through being closer, permitted of larger numbers being employed, was Ferejik junction.

From November 13th until December 1st, we made twelve attacks on Ferejik, with fairly satisfactory results. As I have related, Davies and I did the first two. For the next attempt I set off on my Nieuport with Barnato on a Maurice and Smylie flying a Henri on November 16th.

Two days later I sent off Nicholson on one of the big Henris to see what damage we had done at Ferejik. He had two 112-lb. and two 20-lb. bombs which he was to drop after he had made a careful examination of the results of our attack. He reported that one of the station buildings had suffered severely, the roof having totally vanished.

Next day, November 19th, I set off with four other aeroplanes to attack Ferejik again. This time I detailed each pilot for a distinct objective.

The party consisted of Davies and myself on Nieuports, Smylie and Barnato on Henri Farmans, and Heriot, carrying Captain Edwards, on a Maurice. The attack was most successful; but we lost one aeroplane.

I was the first to arrive at Ferejik, passing Davies *en route*. After letting go my three little bombs I watched the others attack, and saw some really good marksmanship. I then made for home. I got back to Imbros, and awaited the others: Heriot with Edwards arrived, and reported on the damage; they hadn't seen Smylie. Then in came Barnato, who said that he had seen the wreckage of Smylie's aeroplane down close to Ferejik. There were still no signs of Davies, and I was very worried, as he should have been in before the other two, and in any case within ten minutes of my arrival.

I felt extremely sorry over the loss of Smylie; because although he had only been a short time in the squadron, he had done real good work. Davies's loss couldn't bear thinking about. I sat in my so-called office feeling more depressed than I have felt for years, and realising that the squadron without Davies could never be the same again. Here I was now, Collet killed, Peirse, Butler, Marix, Osmond, Bill Wilson, and the older Newton-Clare gone, and only Thomson left of the old crowd.

Suddenly, I heard the familiar sound of the Le Rhone. I didn't go out; but started to make out my report. The next thing that happened was Thomson came in and said Davies had come back with Smylie in his aeroplane.

I was astounded. First of all, how could he have stowed Smylie on board? Secondly, how had he picked up Smylie?

Then Davies came in absolutely unperturbed. What had happened was as follows: Smylie's engine got hit by the enemy's fire and stopped. Smylie was enabled to make a safe landing beyond a bit of marsh about a mile from the station. Davies saw Smylie land, and determined to try to save him, so after flying round at low altitude to look at the ground he landed and picked Smylie up.

The latter being a 6-foot fellow coiled himself up in some mysterious way at Davies's feet, and Davies took the air once more under a very hot fire at close range from a lot of Bulgars, who arrived on the scene.

There are two things that stick out: firstly, Davies's extreme gallantry combined with wonderful pilotage in being able to alight on a dirty little patch of very rough ground with a very fast landing aeroplane. The Nieuports landed at about 60 miles an hour. He ran deadly risk of crashing; in addition, he was fired at the whole time.

Smylie was just as gallant. Immediately he had landed he set fire to his aeroplane; then seeing Davies was going to attempt to land he went close up to his aeroplane and detonated a bomb which was still on it by firing at the fuse with his pistol. He feared that if he didn't explode the bomb, it might go off in the fire and damage Davies's aeroplane. He then took off his flying coat and left a scribbled message in its pocket to say. "Please return my coat, which I have had to leave, to No. 3 Wing."

Davies, for his fine feat, was awarded the Victoria Cross. Smylie richly deserved the D.S.C. which he received.

THE REMAINDER OF THE ORIGINAL EASTCHURCH PARTY, IMBROS, 1915, OUTSIDE OFFICERS' MESS

Chapter 7

The Evacuation

We had a lot of bad weather, and our work with the bombarding ships and reconnaissance was frequently interfered with by the heavy banks of clouds. Vernon and Gardner arrived at the end of November, and Butler was invalided home.

I had a bit of good luck, or good bomb-dropping, whatever one likes to consider it, on December 2nd, as I dropped three 20-lb. bombs from my Nieuport at a 300-foot steamer in Kilia Liman; two of the bombs hit and exploded on her upper deck. Later in the day I saw her being towed up the Straits with a heavy list to port: I wished that they had been 100-lb. bombs.

I forgot to mention our big petrol bomb. We dropped this in August at guns close to Gurkha Bluff, the idea being to burn the gorse so that the guns would be exposed.

For a long time, we had been constructing a real father of a bomb, using an old 26-gallon petrol tank. We made a streamline tail to it, and fitted on a head which contained a fuse constructed out of a Verey light pistol with a cartridge in the barrel. As an extra detonator a 20-lb. bomb was incorporated, the idea being that the explosion of this would disperse the burning petrol and paraffin with which we filled the main body. This 20-lb. bomb was, we discovered, a mistake, as it naturally blew the burning liquid all over the place. The completed bomb looked a most awe-inspiring missile.

I may say that in addition to everything some bright brain made and attached a most efficient whistle to the tail of the bomb, the idea being that the sound of its descent would be more terrifying to the Turks.

Trials made with a dummy bomb fitted with the whistle certainly gave good results, as the bomb emitted the most piercing shriek as it fell. When all was ready the bomb was fitted to a Henri, and we all took the air to watch the hoped-for conflagration. Needless to say, we all took bombs. I kept close to the Nieuport and saw the bomb fall. It went off all right when it hit; but only a tiny little fire resulted, the 20-lb. bomb having no doubt blown the liquid all over the scene before any of it except a small residue had ignited.

It was rather disappointing; but Helles reported that the bomb made a most satisfactory noise as it hurtled through space. On December 1st Vernon, a new pilot, carrying Jopp, was sent to Ferejik junction just to let them see we were still alive; he hit the line with one of his bombs. I had a chase after a hostile seaplane which came over Imbros; but he had a bit too long a start and got down to the water off Chanak just as I got within range.

Busk, with Jopp in the back seat, had a good scrap with a German aeroplane the same day. They were spotting for one of the monitors doing a bombardment when they sighted the German. They got close to him and opened fire before the Germans saw them. Jopp said that the German observer looked round and saw them right on his tail. He flung his arms round the pilot's head, and shoved the stick forward, and the German dived nearly vertically. Busk followed down, but the German could dive quicker than the Henri.

They got the German right down to 20 feet or so of the ground, and chivvied him at that height, firing all the time, until they got to Galata aerodrome. They failed to score a bull's-eye, unfortunately; and they had a rotten time from "Archie" and machine-guns while flying back to Suvla at a very low altitude. Meanwhile, the monitor was rather angry at the shoot being spoilt, and not knowing what had happened to its aeroplane.

One day one of my pilots let go a 100-lb. bomb at some Turks he saw in a gulley close to Anzac. He made a rotten bad shot, and to his horror saw the bomb burst in the Turks' foremost trench at a point where the front lines were only about 20 yards apart. He came back and reported to me that he thought he must have killed some of our own people.

At the instant he reported, I received a message from Anzac to say:

"One of your aeroplanes bombed Turks' trench; bits of Turks seen in the air, remainder of occupants got on to parapet, where we killed a lot with machine-guns; please repeat bombing."

I didn't reply that it was a fluke, and that it was only by the mercy of the Lord that the bomb hadn't hit the Anzacs.

No. 3 lived on this reputation for accuracy for a long time.

STARTING FROM IMBROS ON AN H. FARMAN WITH THE FIRST 500-LB. BOMB EVER DROPPED.

On December 4th the last batch of new pilots arrived, Black, Brinsmead, and Wakeley.

On December 16th I had my bomb accident and lost my Nieuport. On the 18th I took up a 500-lb. bomb on a Henri; this was by far the biggest bomb that up to date had been dropped by an aeroplane in the war. The Henri took it up like a bird, much to my delight.

I searched around for over half an hour between Anzac and Kilia Liman looking for a suitable target at which to drop it; but there seemed to be a lack that day of objectives worthwhile. Finally, I Selected a long building from which smoke was appearing, deciding it must be full of Turks. I let go the bomb and turned round to see the result; but to my chagrin a cloud blotted out the ground. I was terribly disappointed, as I wanted to see the explosion of the first really big bomb. It was only in 1919 that I saw the results. I had scored a direct hit; the building, which was about 60 feet long, was absolutely wrecked, and amongst its ruins I saw no less than three bayonets sticking up between the bricks.

Although I say this myself, it was a really good shot, and only twice before had I ever scored such an absolute bull's-eye.

Nowadays, of course, with the elaborate sights bombing is a fine art; but it must be remembered that in those days we relied solely upon our eye. Practice alone could produce adequate results. I didn't lack practice, as I dropped 4 tons 14 cwt. of bombs at the Dardanelles.

We now had our work cut out to patrol the Suvla and Anzac zones in order to prevent hostile aeroplanes flying over and detecting any signs of approaching evacuation. No. 2 Wing were as formerly working with Helles.

I can safely say that we kept up a continuous patrol during daylight, and no enemy ever came close.

Personally, although I was in full knowledge of all our movements, I could detect practically nothing which would betray us to the enemy. Everything at Suvla and Anzac looked normal.

The nervous strain of the evacuation must have been terrible for General Birdwood and the corps commanders; it was bad enough for me, as an onlooker. It seemed absolutely impossible that we could withdraw without a hard fight; several I know anticipated the worst.

Everything went like clockwork, and the most wonderful example of discipline and splendid organisation was demonstrated to the world.

I remember a certain brigadier, who was, I believe, the last to embark at Suvla, telling me next day that the only casualty he knew of was one keen soul who had mopped up a good many tots of rum, and then fell over Something.

Next morning, I went up early to see if the Turks had discovered our departure. Evidently, they hadn't, because they were shelling the beaches. Later on, I went up again and saw them on the move. I had the keen pleasure of seeing two of our booby traps go up.

With the evacuation of Suvla and Anzac No. 3's time at the Dardanelles was completed, as No. 2 was deemed sufficient to carry on for Helles and the fleet. I was ordered to hurry home with Davies and Thomson, the remainder to follow as soon as the aeroplanes and stores had been handed over.

Little did I think when I left Imbros that No. 3 and I were parted for good. Even if they did good work in France, they did better at the Dardanelles.

When it is seen that we flew for 2,600 hours from March 28th until December 29th with a maximum of eleven pilots and an average of seven, sometimes with only four aeroplanes in action, I think it will be agreed that they one and all quitted themselves like men.

Again, I would like to record that it was because we had such a stalwart band of men on the ground, working under the worst possible conditions practically in the open the whole time, that we were enabled to do our bit to help the Royal Navy and the Army in that glorious display of gallantry called the Dardanelles Campaign.

Aeroplane pilots belonging to No. 3 were not overburdened with decorations for the Campaign, nor were the five observers, Edwards, Hogg, Jopp, Knatchbull-Hugessen, and Walser, who were unrewarded. I don't know how many hours they each did; but if I cared to count them up, it would come to a fine total. They got all the kicks and none of the plums. The three midshipmen were given the D.S.C.

I said farewell to Imbros, I can sincerely say, with regret, although I had had enough. I felt by no means well, and hadn't been right for some time; I was immediately prostrated with jaundice, and had a beastly journey home, lying in my cabin praying for a submarine to end my distressing condition. Davies and Thomson between them got me home—they would have got anything anywhere.

I came suddenly to life in the Pullman car immediately we left Folkestone, and shouted for eggs and bacon.

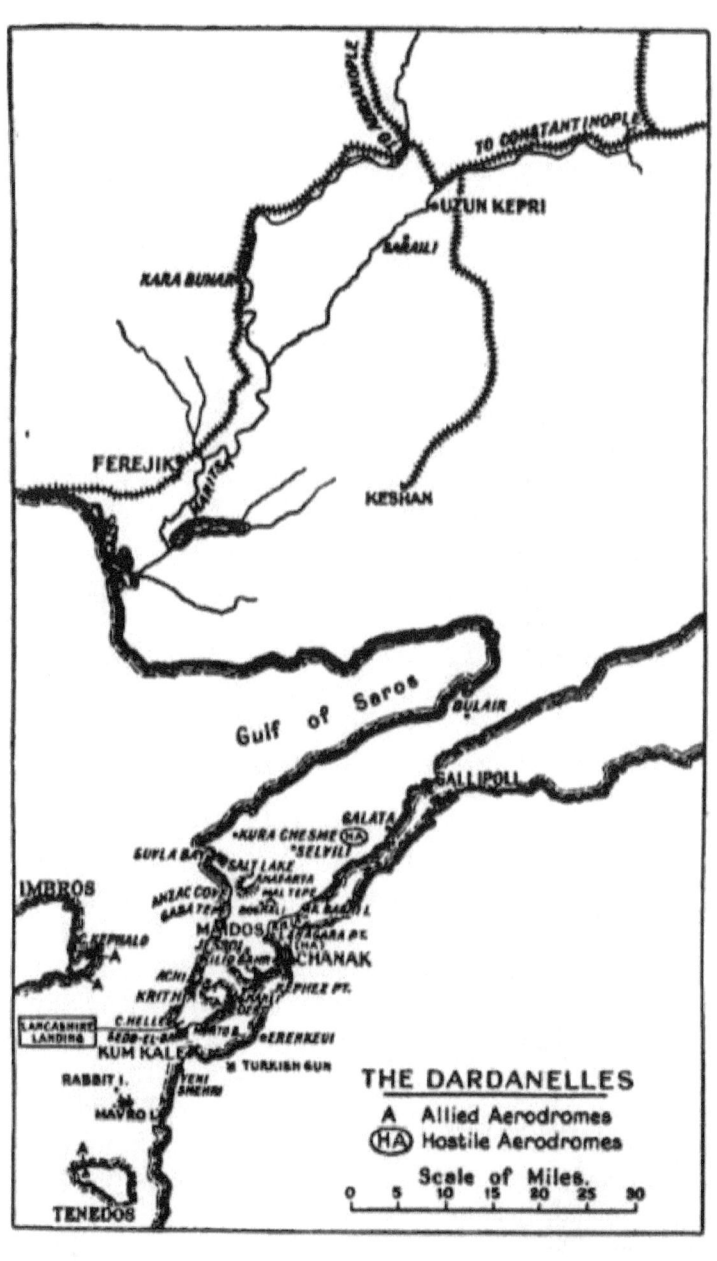

Part 4: The "Ben-My-Chree" (May 1916—January 1917)

Chapter 1

Introducing the Ben-My-Chree

It was wonderful getting back home again and I seeing my father and mother. The latter immediately put me to bed, and sent for the family doctor, although I felt absolutely cured.

I can remember that night so well, with my mother sitting by my bedside listening to my experiences until an early hour in the morning. I felt just like I used to feel the first night of the holidays from School. A rare understander was mother.

Next morning, I went to the Admiralty to report, and found a new regime. Commodore Sueter was no longer in command of the R.N.A.S.; but shelved into an administrative post. At once I felt a different atmosphere. The R.N.A.S. was in the hands of those that knew it not, and the prevalent idea seemed to be that the active pilots were a wild sort of people who should be kept well under.

I was immediately examined by the doctors and dispatched to Haslar Hospital, being transported there by my brother Philip in his car. *En route* at Hindhead, where we stopped for luncheon, I met Sir Max Aitken, Lord Beaverbrook that now is, and had a long talk with him.

I only stayed two days at Haslar, as Sir Humphrey Rolleston personally came to examine me, and, being free from red tape, got me out of the place and sent me home to recoup. If it hadn't been for him, I would have been kept there for months. I now had a long period of sick leave, as each time I went up for examination I was turned down as still unfit for service.

At first, after the strenuous labours and undoubted hardships I had undergone in the Dardanelles I naturally enjoyed life, feeling perfectly well; but I gradually became rather worried, for the old squadron was being consistently split up as they returned home.

As I had understood that the squadron was to be sent to France to carry out bomb-raids into Germany I was naturally anxious to make a start.

At last, I was told to commence work: although still on sick leave I started in with Davies and Frank Maclean, whose generosity in 1911 had started the navy flying, working out the plans.

It all came to nothing, however. Certain undercurrents were under way, and at the end of April I was informed that the project was abandoned, and I was to go to Egypt to take over command of the Seaplane Carrier, H.M.S. *Ben-my-Chree*.

I don't propose to talk about my treatment; but I felt very sad at being sent to what was undoubtedly a minor command. Commodore Sueter, that stout friend of all of us early Naval aviators, strongly advised me to sink my feelings, and quietly depart, as he felt sure that times would change. I hated leaving my own Eastchurch people; but still "orders is orders," as the undertaker said when the corpse came to life, and he went on with nailing up the coffin.

I set sail early in May, saying goodbye to my mother, for what I didn't realise was to be the last time. She meant a lot to her four sons.

She was dead a week before I reached England on my return in 1917. They say she made a gallant fight to live long enough to see me, knowing I had been ordered home.

Brother Bill was sent out to East Africa, where he had some exciting times.

Brother Felix, who had nearly died from dysentery in Egypt, was on board H.M.S. *Riviera*, a seaplane carrier in the Channel.

My youngest brother Philip was in the Yeomanry, stationed in Scotland; but shortly he joined the infantry in France, where he was killed leading a daylight raid in October 1918.

Arriving at Port Said, I found my command consisted of H.M.S. *Ben-my-Chree*, of which I was captain, as well as commander of a little squadron comprising H.M.S. *Anne* and H.M.S. *Raven II*, large cargo steamers, both of them German prizes. In addition, there was a base on an island in Port Said harbour.

The whole had been under the command of Acting-Commander C. L'Estrange-Malone, now a Member of Parliament. He was to stay out as my second-in-command—rather bad luck for him. He was one of my old Eastchurch officers, and he most loyally served under me.

H.M.S. *Ben-my-Chree* had been an Isle of Man passenger steamer. She was a very fine ship that had been converted into a seaplane carrier by the addition of a hangar that could house four big and two small seaplanes.

She was a very fine sea-boat, and could steam at 26 knots. She handled like a destroyer once you got a bit of way on her; but the big hangar, acting like a spanker, made her tricky in a strong wind at slow speed. Once you got to know her you could do what you liked with her. I soon got to love the old *Ben*, and I wouldn't have changed her for anything.

Her armament consisted of four 12-pounder 18-cwt. guns, with two 3-pounders, the latter intended for antiaircraft work. Of course, these were entirely useless. I soon got the Navy to let me have another 12-pounder and a pom-pom, which I mounted for this work. Some months afterwards, as previously recorded, I discovered my old travelling carriage 3-pounder on board H.M.S. *Hannibal*, and asking the captain for it I proudly added this to my arsenal. It went into action several times.

My first lieutenant and navigator was Lieutenant-Commander Barber, R.N.R., a very fine seaman.

The other deck officers were all R.N.R., except for the Gunner, Mr. Greene. He had been torpedoed twice, and sent out to the *Ben-my-Chree* for a rest. He soon found it was hotter work than the North Sea, as we were in action several times, and always had submarines quite handy.

There were a number of R.N.A.S. pilots and about forty R.N.A.S. ratings permanently on board the *Ben-my-Chree*; also, a certain number of seaplanes were always kept on board.

Squadron-Leader England was my chief R.N.A.S. officer. I soon found he was a most sterling fellow, full of ideas, and a very fine handler of a seaplane. Dacre, Wright, Maskell, Bankes-Price, Clemson, and Nightingale were other pilots, all good men. The ship's company were all "hostilities only" men, except for one or two R.N. I never want for a better crowd. One or two of the stokers needed a little stern discipline; but they could make the ship steam like Hades.

Last, but not least, was Engineer-Lieutenant-Commander Robinson, R.N.R. He had been chief of the ship ever since her keel was laid down. He knew every rivet in her. He went ashore three times only in my period of command: once at Port Said, because I made him go ashore for a walk; once at Carmel, when I ran the ship ashore; and the last time at Castelorizo, when the old *Ben* was sunk.

At first, I found Robinson had a little mannerism of easing down or sometimes going faster without orders; but after I had had a heart-to-heart talk and explained that when I put the indicator to a certain number of revolutions, I expected him to go that number and neither faster nor slower, we understood each other, and I always knew that I had a man below who could be relied upon until the bottom fell out.

The *Anne* and *Raven* were manned by R.N.R. Each had a 12-pounder gun as armament, and could carry four seaplanes. Generally, in harbour seaplanes were not kept on board these ships, but were housed at the base. The *Anne*, whose captain was Lieutenant Kerr, had as intelligence officer Captain Weldon. He had been in the Egyptian Survey Department. After the war he became surveyor-general; there was little that he didn't know of the topography of Sinai and Palestine. Great man, Weldon; he is now a farmer in Ireland.

The captain of the *Raven* was Lieutenant Jenkins, R.N.R., a very fine unemotional seaman, who in his quiet way would go anywhere or do anything.

I was extremely fortunate to have such officers. The base was rather a comic mixture of R.N.A.S. and Army, most of the observers being the latter. The buildings were rather ramshackle, but quite serviceable.

The chief observer was Lieutenant Wedgwood Benn, M.P., now (in 1930) Secretary of State for India. I am pleased to say that it was by my pulling of the right strings that I got him the local rank of captain, his first advancement.

I soon realised that in Benn I had found gold. He had a very keen brain, and a distinct flair for the organisation of our intelligence into a quick and accurate system, whereby you could at a glance see the situation in Palestine, Syria, and the Red Sea, which of course altered from day to day. In addition, he shortly devised a service of intelligence boxes which could be got up to date within half an hour, and when any ship went to sea, the box arrived on board complete, not only with the latest state of affairs, but replete with all the charts, documents, etc., required.

He soon became a very fine observer, although he frequently told me he never knew what I wanted, as I used to shout inarticulate remarks to him whilst in the air. There was one thing I always insisted upon, and that was that as soon as we secured ship on our return from a cruise, our full report should be ready, complete with all photographs, etc., for my signature. He never failed me once in this, although it meant sometimes working all night after strenuous flying in the day.

Added to his ability he was a cheery companion, and many was the amusing time we spent on shore. One thing he shared in common with me, was a love of riding. I purchased a pony soon after I took over command, and Benn prevailed upon the military to allot him a charger. We kept these ponies ashore at Port Said in a home-built stable, under the charge of a Yeoman and a Soudanese Syce.

On the arrival of Percy Woodland, he was placed in control of the cavalry. He quickly added a horse belonging to the R.A.M.C. Sanitary Expert, which the latter found too hot for his liking. Riding, with a little gentle golf, provided us with the requisite exercise, which took our minds for a short period away from our duties.

Reverting to my new command, I found that I was very badly off for seaplanes. There were very few actually in the unit, and the majority were in rather a bad state. They consisted of two types. The "Short" with a 225-h.p. Sunbeam engine was of the twin main float and tail float type. It carried pilot and observer; the latter provided with a Lewis gun. The Sopwith "Schneider" was a single-seater seaplane with a 100-h.p. Gnome engine.

It was evident that I required some more seaplanes.

As the commander-in-chief was absent in H.M.S. *Euryalus* at Ceylon, I reported to the senior naval officer at Port Said, and prevailed upon him to send a telegram to the Admiralty stating my opinion of the seaplanes actually in the command, and detailing my minimum requirements. I felt at the time that I was liable to get into trouble with the commander-in-chief; but knew if I didn't start to ask for seaplanes at once, I would weaken my case.

As I anticipated, Admiral Wemyss on his arrival was distinctly annoyed; but as I discovered later his bark was worse than his bite, and he was considerably mollified to discover that the Admiralty had acted promptly on my telegram, and dispatched some additional machines.

My job was a peculiar one: I had to work for both the navy and the army, and also operate in the French naval zone on the Syrian coast.

The army at first required reconnaissance in the Sinai area; but later on, they realised the value of the extended reconnaissance we were able to carry out all along the Turkish line of communications. These latter reconnaissances were, of course, well out of the range of the army aeroplanes. The naval requirements were at first quite scanty, but with the development of the Arab revolt, the Red Sea operations provided me with ample work.

At certain periods I found that no one provided us with work, and I had frequently to proffer schemes for our employment. This required rather careful handling. The admiral at first was extremely doubtful of the efficiency of aerial bombing; but by steady persistence, and by producing photographic results of our work, I gradually converted him, if not into a whole-hearted believer yet into an impartial accepter of the proceedings.

I had at times rather a difficult task in obtaining permission to proceed to sea and carry out various schemes; but having been since 1911 in the position of battling for naval aviation against deep-rooted routine, I sometimes succeeded. I got downhearted on some occasions; but here Wedgwood Benn with his political mind was of great assistance.

Whenever the *Ben-my-Chree* or the other two ships went to sea, except in the Red Sea, we had to have an escort in order to safeguard us against submarines, as naturally we had to stop to hoist our seaplanes out or in. This escort was provided by the French Navy.

Here I would like to acknowledge the enthusiastic whole-hearted assistance I always received from Contre-Amiral de Spitz and his command. They were always full out to help in any shape or form, and never once failed to provide an escort at the shortest notice, although frequently it was most inconvenient and upset their usual routine of patrols and reliefs. The escort ships were (in the case of the *Ben-my-Chree*) destroyers; these were all very old-fashioned ships, which on occasion had difficulty in keeping up with me.

The *Raven* and *Anne* being only 11-knot vessels, were generally escorted by armed trawlers.

Capitaine de Frégate Monnaque, of the *Arbalette*, was in command of the French Flotilla, and I soon found in him a very staunch friend. He generally came to sea with the *Ben-my-Chree*, and keenly looked forward to our trips, as he frequently got into action.

He even sent me one day a little poem about the *Arbalette* and the *Ben-my-Chree* which ended I remember with the line, "Someday we will meet in Paradise." Many was the time he dined with me, and returned the hospitality.

Lieutenant de Vaisseau Picard, of the admiral's staff, was another stout supporter, as were also Capitaine de Fournier of the *Pothuau*, and Capitaine Benoist d'Azy of the flagship. The latter was nearly as bad a golfer as myself, and one day I remember we finished a desperate match under the illumination of a lantern held by his coxswain.

After a couple of days, I started to get used to flying seaplanes once more, a type of flying I had not done for at least two years. I soon got into the hang of it again after four flights on a Short and two on a Sopwith.

In order that anyone may understand the operations that follow, I will explain how we worked the seaplanes.

In the *Ben-my-Chree* the seaplanes were carried in the hangar. When required for work they were run out of the hangar on a trolley and hoisted out by the aid of a derrick provided with a steam winch. They were then lowered over the side and when waterborne the derrick purchase was unhooked and the seaplane was free to start its engine and fly off the water. On the return from a flight, the seaplane alighted on the sea and was hoisted on board.

When I joined the *Ben-my-Chree* the routine was far too slow, thus entailing the ship remaining stopped for long periods. They used to use a motor-boat to tow the seaplane away from the ship, and also to tow it back to the ship on its return.

I altered all this, and by using a slip toggle which could be worked either from the ship or seaplane, I was enabled to keep the ship moving at slow speed whilst actually hoisting out the seaplane. The seaplane was dropped at about 6 to 12 inches above the surface of the water; the ship moving ahead prevented the seaplane fouling the ship when on the water.

The time occupied over the whole operation came to about half a minute.

On the return from a flight the seaplane used to alight to leeward, and then taxi to the ship, which was kept stationary at right angles to the seaplane's track. When close to the side the seaplane pilot stopped his engine, and the observer caught hold of a heaving line which was attacked to the hook of the derrick purchase. Woe betide the observer who missed the line. He used to get abused by the pilot and the officer in command of hoisting in, and finally he had an unpleasant interview with me.

Men were stationed along the ship's side with specially devised long bearing-out spars, while others stood on the rubbing strake to fend the seaplane off the side. Immediately she was hooked on she was hoisted up, and as soon as she was clear of the water the ship went ahead.

It was remarkable how quickly the operation was carried out after I had continuously practised the crew and airmen in throwing heaving lines, etc. I have seen one seaplane hoisted out and a second one hoisted in within forty-five seconds of the signal being given. We thus gave little opportunity for submarines to obtain a sitting target.

CHAPTER 2

Aden and the Red Sea

A week after taking over command I had the pleasure of proceeding to sea as captain of a man-of-war on active service. We set out with the French destroyer *Voltigeur* as escort on May 17th, and at dawn on the 18th joined up with H.M.S. *Espiègle*, a sloop under command of Commander Betts, flying the senior officer's pennant, and the monitors *M 15* and *M 23*. The objective was a bombardment of the forts and aerodrome at El Arish. At first the *Ben-my-Chree* was ordered to keep out of range and to operate her seaplanes in controlling the squadron's fire. I went up on the first flight, but after seeing six rounds fired, I had to alight, as my engine overheated and I lost all my water. This was a common fault with our Shorts in hot climates.

The spotting was then carried on with two Sopwiths. After the monitors had finished, I received permission to take the *Ben-my-Chree* within close range and bombard. We hoisted an ensign at each masthead, and getting in as close as the soundings permitted, we started in with our 12-pounders, much to the delight of the crew, who dearly loved a bit of fighting in place of seeing the seaplanes get all the excitement. The *Espiègle* came in close as well, and I suppose she was one of the few rigged ships that fought in the war.

The operations were fairly successful, as one fort was destroyed and also an aeroplane hangar, while several casualties to personnel were caused. The return fire from field guns was not very fierce or accurate. After the bombardment was finished, I proceeded farther north to a point off Khan-Yunis, where I sent in a Sopwith to make a reconnaissance and bomb any camps and troops seen. The bombing was quite successful, a large camp being located near Khan-Yunis. I then returned to Port Said.

On May 22nd I went once more to sea to carry out a reconnaissance off Jaffa. On arriving there at dawn, I found a very heavy sea running, and against the good advice of England I was hoisted out in a Short with Benn as my observer. I determined to try to get off, as I didn't like not attempting to carry out our mission. Unfortunately, I found that the Short would not face the conditions, and one of the floats collapsed, resulting in Benn and myself having to swim for it. Barber, handling the *Ben-my-Chree* like a small motor-boat, was quickly alongside us, and the pair of us were dragged on board like drowned rats.

The Short unfortunately sank before she could be hoisted in. As it was obvious that no more attempts could be made, I cruised about all day, and then, as the weather showed no signs of improvement, returned to Port Said.

On May 26th we went to sea to attempt again the Jaffa area reconnaissance, which was successfully carried out by myself with Benn and one Sopwith flown by Bankes-Price. Benn sighted some soldiers south of the town, and we let go two 65-lb. bombs at them; Bankes-Price, seeing the same party, came down low, and shot them up with his Lewis gun. He then went on to Ramleh, and bombed the camp there with five 20-lb. bombs.

I then took the ship down farther south to Gaza and Khan-Yunis, and England was hoisted out in the Short to reconnoitre and bomb. He made a good reconnaissance and bombed a large camp at Gaza.

Hoisting England on board, I set off for El Arish. Off this village I hoisted out the Short again to collect information in that area. They took a mixed collection of bombs—two 65-lb., one 16-lb., six petrol bombs, and one incendiary bomb, which they let go at the aerodrome and camps. Whilst they were away a German aeroplane came over us, and from a height of about 5,000 feet let go four bombs: two straddled the ship, one of which did not explode. He then came down to about 4,000 feet, and fired at us with a machine-gun.

We, of course, kept up a hot fire with our inadequate anti-aircraft armament. No damage was done on either side.

This visit made me more active than ever in obtaining some more useful anti-aircraft guns. Next time we went to sea I had a better equipment.

As the situation on the Sinai front promised to be quiescent for some time, I proposed to the commander-in-chief that I should proceed to Aden, and see if the seaplanes could assist in the little war that was going on there. He concurred with my proposals, and on June 2nd the *Ben-my-Chree* left Port Said, after embarking an extra supply of coal.

I left L'Estrange-Malone in command at Port Said, and he went to sea on June 10th in H.M.S. *Raven* to have a look with seaplanes at El Arish.

The situation at Aden was that a force of Turks, under the command of a doughty old warrior, Said Pasha, was threatening Aden. Our advanced post was at Sheikh Othman, and the Turks had their Headquarters at Laheg. The weather was far too hot for any active infantry operations at this time of the year; but it was advisable to keep the Turks occupied, and it was decided to try to see what seaplanes could do. Also, our intelligence required additional details of the enemy to compare with the reports collected from spies.

I knew that our only chance of being able to fly with the Shorts was to try to get off very early in the morning or late in the afternoon, as the severe heat would inevitably not only boil all our cooling water away, but probably affect our lift.

As it was, we had a terrible time getting the Shorts off the water under the existing conditions, and being unable to ascend beyond about 1,500 feet we soon began to lose our water whilst flying.

On several trips it was touch-and-go whether we could get back before the engine seized up through this cause.

As I wanted to surprise the Turks, and knew once I got into Aden harbour the many spies would inform them of my arrival, I hoisted out a Short just before daylight on June 7th whilst we were still well out to sea. I gave orders for a close reconnaissance to be carried out over the Turks, to discover which were the best bombing objectives. The flight was entirely successful, and by the time I had anchored the ship the seaplane had returned. I was thus enabled to report to the senior naval officer, and the acting resident, General Walton, armed with a most comprehensive report and detailed map of the Turks' position.

The general, whose first experience this had been of aeroplane work, was immensely pleased at this demonstration of our utility.

With the approval of the general, I decided that we should carry out as intensive a bombing as my limited resources permitted. I had only three Shorts and two Sopwiths. It can thus be realised we couldn't do very much, but we worked as hard as we could. We carried out no less than fifteen bombing flights in the five days, and dropped three 112-lb., three 65-lb., seventeen 20-lb., four 16-lb., and fourteen petrol bombs, a total of forty-one.

Of course, in addition to the bombing, we provided plenty of information and took many photographs.

The pilots were England, Wright, Bankes-Price, and Paine, and the observers Wedgwood Benn, Middlesex Yeomanry, Lieutenants Widderspoon and Burd, R.F.A., and Lieutenant Clarke, 6th Manchesters.

The Turks were considerably shaken by these attacks, and there is little doubt that they lost prestige, resulting in the consequent reluctance of the tribesmen to throw in their lot with the Turks.

We all had some tough flights, and the seaplanes were constantly hit by shell fragments and rifle bullets. It must be realised that we were fairly easy targets, especially the Shorts, as they were only about 60-mile-an-hour machines, and we were constantly over the Turks at about 1,000 feet and generally lower.

I made my first attack in a Short, carrying Benn, on June 8th. After taking a run of two miles to get off, we wallowed over to Laheg, arriving there at 700 feet above sea-level and actually 300 feet over the town. The air was thick with hate; but fortunately, it was very inaccurate.

Benn was actively engaged in taking photographs, and with his well-known sleight of hand rapidly changing the camera for a bomb on my urgent demands; and then discovering that I wanted him to fire the Lewis gun.

I must inform my readers that we generally carried the 16-lb. bombs loose in the passenger's seat. I leave to the imagination the job the observer used to have. He was in a restricted space with a Lewis gun hitting him in the neck every time he moved, nursing a camera on his knees, with three or four 16-lb. bombs somewhere loose at his feet. Somewhere handy he had to have a pair of binoculars, writing-pad, map, and pencil. Added to this he had to attempt to understand what an excited and, in his view, imbecile pilot wanted him to do. Of course, he couldn't often hear what the pilot said amid the noise of the engine and general turmoil of fight.

I may add as a finishing touch to complete this actual picture of real life, that the 16-lb. bombs had a safety device, consisting of a revolving fan retained by a pin. Once you removed the pin, the fan had a nasty habit of revolving. When it had completed about three revolutions the bomb was liable to explode on the slightest provocation. It will thus be seen that the observer's life was a hectic one.

The pilot, on the other hand, on one of the old Shorts in hot climates had no joy-ride. He had generally a really hard time. First coaxing, or most probably forcing, the seaplane off the water, he then had a tough job trying to make the machine climb in the gradually increasing heat of the atmosphere with the water in the radiator on the verge of boiling. He had to keep the engine at practically full revolutions the whole time to have sufficient power to maintain his meagre altitude, and to have some sort of control in the fierce remous that constantly were encountered. At the same time, he had to seize every chance, when he gained a few hundred feet, to throttle down.

Then when he had reached the required area for work, he had to convey to the observer what he required done. I know I frequently lost my temper with my observer, as he seemed always to miss an opportunity for a bomb or a photograph, through being engaged at his map or writing notes. Meanwhile, when trying to attract his attention I would get hit by some colossal bump, and the old Short used to twist her tail round and I had to fly like a professor for about a minute to keep her from coming down to earth.

Still, we used generally to understand each other, and mutual recriminations were soon forgotten in the feeling that we had done our job to the best of our limited abilities.

On our trip to Laheg, Benn observed a gun which had been firing at us from the roof of the *Sultan's* palace suddenly disappear through the roof, crew and all. I daresay the usual mud and date-palm roof was designed principally for the harem's enjoyment, and not as an anti-aircraft gun platform. We only got hit twice on this trip.

Whilst we were at Laheg, Bankes-Price and Wright were up in Sopwiths bombing the Turks at Waht and Subar; they both were at low altitude, about 500 feet or so above the ground, and were heavily fired at.

On the next day we continued the attacks, this time with two Shorts and one Sopwith. England took one of the Shorts and I took the other. England caused a number of casualties with one of his bombs. Benn and I had a curtailed trip, as we boiled the whole time, and finally got back to the water with our radiator melted.

Bankes-Price in the Sopwith had a trying time, as when well inland over the Turks his engine suddenly stopped dead. He let go all his bombs to increase his glide; but just before he was practically on the ground, with the certainty of a bad crash and imprisonment or worse, the engine came to life again and lasted just long enough to get him to Aden harbour and safety. In the afternoon I took a Sopwith and killed a number of Turks near Darb; the two Shorts also went up and attacked Darb and Waht respectively.

On the 10th we gave the Turks a day off, as I hoped if we gave them a rest they would leave their dugouts, thinking our offensive had ceased.

Next day we commenced once more with two Shorts and a Sopwith: one Short failed to leave the water, owing to engine trouble; but Wright got the other one over Laheg, where he scored two direct hits on some troops.

The total results of our efforts were over forty Turks killed and many wounded; not a great result, of course, but the moral effect was far in excess of the material. One incident that was indirectly caused by us was that a shell fired at one of the seaplanes from Laheg hit the chief's house at Mahalla and killed about sixteen people, including eight Turkish soldiers.

My work at Aden was completed on the morning of June 12th, as it was thought that sufficient had been accomplished, and my time was short. The resident gave me permission to see what I could do against Sheikh Said on my way back to Egypt.

Sheikh Said, which is opposite Perim and within gun range of that island, had been a thorn in our side for some time. An attack had been made on it early in the war; but although a few guns had been destroyed, and several casualties inflicted on the Turks, the enemy had reoccupied the place, and kept up a desultory bombardment of Perim.

It was understood that there were about 500 Turks there with about five guns. Taking Colonel Alexander, G.S.O.I Aden command, as passenger, I left Aden on the evening of the 12th, and arrived off Sheikh Said about 4 a.m. on the 13th. My plan was to bombard the Turks with the *Ben-my-Chree's* guns, spotted by Shorts carrying wireless. At first my programme failed, as the Short refused to leave the water. We had therefore to carry on with a Sopwith, controlling our fire by the use of Verey lights, an unsatisfactory method.

I took the ship to within 2,000 yards of the shore, where I was on the flank of the supposed position of the guns. The Sopwith, piloted by Bankes-Price, gave me a line by dropping an incendiary bomb over the camp. He then dropped five 16-lb. bombs at the tents, which apparently caused severe loss of life. I fired at the smoke of the bombs, with a range of 4,600 yards. Bankes-Price saw four of our shells burst in the camp. As soon as we commenced firing, one gun replied, but its shells all fell short.

From the bridge I now saw troops on the slope of the hills, so I opened fire with two guns at them. England then reported that he had got a Short ready, so I had to cease fire and steam out of range in order to hoist out the seaplane. As soon as this was done and the seaplane in the air ready to observe, I once more steamed close in and opened fire with my little broadside of two 12-pounders. If I may say so, we carried out excellent practice, aided of course by our aerial observation, which reported a direct hit on one gun.

The Turks were replying to my fire from two guns, apparently a field gun, and a large gun, probably a 5-inch; but their shooting was bad, although they once straddled us. A shrapnel burst close enough to hit us with some balls, and we got a shell through the foremost funnel. Altogether the Short made three flights, dropping bombs each time with fairly good results.

After being in action for about two hours, I ceased fire, as the Turks had long since apparently had enough and had not replied for some time.

Hoisting in my Short, on which England, Wright, and Paine, with the observers, had done splendid work, I left for Port Soudan to coal, transferring Colonel Alexander, who had thoroughly enjoyed his first naval engagement, to the senior naval officer, who had arrived on the scene and joined in with his 4-inch guns.

Our little affair at Sheikh Said resulted in the Turks ceasing their interference with Perim, and according to our agents' reports we had shaken them badly, first of all by bombing their camp when they were asleep, and then by catching them with our shells whilst they were in the open on their way to their guns. Reports stated we had killed forty Turks and put one gun out of action. It is needless to relate that the sailors and stokers were in the best of spirits. Looking down from the bridge, I found the upper deck one mass of stokers, who had, between moments of stoking up the boilers, dashed on deck to see the fun, and then darted down below again to shovel on more coal.

Chief Petty Officer Ridley, R.N., my clerk, whose job it was, whenever we were in action or a seaplane was up, to be on the upper bridge alongside me, keeping a record of all that happened, was in his element.

He was a devil for accuracy, and he used to keep absolute data of every bomb that was dropped at us or shell that was fired at us. He also kept me informed about the Biblical history of any place in sight. I often hear from him nowadays as a pensioner, and doing well as an agent for a big business.

We had nearly arrived at Port Soudan to coal ship when I received orders to proceed at once to Jeddah.

I arrived off that port on the morning of June 15th. The passage through the reefs was quite a tricky one, and I was glad when I had got the ship safely through into the outer roadstead, where I found H.M.S. *Fox*, R.I.M.S. *Hardinge*, R.I.M.S. *Dufferin*, and H.M.S. *Perth*. They had been there for some time carrying out a bombardment against the trenches outside the town with apparently little success, as far as making the Turks surrender was concerned.

The situation was that the Arabs, nominally under King Ali, then known as the Shereef, but actually under his son Feisal, now H.M. King Feisal of Irak, were attacking the Turks to the number of about 3,000, who were holding the town and a perimeter about half a mile wide outside the walls.

Orders were that the town itself should not be bombarded, firstly because there were hordes of friendly Arabs living there, and secondly, because although not actually a sacred city, yet there was the chance of religious sentiment being affected. The resulting difficulty for the ships was of course apparent. The trenches held by the Turks were invisible from the ships, and the lack of shore observers to direct their fire, owing to the fact that the attacking Arabs up to the present objected to Englishmen landing, prevented any real accuracy being achieved.

It was obviously a case for seaplanes. The arrival of the *Ben-my-Chree*, as will be seen, immediately solved the problem.

The Arabs were at that time apparently not too keen on attacking Old Man Turk, well dug in as he was, and one could hardly blame them. A Turk in a trench is a tough proposition, as we found in the Dardanelles, and the Russians at Plevna. After a conference with the Senior Naval Officer, Captain Boyle, it was decided that I should bomb and reconnoitre the Turks' position in the evening.

I used the only seaplanes we had in action which consisted of one Short and two Sopwiths. At 5 p.m. we set off. England, on a Sopwith, I detailed to attempt to blow a breach in the eastern wall with a 65-lb. bomb, the idea being that the Arabs would then attack. The bomb just failed to hit the objective and no attack resulted.

Bankes-Price on the second Sopwith I dispatched to attack the Turkish trenches on the south of the town. In his usual gallant way, he attacked right low down, coming in at 100 feet, first letting go his 65-lb. bomb, which must have shaken him up at that height, and then firing his machine-gun at them until he had used up all his ammunition. He shook them badly, as the results proved.

Meanwhile, I took Benn with me in the Short, and after we had flown over the town and taken a series of photographs of all the defences, we concentrated our attack on the north side. Here we found that the Turkish position was very strong, extending to about a mile outside the walls. They were in fair strength. I came down pretty low and dropped the 112-lb. bomb at two guns, missing them, however. I then came still lower down, and Benn did good work with his Lewis gun. The Turks put up a hot fire from rifles and machine-guns. I could see that they were employing volley fire by sections, and that these Turks were evidently well-trained soldiers.

We were hit frequently, and one bullet took off the heel of my right shoe. Finally, the engine received a severe blow and started to vibrate very badly, So I considered we had done enough, and I must make for home before I lost my engine. I was just able to reach the water out of rifle range. As soon as I was down, I stopped the engine, and found that the propeller had been hit twice, and was very badly splintered. Another minute or two and it would have disintegrated.

Our motor-boat got us in tow, and when hoisted in a complete examination of the aeroplane showed that my elevator wire was practically severed and only hanging on by one strand. In addition, we had nine more bullet holes in the seaplane.

After a conference with the captain of the *Fox*, it was decided that on the morrow I should take the *Ben-my-Chree* closer in and bombard the Turkish positions we had now located, with the Short spotting for our fire with wireless.

Unfortunately, at dawn, just as we were about to get under way and move to our bombarding position, the white flag went up, and Jeddah surrendered.

The crew were most crestfallen, especially Mr. Greene and the gun-layers.

There is no doubt whatever that the three inefficient rather antique seaplanes took Jeddah. Anyhow, H.M.S. *Fox* signalled to me "probably the seaplanes decided the matter."

I left Jeddah the next day for Port Soudan, where I coaled and sailed for Egypt, arriving at Suez on the 21st, thus closing a very good voyage. I must here pay a tribute to my stokers, practically all Liverpool men. They had a tough time in the great heat, steaming at high speed continuously in a ship constructed for English waters without any tropical facilities.

I now began to feel quite happy in my new job, and not so much to regret leaving my old Eastchurch men. I remembered what Commodore Sueter had said at the Admiralty.

CHAPTER 3

Castelorizo, Beirut, Ruad, and Gaza

Arriving at Port Said, I found that everything: been going on quite well. The *Raven* was sent out to look at the El Arish zone on the 26th, and a flight was carried out by one of her seaplanes.

On July 1st I dispatched the *Raven* with two seaplanes, under Flight-Lieutenant Dacre, D.S.O., to carry out an extended cruise all along the whole of the Sinai, Palestine, and Syrian coasts. They were accompanied by the French armed tug *Laborieux*, as submarine escort.

They made a reconnaissance of El Arish, the seaplane being exposed to a very heavy anti-aircraft fire. This was Flight-Lieutenant Brook's first experience with us, and he did very well.

The *Raven* then went up to Haifa, and hoisted out a Short, pilot Flight-Lieutenant Dacre, with Lieutenant Ravenscroft, R.F.A., as observer, and Flight-Sub-Lieutenant Man on a Sopwith. The Short brought back a complete report of the situation at Haifa and Acre, and was hoisted in. The Sopwith being long overdue, the Short was sent out again to try to find it. Dacre, carrying Lieutenant Brown as observer, took off and soon located the Sopwith down on the water within half a mile of Acre town, obviously in a sinking condition. Dacre landed close alongside, and Man swam off to the Short. As it was impossible to save the Sopwith in face of the enemy at close range, Brown opened fire at it with the Lewis gun and soon saw it sink beneath the waves.

Dacre with great skill succeeded in taking off again in the Short with Man astride the petrol tank, and regained the *Raven*.

The loss of the Sopwith was due to the *tappet* rod fracturing and breaking two more as the engine revolved.

Jenkins, captain of the *Raven*, then proceeded to Famagusta, in Cyprus, where he unloaded 400 tons of coal, which I had got permission to land there for the use of my squadron.

On July 4th he sailed for Castelorizo Island, off the Asia Minor Coast, arriving there on the 6th. This island, which was only about 2 miles off the mainland, was occupied by the French with a garrison of about 120 sailors under Lieutenant de Vaisseau de Saint Salvy. The French Admiral was very anxious to obtain intelligence as regards Turkish forces on the Asia Minor Coast, and also as to whether any of the harbours were used as submarine bases.

Several very extended flights were made by Brook, Dacre, and Man before the *Raven* left on the 8th for Port Said. Before she had arrived, however, I had gone to sea in H.M.S. *Ben-my-Chree,* accompanied by the French destroyer *Dard,* intending to carry out observations over as large an area as possible. Arriving at El Arish, I sent in a Sopwith, which bombed some trenches, and then got attacked by two German aeroplanes, who gave up the chase when within 4 miles of the *Ben-my-Chree.*

I then steamed through the night for Beirut, reaching that place at dawn. The first Short in trying to take off in the fairly rough sea had its propeller broken, so Benn and I went off in another one. We found the surroundings of the town well entrenched, and a certain amount of shipping in the harbour.

As the Turks used schooners and *dhows* to carry food and ammunition, it was important to destroy any we saw.

We made a rule of not bombarding the coastal towns, so we bombed these ships; but our shooting was not good. Proceeding in the ship farther north and keeping as close in to the coast as Soundings permitted, we saw a large convoy and caused serious loss of life with the ship's guns.

Farther on, at the entrance to the Nahr El Kebir River, a Turkish redoubt was sighted and demolished by our 12-pounders. Whilst we were dealing with the redoubt a Short was sent off to try to get to Tel Keli, a station on the Tripoli-Homs railway. Unfortunately, however, England could not coax it high enough to climb over the mountains, and had reluctantly to give it up and return.

On his way back he saw two large tugs in the Nahr El Kebir River. I then went off to Ruad Island, which was occupied by the French with a small Naval garrison. Ruad, which is about 25 miles north of Tripoli, was the last stronghold of the Crusaders in the Holy Land. It is only about half a mile by a quarter of a mile in extent, and is almost completely covered with houses, some of them quite large. The inhabitants who were still there looked quite prosperous and contented

CASTELORIZO.

under the French rule.

I anchored between the island and the mainland, which was only about 1½ miles away, and hoisting out the seaplanes we made a survey of the neighbouring country; also, two Sopwiths were sent off to bomb the two tugs we had seen in the Nahr El Kebir.

On July 8th, my birthday funnily enough, as I was on my way to Famagusta to coal, at 11 a.m. a submarine broke surface about a mile astern of us. We immediately altered course, followed by the *Dard*, and made towards her, opening fire; but she crash-dived before we could reach her. As I didn't care to risk my big ship, I then increased speed, and carried on towards Famagusta, leaving the *Dard* to carry on the hunt. The sea unfortunately was too rough for seaplanes.

Arriving at Famagusta, I much astonished the English harbourmaster, who came off to pilot me in. Refusing his aid, I took the ship in stern first at high speed through the 90-foot wide harbour entrance. He thought I was some ship handler until I explained to him that the *Ben-my-Chree* was fitted with a bow rudder.

The *Dard*, who had given up the hunt, and I then coaled ship. If it had not been for the coal at Famagusta, we would have had to curtail our cruise and return to Port Said.

On the 9th we set sail, and arriving off the Nahr El Kebir we attacked the tugs and the Turkish garrison, using all the seaplanes and the ship's guns controlled by wireless from a Short. We severely damaged the tugs, and finished off the redoubt and block-house.

Having completed this minor operation, at the request of the French I then went to Beirut to carry out further reconnaissance. Lieutenant Picard, French Navy, who was on board as my guest, made a trip over the area as my passenger, in order that he could give first-hand information to Admiral de Spitz.

The same afternoon we reached Haifa, and a Short was sent on reconnaissance. That night it came on to blow pretty hard, and as this would continue probably for two days at least, I returned to Port Said. The *Ben-my-Chree*, always a splendid seaboat, kept up 20 knots the whole time; but I had to part company with the *Dard*, who couldn't naturally risk high speed in the heavy seas. It was inadvisable in view of the known presence of submarines in the vicinity to reduce speed, so I kept on, and arrived off Port Said on the evening of the 11th.

The presence of the submarines in the Eastern Mediterranean made it important for every step to be taken to guard the entrance and approach of Port Said from actual attack or from mines laid by the submarines.

During the next eight days we made twenty-seven patrol flights for this purpose. Meanwhile, the ever-active R.N.V.R. motor-launch flotilla kept up continuous guard.

Sometime later mines were actually laid off the Channel, and as we returned from a cruise one morning, we passed a Russian battleship coming out. She struck a mine and sank with fairly large loss of life.

On July 23rd I again proceeded to sea, accompanied by the *Arbalette*. Arriving off Gaza at an early hour next morning, we carried out reconnaissances to look for troop movements westward. Taking Benn as passenger, I went to Beersheba and Shellal. A low-lying mist made observation difficult, and we saw nothing important; but found the large Shellal camp deserted. England, on another Short, with Smith made a practically similar flight. Whilst we were away a German aeroplane came over to look at the ship.

After hoisting the two Shorts in, I steamed down to El Arish, and dispatched a Short carrying Maskell with Stewart as his observer. They found a camp near El Maadan and bombed it; but could detect no large movement of troops in this area. After they got back a German two-seater aeroplane came out and bombed the ship. He dropped three bombs from a very high altitude, and made fairly good shooting, as one fell within 20 yards and one within 50 yards. The third nearly hit the *Arbalette*. We of course kept up a heavy fire at him from my anti-aircraft artillery. The pompom would pom, but not pom-pom.

I then received orders to return to Port Said, as submarines had been reported.

On July 25th I went to sea again, however, with our old friend the *Arbalette*. The object of the cruise was a request from the Army to observe troop movements on the roads between Nazareth and El Arish.

I was always very keen on doing all we could for the army, as General Sir Archibald Murray, whom I knew before the war, was always interested in our work, and would immediately supply me with observers whenever I asked for more. He helped me in other ways as well. I never think sufficient credit was given to Sir Archibald for the tremendous amount of organisation and elaborate preparations he carried out for the hoped-for advance against the Turk. He was handicapped for men, and the battle of Gaza failed to be a complete success; but he produced water in Sinai from the Nile, and made Lord Allenby's task far easier than it would have been.

In the afternoon a couple of flights were made, and at 4.30 p.m.

we had a change from our ordinary routine, as three schooners were sighted heading south. The *Arbalette* and my ship immediately gave chase. As soon as they sighted us the sailing-ships made for the shore, so I stopped, and hoisting out a seaplane sent it off to prevent this happening if possible, by using bombs and machine-guns. As soon as I got within range and fired a shot across the bows of the biggest one, a vessel of about 250 tons, she headed straight for the beach, and when close the crew took to their boats.

Waiting until they were clear, I opened fire, and we soon set her on fire. The final break up was caused by a large explosion. This showed she had ammunition on board. The seaplane meanwhile had dealt with the second one, which was soon a wreck in the surf. The *Arbalette* was firing at the third ship, and was quite close in to the coast. She reported that she was being fired on from the land by rifles and machine-guns, so I steamed in close to help deal with the opposition, which we soon dispersed by the aid of our guns. Several shots hit the ship; but no one was hurt.

I was very pleased at this little incident, as were the French, because this red schooner was a well-known vessel that had hitherto eluded their patrols.

Next morning found us off Haifa, whence I set out in a Short with Benn, as usual. We went along the railway line to El Afuleh junction, flying the whole time at about 800 feet, which was as high as we could get. We soon ran into a heavy bombardment from several guns, and encountered rifle fire from troops on the hillside, who were actually higher up than we were. Arriving at El Afuleh, we found about 1,500 Turks in a large camp; also, a train in the railway station. To our delight we scored a direct hit on the train with a 16-lb. bomb, which set a carriage on fire. We got safely back to the ship, although at one time I thought we were in for trouble, as some shrapnel hit one of our main struts and carried it away. There were several holes in the seaplane.

Proceeding south once more, we had the good luck to sight and destroy another schooner and a *dhow*, and to shell a large convoy; on the road close to Hammam we severely damaged the bridge with our fire.

Later in the morning I sent off a Short, piloted by England with Smith as observer, to try to get over the mountains to Samaria and Nablus. They failed, however, as the Short couldn't climb high enough. In the afternoon Maskell carrying Steward on a Short with Bankes-Price on a Sopwith went on reconnaissance in the coastal zone. They were heavily fired at from a Turkish post, which Ridley was sharp enough to locate from the ship. I therefore went in close, and silencing their gun, destroyed the post.

At 4.47 p.m. England made another attempt to get to Samaria and Nablus, taking the same Short with Smith as observer. This time, after strenuous efforts, he succeeded. It was a noteworthy flight, and showed what a determined and skilful pilot can do. He was constantly under heavy fire, and it was remarkable that he was not hit, considering the low altitude at which he had to fly.

I arrived back at Port Said on the morning of the 27th after what was undoubtedly a very good voyage. The *Arbalette* had been a most useful ally. She used to go within easy rifle range of the shore to fire at guns and patrols who were attacking our seaplanes.

I was determined, after what I had observed at El Afuleh, to attempt a big attack on this place, as it was evidently an important point in the Turkish line of communication. Also, there were the large camps and piles of stores simply asking to be bombed; but some time elapsed before I could obtain permission to proceed with this mission.

Meanwhile, a welcome addition in the person of Lieutenant Percy Woodland, R.N.V.R., the well-known cross-country jockey and trainer, joined up as an observer. I appointed him to the *Ben-my-Chree*, where he immediately settled down to learn Morse and wireless telegraphy. Incidentally, I taught him to play golf—rather a case of the blind leading the blind.

Some new Sopwiths arrived about this time. As they had 110-h.p. Clergets in place of the 100-h.p. Gnome, they had a better performance.

Meanwhile, L'Estrange-Malone had gone in the Raven to the Gulf of Suez and the Red Sea to carry out work for the Navy and investigate Akaba. They did some excellent work with their seaplanes, and made a very fine photographic map of Akaba. Malone made two landings, and on one occasion the Turkish sergeant in command of a post offered to surrender it for 100 *piastres*.

He returned to Port Said on August 7th.

Chapter 4

El Afuleh, Homs, and Adana

During the early part of August, the *Ben-my-Chree* had to be docked at Suez.

The *Raven* sailed on August 9th with orders to spot for Monitor No. 21 on to the enemy at Bu El Mazas.

The resulting shoot was not successful, as although the *Raven* clearly heard all the signals, yet the monitor, probably through lack of practice, failed to receive them. Whilst Clemson was observing for the monitor, another Short piloted by Brook with Smith as observer attacked a large camp. They were themselves attacked by a German Fokker, which of course was more than a match for a slow old Short with only a Lewis gun. The Short finally drove off the Fokker; but suffered severely, having holes in the petrol tanks, radiator, and floats.

On alighting she began to sink; but smart work on the part of Lieutenant Jenkins, R.N.R., enabled her to be hoisted in.

Whilst Jenkins was thus occupied a second German aeroplane arrived on the scene and dropped five bombs at the *Raven*, whilst a third bombed the monitor.

The *Anne* was sent to sea on August 8th, escorted by the French destroyer *Voltigeur*. She arrived off Messina on August 10th, where she joined the French cruiser *Pothuau*, three French destroyers, the *Laborieux*, and five trawlers. The objective of this little fleet was an attack on barracks and factories at Messina.

The seaplanes made four flights, directing the ships' fire, and good results were obtained.

Whilst the bombardment was going on, a German aeroplane arrived and dropped four bombs; but, as usual, he remained at a very high altitude, thus taking no chances of being hit, and incidentally making his bomb-dropping perfectly futile in those days of inaccurate bomb sights.

SEAPLANE WRECKED OFF KALPENI.

HOISTING IN A WRECKED SEAPLANE, H.M.S. *RAVEN II*.

The French were very pleased at our co-operation, and I received a most complimentary letter of thanks, which especially mentioned Dacre and Stewart.

Once more we went to sea in the *Ben-my-Chree* on August 14th with El Afuleh as our objective. This time we made an attack with two Shorts and a Sopwith on El Afuleh and Tubaun camps. There should have been three Shorts, but one failed to get off the water, owing to engine trouble.

It was not often we had actual engine trouble causing us to fail to start, as Mr. Whitmore, my engine officer, was a very fine engineer, and little escaped his eagle eye.

Benn and I hit two trains with bombs, damaged the line, and blotted out a tent which got in the way of a 16-lb. bomb. We also started a big fire amongst some stores, which we could still see burning when we were nearly over the sea on the return journey.

The second Short dealt with the large camp at Tubaun most satisfactorily, and England amongst other damage demolished a large building. We were heavily fired at from six guns as well as rifles and machine-guns; but suffered very little damage, although we were all very low down. On our way back we steamed along the coast and three flights were made, covering the whole area from Ramleh to El Arish.

We arrived back at Port Said on the evening of August 15th, a pretty quick bit of work.

I received a letter from the Admiralty requiring to be informed why H.M.S. *Ben-my-Chree* had expended so much ammunition in the last three months in comparison with earlier periods. I am afraid I replied "that there was unfortunately a war on."

We were a very happy ship now, and had an excellent amateur band. It was started by one of the stewards, who had been first violin to a large London theatre. It started as a string band; but I made him most reluctantly and against his best musical ideas enrol some amateurs and make it a brass band. They got quite good in time, although their programme was rather limited. They always played as we came in or out of harbour, and they used to play "The Green Grass grew all round" as we passed H.M.S. *Hannibal*, which never went to sea. I am afraid my men rather spread themselves ashore, as certainly we used to keep the sea whilst the rest of the East Indian Squadron stayed in port, except for the monitors and the motor-launches.

I now had my plans ready for as powerful an attack as I was able to make with my limited resources on the Turkish communications at El Afuleh.

On August 21st I flew up to Ismailia, and went on board H.M.S. *Euryalus* with my prepared scheme. Admiral Sir R. Wemyss approved of my plans, and with the ready assistance of the French Navy everything was satisfactorily arranged.

My force consisted of:

H.M.S. *Ben-my-Chree*, carrying three Shorts and two Sopwiths.

H.M.S. *Raven*, two Shorts and two Sopwiths, with L'Estrange-Malone in charge.

H.M.S. *Anne*, one Short and one Sopwith; Captain Weldon in charge of operations.

The trawler, *Paris II*, and *Hache*, destroyer, escorted the *Raven* and *Anne* respectively, and this little armada sailed at dawn on August 24th.

I sailed on the evening of the same day, escorted by that fine old sailor Monnaque in the *Arbalette*.

I gave orders for all to rendezvous at dawn off Haifa. I had issued detailed orders for the targets to be attacked by each section, and everything went off like clockwork. We proceeded in one formation until we had passed Tubaun Camp, where we separated in order to attack from various directions.

The orders were for the *Ben-my-Chree* seaplanes to attack El Afuleh station and rolling-stock at between 1,000 and 1,500 feet.

The *Raven's* party were to attack the railway line 3 miles south of Afuleh at 700 feet, whilst *Anne's* seaplanes were to devote themselves to the stores at El Afuleh from 1,700 feet. The Sopwiths, after dropping their bombs, were to look out for and engage hostile aeroplanes if any arrived.

After the bomb attack had been made each seaplane had an allotted reconnaissance to carry out.

I felt once more a happy man when I looked back and saw my little Squadron of nine seaplanes keeping perfect station on me. Splitting up in accordance with plan, I went on to El Afuleh, and was received by a hot fire. As we approached a train steamed out of the station; but ran into L'Estrange-Malone's party, who hit the last coach with a 65-lb. bomb and also destroyed the permanent way.

Altogether we destroyed one engine and fourteen carriages and trucks, and set fire to a large amount of stores.

In all we dropped thirteen 65-lb. and 112-lb. bombs, and thirty-

SIXTY-FIVE-POUND BOMB BURSTING BETWEEN TRAINS AT EL AFULEH JUNCTION.

one 16-lb. One of my big bombs exploded between two trains on parallel lines. Benn took a photograph of it, and it distinctly shows the accuracy of our bombing. Benn had a most busy time, as besides having to heave over the small bombs, he had to take photographs of each bomb explosion. He kept on demanding me to go lower, but I struck at about 700 feet. I remained over El Afuleh until I saw all the seaplanes had left, and I can still remember one old Turk standing in the open and firing at us each time we came over his head.

He had apparently an old Snider, as when he discharged it, I could see a puff of black smoke. I was so low I could see his face distinctly, and I am certain I would recognise him again. There is little doubt that the constant hail of bombs and seaplanes arriving from three different directions totally disorganised the defence, as the firing was very wild, and after a bit died out altogether, except for our old pal. Some of my seaplanes came in very low indeed, and these made really good shots with their bombs. We suffered no casualties, although most of the seaplanes were hit. Mine had only four holes in it, but the others had far more.

The pilots engaged were: Dacre, Clemson, England, Maskell, Bankes-Price, Brook, Man, Paine, and Smith; the observers: L'Estrange-Malone, Wedgwood Benn, King, Williams, and Millard. So, we had a good combination of the two services.

After we got back to the water, all the seaplanes were rapidly hoisted on board. This was of course a ticklish moment with a number of seaplanes, as the ships had to remain stopped for much longer than usual. However, with our active French friends it would have been a very good submarine that could get at us.

Whilst the slower ships went off to the next rendezvous, I sent in two seaplanes again to El Afuleh to check the damage. They came back with a full report, and said the stores were still burning most satisfactorily.

Steaming southward, we came across two *dhows*. One of them ran ashore, chased by the *Arbalette*, who went close in to fire at twenty soldiers who swam ashore from her. The other one, quite a small one, I intercepted, and hoisted in to take back as a prize. She had a crew of five. They informed us that our first attack on El Afuleh had suspended railway traffic for five days.

Our next objectives were the large camp at Bureir and the railway viaduct over the Wadi El Hesy. I sent off seven seaplanes for these jobs, and as Dacre's seaplane had engine trouble, I gave him mine instead of going myself; he was a keen fellow, and bitterly disappointed at the thought of losing a chance.

Unfortunately, he had engine failure over the enemy's country, and was made prisoner; which fact we heard later. His loss was a great blow to the command, as he was a most dashing pilot, with a splendid war record.

Some casualties were caused to the camp; but although the railway embankment and permanent way close to the viaduct were destroyed, the viaduct was untouched. Leaving the *Anne* to search for Dacre, as there was just a chance, he might reach the shore and so be rescued, I sailed north to carry out a further mission, which was an attempt to get to Homs.

Arriving at dawn on the 26th off Nahr el Kebir, I set off, taking Benn, whilst England took King. The conditions were very bad, cloud at 1,500 feet, and a very strong wind blowing from the Lebanon Mountains, which caused really fierce remous amongst the high hills. I totally failed to get over the pass, and had some very anxious moments, as there were times when the machine was practically uncontrollable.

England, however, succeeded in scraping over the hills after three or four narrow escapes of hitting the hillside obscured by the low clouds; he got to Homs, and returned with most important information. This flight was quite one of the finest I have seen.

After England's return, I took the ship to Ruad Island, where we attempted to carry out flights over the neighbourhood on request of the governor; these failed, however, as the high sea prevented the seaplanes getting off the water.

I therefore proceeded to Famagusta to coal. Having completed with coal, I spent the next day in harbour giving the seaplanes a thorough overhaul. We carried a 24-h.p. Wolseley tender on board, one of my old No. 3 Wing transport vehicles I had found at Alexandria, and claimed, as it had R.N.A.S. on it. Hoisting this out on to the jetty, I set off for a trip over Cyprus, taking Captain Monnaque, Benn, Woodland, and England.

We spent a most enjoyable day, going to Larnaca, Nicosia, and Kerenia. The scenery was gorgeous, and the whole countryside seemed steeped in the romance of the Crusades. There are countless legends in the country, which the old castles on the hills seem to keep alive. Famagusta has tremendous fortifications, which the Turks besieged for nearly three years; finally, they took it, and flayed the defending commander alive. Looking at the walls, which are quite 12 feet thick, it

FAMAGUSTA. THE FUNNELS OF H.M.S. *BEN-MY-CHREE* IN THE FOREGROUND.

seemed impossible to take it. Apparently, the Turks constructed a ramp outside the walls, and thus gained the fortress.

Encircled by these massive fortifications are several old churches. I went into one, and there in the dim light of a candle was an old Greek priest reciting the service with no other congregation but himself. Probably he never had any—anyhow, I felt I was looking on at a relic of a bygone age.

Setting out to sea on August 29th, I steered for Karatash Burnu, with the object of making flights to Adana and the surrounding area to find out what troops were in the vicinity and to bomb any military objective, especially the railway bridge over the river. I took Benn with me in a Short, and we had rather a difficult flight, as there was a considerable downward trend of air in the cup formed by the Taurus Mountains on one side and the Amanus Mountains on the other. I could never get above 1,100 feet; in fact, I arrived over Adana at only 700 feet, probably actually only being about 500 feet above the land. I had all my work cut out to keep the Short in the air at all. We let go one 65-lb. and one 16-lb. bomb at the railway station, where we actually saw a troop train, and one 65-lb. and one 16-lb. at the railway bridge, which we missed; but this was easy to miss, as the bumps were terrific, and the old Short was wallowing about all the time.

In the middle of one bad spasm, when, as the saying goes, "all hands man the pump," Benn lent over me and shoved a bit of paper into my mouth. Thinking he had seen something highly important, I let go of the wheel with one hand, and after some struggle managed to spread out the paper and decipher what he had written. It read as follows, "Aren't the shadows on the mountains lovely?" I never felt nearer killing anyone in my life, and when we got back to the water I hadn't cooled down; but Benn took it all in good part. There was little that he missed as an observer, and I was delighted to read the voluminous report he had written. Personally, on that trip I had seen little, being otherwise occupied. I still look back upon this Adana trip as one of the toughest bits of piloting it has been my lot to undergo.

I returned to Port Said, arriving there on the afternoon of August 30th.

After separating on the 25th, the other two ships had been by no means idle. The *Anne*, after cruising off the coast until 3 a.m., hoping for Dacre to appear, left for a position 30 miles north of Jaffa. Arriving there, Brook, carrying Williams, 2nd Rajputs, made a fine reconnaissance to Nablus and Samaria. He bombed Tulkeram station with effect, and brought back a very full report, which was considered extremely interesting by G.H.Q.

The *Anne* arrived back at Port Said on the 27th.

The *Raven* was up north reconnoitring Adalia and Fineka Bay, looking for mines and submarines. She arrived at Port Said on the 28th.

It will thus be seen that we kept the Turks busily engaged from August 25th until 29th, dealing blows at widely separated points on their lines of communication. There is little doubt that we not only did a good deal of actual damage, but gained important information, and made them doubtful of the security of their communications.

The seaplane carriers were certainly proving their utility. The *Ben-my-Chree* was of course the best, as her high speed enabled her to launch seaplanes at widely spaced objectives within the same day.

I returned to Port Said well satisfied with our work; but wishing I had more efficient seaplanes. My little command were in fine fettle, and anxious for further work. A new acquisition in the person of Lieutenant C. E. Hughes, Wedgwood Benn's brother-in-law, arrived. He was appointed Assistant Intelligence Officer, and did yeoman service.

H.M.S. *Raven* was to have sailed for the Red Sea on September 1st, but unfortunately a German aeroplane came over and one bomb dropped by it struck the *Raven* just abaft the forecastle: one officer was wounded, three men were killed, and five wounded; in addition, the windlass was put out of action. As it meant a delay of at least forty-eight hours, I dispatched the *Anne* in her place.

As it was certain that the German aeroplanes were getting more active, I started training my pilots in fighting formations, the idea being for one Short to be escorted by two Sopwiths. We also carried out intensive machine-gun fire from the air against a towing target.

I knew that singly any one of my seaplanes stood a poor chance against an aeroplane; but I considered that if we carried out well-drilled tactics to protect our reconnaissance or spotting Shorts, we would be able to carry on in dangerous zones like El Arish.

We also practised WT with the navy, in readiness for any bombardments they might carry out.

L'Estrange-Malone sailed in command of the *Anne* on September 1st, and was actively employed all September and October in the Red Sea. He carried out most useful work with his seaplanes, and greatly assisted the Arab Army in their war against the Turks.

CHAPTER 5

A Failure and a Success

I took the *Ben-my-Chree* to sea on September 13th, and the following morning we carried out a reconnaissance to Beersheba, using one Short escorted by two Sopwiths in view of the extreme probability of having to fight German aeroplanes. As it happened, we met no opposition, but encountered very heavy anti-aircraft fire at Beersheba, the Short being hit in one of its floats by a fragment of a shell. For the last half-hour of the journey the engine of my Sopwith had been vibrating very badly, and it was getting worse every minute. I got back, however; but after alighting and whilst taxiing to the ship the engine fell out of the bearers and the propeller flew off into space.

Subsequent examination showed that the front spars of the fuselage were rotten with age and usage. Of course, like the majority of our seaplanes, it had seen hard service for some time in hot climates. I was glad it was kind enough to wait until I landed.

Returning to Port Said, I was called to a conference with the commander-in-chief. It was the intention to carry out a bombardment of El Arish and the neighbourhood with H.M.S. *Espiègle* and Monitors Nos. 15 and 31. I pointed out to the commander-in-chief that our fleet would certainly bring out the full force of the enemy aeroplanes, and that my seaplanes would be bound to be attacked; thus, unless I could concentrate on spotting for one target with a strong formation, the fire control would be spoilt, and probably my seaplanes would be shot down. I was overruled, however, and ordered to divide my small force into two parts, and carry out simultaneous fire control at two targets 10 miles apart. I viewed the future with misgiving. However, one has to obey orders.

I sailed on September 16th, and at dawn I reached the rendezvous.

(A) flight, consisting of a Short flown by Maskell with Kerry as observer, was to spot for the monitors at El Arish. It was escorted by

Bankes-Price and Nightingale on two Sopwiths.

(B) flight, made up of England with King as observer, was to locate a target about 8 miles south of El Arish for H.M.S. *Espiègle*. Man and myself in Sopwiths provided the escort.

We all expected a fight, and I am afraid I for one didn't think much of our Sopwiths, with their Lewis gun inadequately mounted for combat, as a match for a good aeroplane; but I hoped that our well-drilled tactics might surprise the Germans and pull us through.

Exactly what I had feared happened. (B) flight set off, and after a good search we found no target worth shooting at. The Short therefore returned, and Man and I flew up to El Arish to join up with (A) flight.

Arriving there, Man had engine trouble, and had to alight on the water, but unfortunately, he hit the water too hard and sank, being picked up by a trawler. I couldn't see any signs of (A) flight; also, the monitors were not firing. I hunted round for a good time, and went over the German aerodrome, and saw some aeroplanes on the ground. I then returned to the ship, and alighted to find the worst had happened.

(A) flight, which had started at the same time as we had, flew to the north-east of El Arish and observed for one round from a monitor. They were then attacked by an aeroplane, which, getting between Bankes-Price and England, shot Bankes-Price down in flames.

Nightingale immediately engaged the German; but the latter flew rings round him, being immensely faster and far handier. Nightingale put up a stubborn fight; but he was soon forced to alight on the water with his petrol tank riddled with holes. It was only by the mercy of God he didn't get on fire.

The German then went for the Short, attacking from below; but Maskell, diving at 75 knots, by a skilful manoeuvre got under the German's tail, where Sub-Lieutenant Kerry got a real good burst from his Lewis gun into the enemy. Several tracers were seen to hit him, and the German made for home, chased for some distance by the stouthearted Short, which of course was soon outpaced. Whilst this was happening three other Germans were bombing the ships. I may add that low clouds made it difficult for both sides to sight each other.

The whole expedition was of course a complete failure. I had lost quite the best Sopwith pilot I had in Bankes-Price. He was only a youngster; but he had perfect hands, and was as plucky as they are made. He had a brilliant future in front of him. I felt his loss immensely, as did we all. The Sopwiths were of course absolutely useless for combat; but as they were the only seaplanes available, I had to use them.

I returned to Port Said, feeling that two seaplanes had been lost, and one gallant pilot sacrificed for nothing. The commander-in-chief sent me a letter, which showed that he had now come to the same conclusion. It was a pity that I couldn't get on the scene quicker, as my greater experience may have been of assistance; but probably I might have been included in the bag.

The rest of September and most of October was a quiet period, firstly because we were given no work to do, secondly, because I was very short of seaplanes. I kept my pilots and myself, however, hard at it firing at targets, and we had a certain amount of anti-submarine patrols to carry out. I was also busily employed in attempting to improve the performance of the Short seaplane, and my experiments were entirely successful.

I cut off a good deal of the lower plane, and poked about in other ways, converting one of the old ones into a better performer than a new one. I gained six knots in speed, and about 15 *per cent.* in climb. We termed this altered seaplane the "Experimental Short."

Towards the end of October, I sent the *Raven* to relieve the *Anne* in the Red Sea, where L'Estrange-Malone was still doing excellent work, although his seaplanes were on their last legs.

I left Port Said in H.M.S. *Ben-my-Chree* on November 2nd to rendezvous with Admiral de Spitz off Adalia. Arriving there on the morning of the 3rd, I found the Admiral on board his armed yacht, with the destroyer *Dard* and three armed trawlers, one of which had a 5.5-inch gun.

The general idea was to locate and engage hostile batteries that had been recently firing at the French patrols. I sent up two seaplanes, which found some entrenchments and empty gun positions.

At 1 p.m. the trawler *Canada* and *Ben-my-Chree*, spotted for by a Short, fired at the entrenchments, which the Short soon reported as destroyed. As we could find nothing else, the little fleet was ambling up the coast about 2,000 yards to seaward when suddenly shells began to fall all round us, coming from the direction of Adalia.

I immediately hauled out of the line, stopped, and hoisted out a Short in order to locate the guns. This was only a matter of about thirty seconds, as we were well trained in those days. I then headed for the shore, and opened fire at the estimated position of the guns.

The Short soon located the enemy, and I then carried out a deliberate bombardment, spotted for by the aeroplane, which soon caused the enemy to cease fire. The Short reported four guns, and signalled that we had hit one. We were straddled on at least eight occasions, and being the biggest ship naturally drew the most fire. I had to keep close in, as my 12-pounders didn't have the range of the enemy. The fight was quite hot whilst it lasted, and the tough old admiral, in his little ship, gave us a fine example by going close in and blazing away with his little 6-pounders. I saw him hit twice, and shells fell all round him.

As soon as the Turks' fire ceased, I hoisted out a Short with bombs, and Percy Woodland as observer displayed his marksmanship by scoring a direct hit on one gun.

The squadron then proceeded to Castelorizo. Afterwards Admiral de Spitz was kind enough to send in the following report, which said amongst other things:

> The assistance of the *Ben-my-Chree* has under the circumstances been precious to me. The various flights effected by the planes enabled us to regulate our fire, and to ascertain exactly the position of an important system of trenches.
>
> The *Ben-my-Chree* also came spontaneously to the assistance of one of our torpedo-boats engaged by an enemy battery, and by its well-directed fire contributed to reducing it to silence.

Arriving at Castelorizo, I spent the night there, and in the morning sent off two flights to try to locate some guns which were reported as being mounted to fire at the harbour. My seaplanes saw no signs of any guns or preparations. This was sad, as later on these were the actual guns that sank the old *Ben-my-Chree*. I returned to Port Said that day.

Strictly speaking, of course, I suppose I never ought to have taken the *Ben-my-Chree* into action, as she was not by any manner of means a fighting ship. The big hangar made her a very fine target, and the presence of the seaplanes, and the upper-deck petrol stores made her very vulnerable. One shell in the hangar would have set her on fire, just like a match in a puddle of petrol; but still, if one always thought about this sort of things no one would ever fight, and the crew thoroughly enjoyed a scrap.

Our next cruise took place when we left Port Said on December 1st with the French destroyer *Dard*. I arrived off Haifa, and sent two Shorts off to look at Nazareth, El Afuleh, etc.; also, a Sopwith to reconnoitre the Samaria-Tulkeram road. I next steamed south to scout over the Jaffa-Ramleh area.

Arriving off Jaffa, I sent in a Short piloted by Nightingale and carrying Percy Woodland as observer. When over Ramleh, we saw the Short come under heavy shellfire, and Ridley saw her actually hit. I saw the seaplane diving down practically vertically; but I distinctly saw that it levelled up as it disappeared from sight behind a sand-hill. I therefore had a glimmering of hope that it had been able to make a fairly safe alightment, although of course landing a seaplane on *terra firma* is not a particularly safe performance.

Yet I felt that as the machine seemed under control, the crew were still alive. I immediately stopped and sent in another Short to see if they could discover what had happened. They returned without being able to see Nightingale's seaplane. Late that evening we got a German wireless to say that a seaplane had been shot down, and the crew captured. This relieved my mind, as Percy Woodland was a great friend of mine who had done well during his service in the ship.

It was very sporting of the Germans to give us this tip. We were all rather downcast over the loss of our two officers; but we knew we couldn't make bricks without straw, and we had been fairly lucky up to date. Nightingale and Woodland landed fairly well; but both were badly hurt. The first people to arrive on the scene were some Arabs, who in the usual manner of that nasty race started to tear off all their clothes and look for loot. One was just about to cut off Percy's finger to get his signet ring when some Germans arrived, who, laying about with cudgels, drove the Arabs away. The Germans behaved very well to the pair of them.

The average Palestine Arab is by no means a desirable person, and I can never understand how in the many Palestine troubles nowadays we take them seriously.

We made further flights along the coast, and got rather heavily bombed by a German aeroplane near Gaza. I arrived at Port Said on December 3rd.

The loss of Woodland rather spoilt my simple recreations on shore of golf and riding, and I missed his cheery companionship. It cast quite a gloom over the wardroom also, where he was a great favourite. My brother Bill Samson had arrived early in November, and, as a well-experienced observer, he was most useful.

He had undergone considerable hardships in East Africa, but was pretty fit and well. The next cruise was for the attack on the railway bridge at Chicaldere.

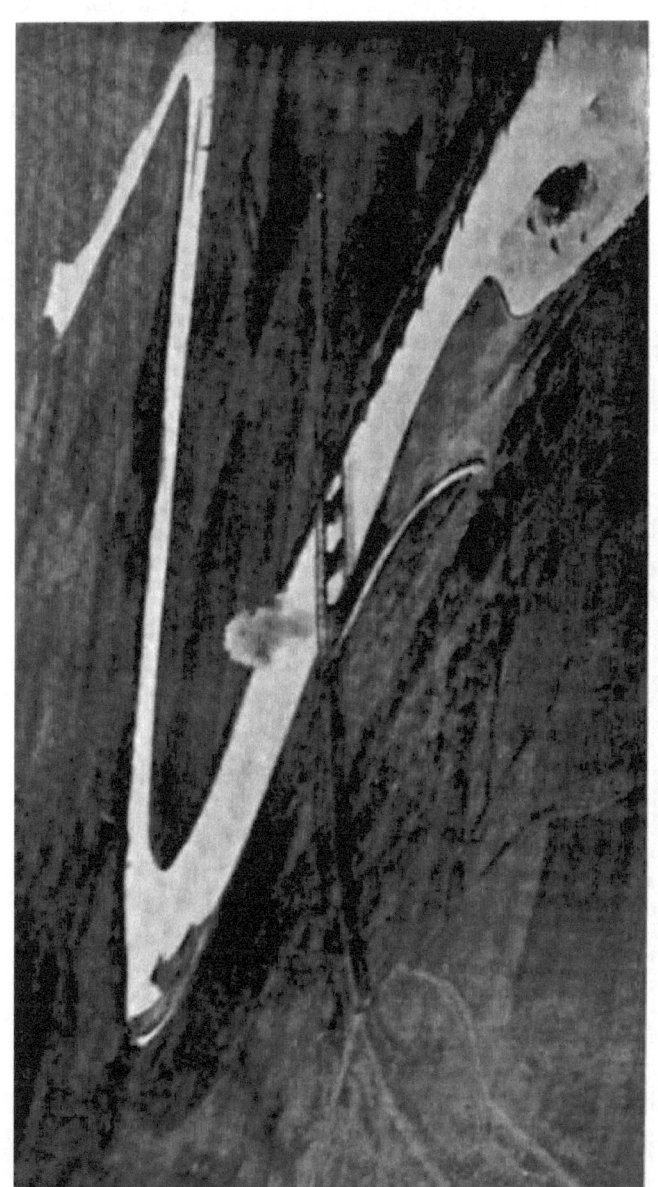

BOMB BURSTING ON CHICALDERE BRIDGE, DECEMBER 1916.

This was about 30 miles inland from the Gulf of Alexandretta, and I had been endeavouring to obtain permission to bomb this important link in the Turkish lines of communication for some time. At last, the powers that be gave permission, so I set off with the *Ben-my-Chree* and the *Raven*. I decided that I would rely upon the Sopwiths to attack the bridge from low altitude, and use the Shorts to cover our attack by bombing and machine-gunning the guards, thus hoping to attract their attention away from the Sopwiths.

The whole scheme worked admirably.

The Shorts dealt out hate to the guards, whilst the three Sopwiths, attacking at 400 feet, had an undisturbed approach. My bomb fell between the girders; but Clemson obtained a direct hit with his; and Smith's also damaged the bridge. The second phase of the attack was then carried out, and a second hit on the bridge was scored.

The third attack also scored another hit, the successful bomber being Clemson once more. Bill Samson bagged Some Turks with his machine-gun from a Short.

The attack had succeeded beyond my expectations, as I thought it would be at least two days' work.

As it was undesirable to remain in these submarine-infested waters too long, I steamed away, expecting to renew the attack on the next day; but the commander-in-chief considered we had done enough. Reports were received that we had put the bridge out of action for a week. Burling made a very fine flight on this occasion, as he covered the second phase most efficiently.

CHAPTER 6

The End of the "Ben-My-Chree"

On January 2nd I sailed once more for Alexandretta make a further attack on the bridge; but a gale sprang up, and I had to seek shelter in Famagusta. From there I was recalled to Port Said.

On January 8th I left Port Said for what was the last cruise I was to make in the good old ship, though I did not know it. The programme was to go to Castelorizo and carry out some operations with the French. It was blowing pretty hard the whole time, and on arrival off the harbour the weather got too bad for my French destroyer to keep the sea except at dead slow. Since it was impossible to work seaplanes and dangerous to cruise about in this happy hunting-ground of submarines, I came inside between the mainland and Castelorizo Island.

Admiral de Spitz was in harbour in his yacht, with my French destroyer and a torpedo-boat. He sent out a request for me to bring the *Ben-my-Chree* into the harbour. I didn't care to do so very much for some reason, although the *Raven* had been there previously, and the harbour was guarded by a boom; also, it was extremely difficult for a submarine to enter the channel undetected.

Still, some inner feeling made me feel inclined to stay cruising up and down in the narrow channel; but on thoroughly considering the matter, it seemed more dangerous in the channel than it would be in the harbour, so I followed the admiral's request and entered. I lay with my head to seaward with the shore about 60 yards off my port side. I had one wire astern and a second wire to a buoy on my starboard hand. The boom was rigged, and we were reasonably safe. I kept steam up ready for full speed at five minutes' notice, and kept my two foremost guns'-crews closed up at their guns.

As I had a certain amount of stores for the French, they sent off a lighter to transport them ashore. Before the lighter had shoved off from the ship the Manx cat which had been in the ship since she was built got into the lighter and refused to be coaxed on board again.

This seemed a sinister sign, and I went to lunch with the admiral, feeling distinctly uneasy for some reason. I got away as soon as I could, and returned on board. After a look round, I went to my cabin.

At 2.10 p.m. I heard an explosion close at hand, and thought this was a German aeroplane bombing us. I rushed up to the bridge and ordered anti-aircraft stations. A further explosion took place, and then I realised we were being shelled. At first, I thought it was a submarine firing over the island from seaward, until I heard a shell coming from the mainland. I immediately ordered stand-by to the engine-room; and ordered the boats away to slip the two securing wires. I also went to general quarters.

At 2.13 the fourth shell came and hit the hangar; immediately an intense fire started. I went to fire quarters, and ten hoses were led to the hangar; but it was soon evident that we would never be able to put the fire out. The after end of the ship soon became a sheet of flame, the petrol in the seaplanes being, of course, the principal cause.

Meanwhile, we were struck again, this time by a shell that hit the bridge, where we all had a narrow squeak, as the steering wheel and telegraphs were wrecked by it. A second shell hit the bridge, and others hit the hangar, the engine-room, and the forward mess-deck. The shells were 6-inch and 17-pounders.

The engine-room at 2.30 had become untenable, owing to the heat and fumes from the fire in the hangar. I couldn't steer the ship, as the wheel was wrecked and the hand-steering wheel aft couldn't be got at owing to the raging fire. There was nothing to be done except carry on trying to put the fire out, which I knew was beyond our powers; but we kept on at it. The only thing was to keep the crew in shelter as much as possible, which I did by ordering all hands to muster on the port side amidships.

I gave orders to land the sick, and to clear lower deck. The crew behaved admirably, although we were hit by six or seven shells a minute. Some obviously were hitting us under water, as water was beginning to come in below. It was distinctly unpleasant standing there being shelled from unseen guns.

Benn and I had a narrow squeak as we were standing on the upper deck, as a shell hit the whaler directly over our heads, and only a bit of wood about 1 foot long remained hanging at the davits.

At 2.45 I gave the order to abandon ship, as it was only senselessly risking the men's lives keeping them on board. The boats soon landed

H.M.S. *BEN-MY-CHREE* IN FLAMES.

H.M.S. *BEN-MY-CHREE* A WRECK.

the lot, as the shore was only about 50 to 60 yards away. The ship by now had a heavy list; but I knew she couldn't sink more than about six feet or so owing to the shallowness of the harbour. After everybody had gone and I had seen the confidential books destroyed, I left the ship. She was a sorry spectacle, as bombs were constantly exploding, the fire having reached the bomb store. The hangar and stern were practically burnt out.

Everybody behaved very well indeed. Lieutenants Allingham, First Lieutenant, and Braithwaite gave a wonderful example to the men. Wedgwood Benn and Ridley, who kept with me, were calmness personified. Clemson and they made a thorough search below to see that everybody was out of the ship.

On shore the conditions now became rather hectic, as the guns, which consisted of two 6-inch, one 4-inch, and three 17-pounders, ceased firing at the ship and started at the town. The torpedo-boats and the admiral's yacht were sheltered from the fire and got away to sea untouched.

Bill Samson displayed a good deal of gallantry, going all over the town under the heavy shell fire and collecting the various parties of my men, who naturally had got pretty well scattered. I finally selected a monastery in which to stow the crew.

Our casualties were remarkably small.

Surgeon Goss, assisted by officer's steward Riddington, soon organised a hospital ashore, where they attended our wounded and those of the inhabitants.

The old ship went on burning until the forenoon of January 10th, and explosions continued until the morning of the 13th. Each night I used to go on board with a small party and salve all the gear we could. The majority of the crew were transhipped to Egypt on the 10th at night. I remained with a small party Salving the stores, and we had a bad time generally, as we frequently got shelled. Parker, the Assistant Paymaster, made a most gallant effort, by diving under water and getting through a port hole, to get at the ship's safe.

I returned to Port Said with the remainder of the crew ten days after the ship was lost.

The subsequent court-martial acquitted me and the crew, and we were commended for our behaviour, but I felt the loss of the ship very much. I had got very attached to her. Poor old Robinson was like a father bereft of his child.

In 1919 I rescued a Turkish major from the Greeks at Smyrna; I then discovered quite by chance that he was the actual battery commander who had sunk the ship. I think this is an extraordinary coincidence.

In 1922, whilst flying from Malta to Constantinople, I saw the old *Ben-my-Chree* in Piraeus: she had been salved and towed there.

Meanwhile, the *Anne* was carrying on with work in the Red Sea. On January 23rd we lost a very fine observer, who had continuously done sterling work, in Lieutenant Stewart, Royal Scots, who was shot whilst spotting for H.M.S. *Fox* at Wej. The *Anne* returned to Egypt on January 26th.

February found me still at Port Said with the *Raven, Anne*, and the base. Some new Short seaplanes arrived at the end of January. These had a 240-h.p. engine; thus, they had a slightly better performance than the older ones; however, the Experimental Short was a better performer than even these new ones.

Rumours of a German raider in the Indian Ocean, and mines being found off Colombo and Bombay, led the Commander-in-Chief to dispatch me in search of this craft, especially as she was reported to carry a seaplane. As a matter of fact, the ship in question was the German raider *Wolf* and, as history relates, she did carry a seaplane.

I immediately selected the *Raven*, as she was slightly faster than the *Anne*, stowed as many Shorts as I could on board, and took the pick of the pilots and observers, including, of course, England.

We left for Aden early in March, where we were to join up with the French Cruiser *Pothuau* and hunt the seas for the *Wolf*. Thus, started rather an interesting cruise, leading us to many coral islands.

I said farewell at Port Said to Wedgwood Benn and most of the crew of the ill-fated *Ben-my-Chree*, who left for England. My brother was amongst the party. Benn, with whom I was sorry to part, went home to learn to fly. My brother was soon sent out to Italy to join Commodore Sueter in command of the R.N.A.S. at Otranto.

After an uneventful journey down the Red Sea, we arrived at Aden on March 16th. Our arrival was rather unpleasant, as through some error we had hoisted the old signal instead of the new one, and were greeted with three large shells, one of which passed unpleasantly close. Aden was a bit perturbed owing to a captured prize called the *Turbantia*, with some Germans on board, having laid some mines three days previously. She was intercepted by one of the sloops under Captain Palmer, however, and the prize crew were brought into Aden.

Whilst awaiting the *Pothuau*, flights were made over Said Pasha's

Turks, and we carried out several bomb attacks. I took up Colonel Alexander and General Stuart, the Resident. It was the latter's first experience of aeroplanes. At his desire I took him over the whole Turkish position and over Laheg, so that he returned with a good appreciation of the situation.

I found that with our new Shorts, provided as they were with about 30 more horse-power, we could fly much higher than on our previous visit.

As a change from my ordinary routine, I had a day with the Aden troop, and in company with Captain Handley and seventeen sowars got into a little skirmish well beyond our lines.

When Capitaine de Fournier of the *Pothuau* arrived we had a consultation, and decided that we would make for the Laccadive Islands, carrying out as many flights as possible *en route*.

Arriving at these islands, a thorough search was to be made with the seaplanes. Then after completing with coal at Colombo, we would search the Maldives.

The *Pothuau* was a very old cruiser of not very high speed, and I felt that we were not so certain to capture or destroy the *Wolf* if we were lucky enough to meet her, especially as she was reported to be armed with at least four modern 5.9-inch guns, which could far outrange the Frenchman's. We in the *Raven* with our two 12-pounders were of little fighting value. I considered that our main hope lay in the seaplanes with their bombs.

We sailed on March 19th, and after passing Socotra Island ran into very fine weather. On the 22nd I was hoisted out in mid-ocean on board the Experimental Short, carrying Captain Knight-Bruce as my observer. The Short in the very heavy swell left the water in fine style, after one or two anxious moments, and we set off to make a sweep on a radius of about 50 miles from the ships.

It was a lonely feeling, once we lost sight of our Squadron, as the Indian Ocean is a large space and no ship was in sight. After completing our journey, I returned to what I had estimated would be the new position of the *Raven*, allowing for her speed, and I was a little relieved to discover that my navigation was correct. As a matter of fact, I saw her when still about 20 miles away. Landing was difficult, as the swell was very heavy, but I managed it safely by getting down just below the crest of a wave.

When on the water, the waves were so huge that frequently when in the trough I could not see the ship. Getting alongside and being hoisted in were both ticklish operations.

We made several more mid-ocean flights, all of which called for great care on the part of both the crew of the seaplane and those on board the *Raven*.

Arriving off the Laccadive Islands, we made a thorough search of every island and atoll. Flying amongst these islands was most exhilarating, as you could see for miles when in the air, while below you saw the bottom of the sea, and hundreds of islands of all shapes and sizes, some above water, others being made beneath the sea, some day to rise above the waves. Most of the time we used to take the *Raven* inside the outer reefs whilst the *Pothuau* cruised outside. Inside we had sheltered water to work the seaplanes.

We had one or two close shaves of losing seaplanes, owing to the floats giving way. We had undoubtedly a bad batch of floats; they were far too weak for the job, and were inferior to our old original ones. It was an unpleasant sensation feeling the seaplane sinking under you, with sharks close alongside awaiting their chance.

The Experimental Short was unfortunately sunk through the floats giving way, but the crew were rescued in the nick of time.

After thoroughly hunting through the Laccadives we explored the northern part of the Maldive Islands, and then set sail for Colombo, as coal was beginning to run short.

We arrived at Colombo on April 2nd, having carried out a tremendous amount of flying and covered a big area.

We spent a fortnight in Colombo having a well-earned rest. At least the pilots had, but the remainder of the seaplane hands had hard work in order to overhaul all the seaplanes and rebuild all our floats.

Sailing again on April 14th, we started on a hunt over the Maldives and Chagos groups. We went through the whole of them most thoroughly; but unfortunately, we didn't locate the *Wolf*, which, as a matter of fact, didn't visit this area until sometime after we had been recalled from our search.

A number of the flights we made called for a good deal of navigational skill on the part of the pilots and observers, and there is little doubt that we all gained a great deal of experience.

On April 30th we returned to Colombo, whence I was ordered to terminate the hunt, to return to England myself by mail steamer, and dispatch the *Raven* back to Egypt.

Part 5: The North Sea

Chapter 1

Yarmouth and Felixstowe

I arrived home at the end of May, and was immediately appointed to the Air Department to reorganise the numbers of men in each station and squadron. This was quite a difficult task, as there was no standard to go by.

It entailed personal visits to most units at home and in France, and I am afraid that I was not any too enthusiastically received at one or two soft billets, like Wormwood Scrubs and the White City, where quite a number of men were stationed doing practically nothing. I can claim to have saved a good many men, and built up the strength of our fighting units, by having had a number of men removed from quiet peaceful jobs to active units overseas and on the coast.

I had a fair amount of flying, having a rather shaky 1½ Strutter allotted to me. I took the opportunity of changing this for a new one at Manston, where Butler was in command.

Having in mind the great wastage of man-power in certain types of work, I urgently impressed upon the authorities the scheme of replacing a number of our men by the fairer sex. I met with a good deal of opposition, but kept hammering away, and finally it was decided to employ women at the coastal air stations for numberless jobs like transport work, office staff, cleaning of aeroplanes and seaplanes, etc.

I was very keen to get overseas again, but the only commands suitable were already filled up. However, I kept on applying to be sent on active service once more.

By October I had completed my special work. Then, just as I was beginning to think I would never get a chance of further active service, but would be kept on for months in the office at the Hôtel Cecil, I was offered the command of Great Yarmouth Air Station. I, of course, accepted this post with alacrity, as I knew that this station had plenty of work.

I took over command in November 1917, and immediately entered into a most interesting period of active operations in the North Sea. At Yarmouth there were large flying-boats, seaplanes, and a great number of aeroplanes. I don't intend to write very much about Yarmouth or No. 4 Group, which was formed in April 1918 when the R.A.F. came into existence, and which I then commanded until the end of the war, as it is so well described in the *Story of a North Sea Air Station*, written by V. Gamble.

The work that Yarmouth had to do was:

(1) Protection of our shipping against attack from submarine and aircraft on a long stretch of coast.

(2) Protection of our bases against aircraft attack.

(3) Reconnaissance over the North Sea as far as Germany.

(4) Anti-Zeppelin work. We were always busily engaged, and numerous were the fights we had with German seaplanes, not only in the North Sea, but right on their own doorstep, so to speak, off Borkum and Emden.

We lost a number of flying-boats and seaplanes, and also destroyed a number of German seaplanes.

At some periods practically every long patrol we made terminated in a fight.

Thus, it will be seen that although we had the advantage and comfort of a home station, yet we had constant fighting miles away from our base. Personally, I consider that the flying-boat fighting near Borkum, entailing as it did flights of over six hours and sometimes even eight hours, was more desperate work than most of that carried out on the French front. I say this, because added to the ordinary chances of combat you had the long journey over a deserted sea both before and after your flight.

It can be readily understood that generally in winter the North Sea is a nasty customer—fog, high seas, low cloud, etc., being more the rule than the exception. You always knew that if you got engine failure or some trivial mishap you had the ever-present chance of being drowned, with only the smallest chance of rescue.

Yarmouth shot down five Zeppelins. The last one we bagged was within 20 miles of the German coast.

Leckie and Cadbury each shot down two apiece. In addition, we claimed many submarines, although like other submarine sinkings that were imagined successful after-events proved that the submarines frequently got home. Yet we did actually sink some.

To give some idea of what the usual flying-boat long patrol was like, I will picture an average one. Flying-boats, called F. 2A.'s, which had two Rolls Royce engines, fuel for eight hours, two pilots, one engineer, one wireless rating, and one gunlayer with four Lewis guns, were sent off in a formation of five from Yarmouth on a nasty morning with a visibility of about half a mile to fly over to about 30 miles west of Borkum. This was about 200 miles off, or a total flight of 400 miles, which meant about 6½ hours' journey, thus leaving little margin of fuel for the reconnaissance in the area ordered, probable fight, and navigational errors.

The difficulties of navigation were of course immense. There were no lightships once you left the proximity of the English coast, and until you reached the Dutch coast; but generally, you had to proceed out of sight of the Dutch coast. Your navigation was therefore guided by accurate estimation of your speed and drift, and by close attention to your compass.

At any time past the first 90 miles, you might run up against a German seaplane patrol, which generally extended to a line taken due north through Texel.

Once they sighted you, they used to wireless in, and reinforcements soon arrived. When they were in vast superiority of numbers they attacked, and never, I am proud to say, did our formations turn back when sighted or fail to take them on, however great the odds. Many epic combats were recorded, and on every occasion, I can safely say the enemy left the fight first.

Their seaplanes, although less heavily armed than ours, had the advantage of higher speed and better fighting qualities; also of course they were nearer home and constantly receiving reinforcements. In addition, as the fights were generally inside the German minefields, they had the moral support of their destroyers and trawlers to come to their aid when they were shot down.

We lost several boats; but very rarely did this occur when we were in formations; generally, our losses occurred when a single flying-boat was on reconnaissance. Our success was due to our well-drilled fighting tactics, close formations providing material support and zones of intense fire; also, to the intrepid leadership of men like Leckie, Nichol, and Livock, who always made a rule of going directly at the enemy and breaking up their line.

Our leaders had to combine dash with coolness, as they had to allow sufficient margin of time to enable our formation to get back across the 200 odd miles or so of nasty-looking sea.

The boats used to come back full of holes, and with dead on board. One pilot flew for four hours with the dead body of his second pilot alongside him.

Of course, it wasn't on every patrol that you got into a fight; very many were uneventful. Probably all you saw were German ships on patrol, or mine-sweepers at work. But generally something happened.

Once I was going with a big patrol, acting as second leader; but we had engine trouble, one of the rare times we were let down, and it being impossible to delay the others, Featherstone, who was first pilot, and I got into another boat, which had an engineer and wireless telegraphist, but no gunlayer. This reduced our fighting efficiency of course.

We started off an hour behind the formation, intending to proceed to off the Texel, then go up north, and hope to intercept them on their way back home. We sighted the Haaks Lightship, which is off the Texel, and then altered course to the north. Suddenly we saw a Zeppelin about 7,000 feet up. We immediately gave chase, and climbed as fast as we could.

Obviously, they didn't see us. I began to think we might get close enough to attack, and changed the charger of the Lewis gun, which was in the front cockpit, to a charger of anti-airship ammunition. We actually got within a mile of her, and only about 500 feet below, when she evidently saw us, as she went up like a high-speed lift, at a rate, of course, that we couldn't touch. We continued after her, not worrying much where we were, but at last found we had reached the limit of our climbing powers, and gave up the chase as futile.

Featherstone and I were trying to estimate our position, when the wireless man touched me on the shoulder and pointed to starboard. There I saw the sky one mass of German seaplanes, most of them their latest monoplane type. There was only one thing to do, and we did it at once: we shoved our nose down and dived for the sea. Our weak spot was, of course, under our tail; if we got down and flew about three or four feet off the water, we had a chance.

We got down that 10,000 feet or so in record time for an F. 2A. Every minute we expected to be attacked by at least a dozen machines; but nothing happened, and we got down and turned for home. To this day I feel certain that they lost sight of us, as we dived into the

WAR FLIGHT OF F2A'S READY FOR PATROL AT FELIXSTOWE, 1918.

sun. Obviously, the Zeppelin had signalled to them to come out and bag a solitary F. 2A.

It was an unpleasant situation, and we were glad to be out of it.

We had many patrols miles out to sea, hunting for German seaplanes, using a formation consisting of one F. 2A with two or three Camels which were single-seater fighter aeroplanes. The F. 2A acting the triple part of (1) navigator, (2) lifeboat in case a Camel had to go into the sea through engine trouble, (3) bait to draw the enemy, as we hoped all they would see would be the F. 2A and miss the little Camels which flew at much higher altitude.

I took part in several of these patrols, flying one of the Camels; but I never got a fight, although very often we had set off to intercept an enemy formation which had been sighted by some surface craft. The Camels would have made short work of the German seaplanes. One hour and a half spent on a Camel miles out to sea was a trying trip, and the sea used to look most uninviting.

On one occasion, on my return from one of these trips and when over the land a flying wire broke, and the wing began to vibrate in a most alarming manner; every minute I expected the spar to break. I was about 7,000 feet up, and I had to choose between coming down slowly, thus hoping to reduce the strain, and coming down rapidly and getting it over as quickly as possible.

I landed in the first place I saw, which was unfortunately a ploughed field. I landed all right, ran about 10 yards and then the Camel turned over, and I was suspended by my belt head downwards. Like an idiot, I let go the quick release, and I fell plunk on my head, which knocked me out for a few seconds. One does silly things sometimes.

There were many exciting times at Yarmouth between November and April 1st when, with the formation of the Royal Air Force, I was transferred to Felixstowe in command of a group, which consisted of Yarmouth, Felixstowe which had a large number of flying-boats, Westgate seaplane station, and an aeroplane Squadron at Manston. In addition, I had small units at Covehithe, Bacton, Holt, and Brough Castle, with Kite Balloon sections at Lowestoft and Shotley.

The office work was, of course, immense, and gradually I had to take a less active part in the actual flying.

I had a good many trips though in the flying-boat formations, and also was enabled to go on several of the fighting patrols in my aeroplane, which I kept at Martlesham Heath.

I was immensely keen on devising some method of getting the

Zeppelins which made flights over the North Sea. The flying-boats and seaplanes couldn't, of course, reach the altitude the Zeppelins now kept. There was only one thing to do, and that was by some method to get a Camel which could climb to about 20,000 feet, close enough to them.

It was obvious, however, that the fuel capacity of a Camel would not allow a flight over to the Zeppelins' beat. After great thought, I struck on the following scheme.

I had several special towing lighters. These were craft about 60 feet long of special construction, which enabled them to be safely and easily towed at high speed. They were intended to carry F. 2A's.

I decided to construct a runway on the lighter, put a Camel on it, and get a destroyer to tow at full speed. We could thus be taken fairly close to the Zeppelin's patrol, fly off and bag the Zeppelin.

As time pressed, I made a double trackway and fitted skids on the Camel in place of wheels.

Admiral Sir R. Tyrwhitt, who was in command of the famous Harwich Light Cruiser Squadron, was most enthusiastic over the idea.

I set off one day, really before everything was absolutely ready.

It was not certain, of course, if the Camel would get off. The run was extremely short, the difficulties mostly unknown. They were: (1) Uncertainty of being directly head to wind, therefore the Camel might slew when it started; (2) uncertainty as to the air conditions immediately in wake of a destroyer going at 30 knots.

Unfortunately, through some unforeseen error we only had a 50-feet tow-line; therefore, we were far too close to the destroyer. I got into the machine, and the destroyer got roughly head to wind and worked up speed to 30 knots. Sitting in the Camel the destroyer looked within 3 or 4 yards off me. My engine was started, and Cadbury, who of course couldn't be kept out of anything, standing on the slippery planking, tried to lift my tail up.

I had fitted a quick release by which I could slip the machine when ready to go.

I am afraid I had to steel myself to pull that toggle before I dashed into the unknown. I pulled the toggle and off I went. I ran only 3 or 4 feet when something caught up, and the next thing I knew Camel and I fell over the port bow of the lighter, and the lighter passed over the top of us.

Fortunately, I wasn't hurt; but I was rather uncomfortable, being under water upside down, and jammed into the wreckage. I tried

CAMEL ON LIGHTER AT FELIXSTOWE AIR STATION.

desperately to escape to the surface, but found myself entangled with wires. I then pulled myself together, and said to myself, "Keep quiet and go slow; if you cannot get up, go down." I tried this, and after a fierce tussle I got clear of the machine and swam down and away; then with my lungs bursting I struck for the surface. I was very pleased to see the light, and popped up to find the wreckage awash with the tail sticking up. I clung to this until rescued.

I then completely altered the design, as it was apparent my skids had jumped out of the trackway and fouled one of the cross-bars. Photographs taken from the destroyer showed fairly well what occurred.

I constructed a complete deck over the lighter, and altered the angle of the deck so that it was parallel to the water when the lighter was at full speed.

A tail guide was made to keep the tail up and also straight for the first 4 feet of the run. Wheels were used as usual on the chassis instead of skids.

Culley, whom I had selected out of all the volunteers, made the next attempt with complete success, and as is written in history we went out with the light cruiser force, and there, on Germany's threshold, he at 19,000 feet shot down a Zeppelin. For this feat he was given the D.S.O., and I was delighted to receive a telegram of congratulation from the Admiralty.

I never forget the moment when, standing on the destroyer, I saw miles away a cloud of smoke descending to the sea, and knew that our experiment and labours had not been in vain.

Culley had a tough job, and I was relieved when he came alongside the lighter and landed in the sea. We salved the aeroplane, and steamed back to Harwich rejoicing.

Once more Yarmouth had destroyed a Zeppelin.

I ended the war in the same command.

I was lucky to have served with the very cream of the R.N.A.S., the finest service that ever was.

ALSO FROM LEONAUR
AVAILABLE IN SOFTCOVER OR HARDCOVER WITH DUST JACKET

WINGED WARFARE *by William A. Bishop*—The Experiences of a Canadian 'Ace' of the R.F.C. During the First World War.

THE STORY OF THE LAFAYETTE ESCADRILLE *by George Thenault*—A famous fighter squadron in the First World War by its commander..

R.F.C.H.Q. *by Maurice Baring*—The command & organisation of the British Air Force during the First World War in Europe.

SIXTY SQUADRON R.A.F. *by A. J. L. Scott*—On the Western Front During the First World War.

THE STRUGGLE IN THE AIR *by Charles C. Turner*—The Air War Over Europe During the First World War.

WITH THE FLYING SQUADRON *by H. Rosher*—Letters of a Pilot of the Royal Naval Air Service During the First World War.

OVER THE WEST FRONT *by "Spin" & "Contact"*—Two Accounts of British Pilots During the First World War in Europe, Short Flights With the Cloud Cavalry by "Spin" and Cavalry of the Clouds by "Contact".

SKYFIGHTERS OF FRANCE *by Henry Farré*—An account of the French War in the Air during the First World War.

THE HIGH ACES *by Laurence la Tourette Driggs*—French, American, British, Italian & Belgian pilots of the First World War 1914-18.

PLANE TALES OF THE SKIES *by Wilfred Theodore Blake*—The experiences of pilots over the Western Front during the Great War.

IN THE CLOUDS ABOVE BAGHDAD *by J. E. Tennant*—Recollections of the R. F. C. in Mesopotamia during the First World War against the Turks.

THE SPIDER WEB *by P. I. X. (Theodore Douglas Hallam)*—Royal Navy Air Service Flying Boat Operations During the First World War by a Flight Commander

EAGLES OVER THE TRENCHES *by James R. McConnell & William B. Perry*—Two First Hand Accounts of the American Escadrille at War in the Air During World War 1-Flying For France: With the American Escadrille at Verdun and Our Pilots in the Air

KNIGHTS OF THE AIR *by Bennett A. Molter*—An American Pilot's View of the Aerial War of the French Squadrons During the First World War.

AVAILABLE ONLINE AT **www.leonaur.com**
AND FROM ALL GOOD BOOK STORES

www.ingramcontent.com/pod-product-compliance
Lightning Source LLC
Chambersburg PA
CBHW031559170426
43196CB00031B/234